DEVELOPMENT SUCCESS IN ASIA PACIFIC

By the same authors

A. H. Somjee

VOTING BEHAVIOUR IN AN INDIAN VILLAGE
POLITICAL THEORY OF JOHN DEWEY
DEMOCRACY AND POLITICAL CHANGE IN VILLAGE INDIA
DEMOCRATIC PROCESS IN A DEVELOPING SOCIETY
POLITICAL CAPACITY IN DEVELOPING SOCIETIES
POLITICAL SOCIETY IN DEVELOPING COUNTRIES
PARALLELS AND ACTUALS OF POLITICAL DEVELOPMENT
REACHING OUT TO THE POOR (*with Geeta Somjee*)
DEVELOPMENT THEORY: Critiques and Explorations

Geeta Somjee

NARROWING THE GENDER GAP
REACHING OUT TO THE POOR (*with A. H. Somjee*)

Development Success in Asia Pacific

An Exercise in Normative-Pragmatic Balance

A. H. Somjee
Professor Emeritus
Simon Fraser University

and

Geeta Somjee
Adjunct Professor of Political Science
Simon Fraser University

St. Martin's Press

First published in Great Britain 1995 by
MACMILLAN PRESS LTD
Houndmills, Basingstoke, Hampshire RG21 6XS
and London
Companies and representatives
throughout the world

A catalogue record for this book is available from the British Library.

ISBN 0–333–62696–6

10 9 8 7 6 5 4 3 2 1
04 03 02 01 00 99 98 97 96 95

Printed and bound in Great Britain by
Antony Rowe Ltd, Chippenham, Wiltshire

First published in the United States of America 1995 by
Scholarly and Reference Division,
ST. MARTIN'S PRESS, INC.,
175 Fifth Avenue,
New York, N.Y. 10010

ISBN 0–312–12859–2

Library of Congress Cataloging-in-Publication Data
Somjee, A. H.
Development success in Asia Pacific : an exercise in normative
-pragmatic balance / A. H. Somjee and Geeta Somjee.
p. cm.
Includes bibliographical references and index.
ISBN 0–312–12859–2 (cloth)
1. Asia, Southeastern—Economic policy—Case studies. 2. Asia,
Southeastern—Politics and government—1945— —Case studies.
3. Asia, Southeastern—Social conditions—Case studies. I. Somjee,
Geeta, 1930– . II. Title.
HC441.S66 1995
338.959—dc20   95–17963
                                                          CIP

Contents

Preface

Many new 'capitalisms' or social and economic organisations are emerging in different parts of Asia Pacific which have skilfully adapted the earlier Western capitalism to suit their own specific requirements. Not only that, they have also put their own social and cultural values to effective use in order to get the best results. Japan has brought to its work-place its own heritage of associated living to overcome proverbial adversarial labour and management relations; Singapore has made use of Confucian emphasis on social discipline and respect for merit to build a meritocratic society; Indonesia has made use of its genius for eclecticism to build its own brand of social pragmatism and then use it for economic growth; Thailand has made use of the concept of merit in Theravada Buddhism to accelerate economic growth; and, above all, the Chinese minorities, from the Philippines to Malaysia, have developed their own pragmatic approaches not only to survive in socially and politically adverse conditions but also to become the pillars of economic prosperity in the region by an adroit use of their own traditional values. And when China and India become the major players in Asian economic growth, scholars will have to probe into the relationship between the cultural background of their different regional and social groups and the kind of economic initiatives and organizations they gave rise to.

Within such an overall concern, whereby background factors were made to contribute effectively to development processes, this book concentrates on the search for and exercise of normative–pragmatic balance on the part of the societies in ASEAN countries which triggered off their many-sided development. These societies, in other words, exercised a keen sense of judgment between what was normatively desirable and what was pragmatically possible, given their resources, nature of constraints and political problems. But more than that, invariably each of these societies also had to find a homegrown, and effective, solution to its problem of economic growth, social development and political change. As a senior Indonesian economist put it: it was not enough to be right, we also had to be effective.

This book, then, is an attempt at understanding the problem of their development in the wider contexts of their historical legacies, cultural background, vision and commitment of leaders, and the highly pragmatic manner of approaching their problems. In each of the six societies examined in this volume an attempt has been made to concentrate on the nature of the specific core development issue which influenced the rest of its development process. The core issue for Singapore is its micro dimension; for Malaysia it is its tangled ethnic problem; for Indonesia it is its archipelagic character and eclectic social systems; for Thailand it is how to balance its deep religiosity with the need for material achievement; for the Philippines it is the inability to check political cynicism; and for Brunei it is affluence and paternalistic rule. Such core development issues are examined against the background of their own attempts at normative–pragmatic balance. We have also tried to view the importance of those core issues through the perspectives of indigenous scholars and their writings.

We began doing field research for this volume in 1988. And since then every year we have spent a period ranging from two to six months interviewing people in various walks of life in the urban and rural communities of ASEAN countries. During the past six years what also helped us the most was academic affiliations in those countries. We are particularly grateful to the National University of Singapore for a Visiting Professorship, in 1988–9, for A. H. Somjee; and a Visiting Fellowship, in 1988–9, for Geeta Somjee at the Institute of Southeast Asian Studies (ISEAS), Singapore. The ISEAS has also done us a great honour by extending Visiting Fellowships to both of us since 1989. Our thanks are also due to Universiti Kebangsaan Malaysia, Sabah Campus, for their Fellowships. Finally, Chulalongkorn University, Bangkok, also did us a great honour by inviting us as Visiting Professors in 1990–1. During the course of our visits, which are still continuing, we have benefited immensely from the exchange of scholarly ideas with more scholars than we can possibly remember or thank.

We are grateful to the Social Sciences and Humanities Research Council of Canada and Simon Fraser University for their travel grants for making our field reseach trips to the countries of Asia Pacific possible. We also wish to thank the librarians and staff of Simon Fraser University; the National University of Singapore; the Institute of Southeast Asian Studies, Singapore; the University of Malaya, Kuala Lumpur; Universiti Kebangsaan Malaysia, Bangi as well as Kota Kinabalu; the University Sans Malaysia, Penang; Chulalongkorn University, Bangkok; the University of the Philippines, Diliman; Social Sciences Research

Council, Quezon City; Cambridge University; the University of Brunei; and Gadjah Mada University, Yogyakarta, Indonesia.

In this ambitious work, which encompasses six very diverse societies, we are fully aware of the fact that we have barely scratched the surface as to how background factors contribute to the determining and shaping of the development which those societies will finally achieve. Scholars are now beginning to reach an understanding of such factors and to cut across rigid social science boundaries. Towards such an understanding of development processes in societies of Asia Pacific, this is one small contribution.

University of Cambridge A. H. SOMJEE
1994 GEETA SOMJEE

Introduction

I. AN EXERCISE IN NORMATIVE–PRAGMATIC BALANCE

The rapidly developing countries of Asia Pacific, each in its own way, have learnt the dos and don'ts of economic growth, social development and what they think is a manageable proportion of political development. In crystallising their goals within these categories, they depended initially on what their academic training, the advice of the international development personnel, and the emulation of the ways of the more developed countries had achieved. But they soon realised that unless all these were suitably adapted to serve the specific nature of their own problems, and also supplemented with their own context-effective approaches, their efforts might not produce intended results. Academic training and the advice of international development personnel often assumed the character of a universal prescription even when they were based on the social and historical experiences of few industrialised societies in the West. Consequently, apart from attending to their own development problems, what these societies have also succeeded in putting across to students of development studies is the message that only up to a point can they rely on the universal-effectiveness claiming development strategies which have come through external sources. That in the final analysis they will have to depend on their own strategies after gaining a clear idea of the specific nature of their own problems.

But within such an overall adjustment of what was borrowed and then used only if it served their particular needs, these countries also developed their own normative structures indicating what should constitute their necessary goals. The inspiration for such structures, and the values implicit within them, came, and continues to come, from the cultural and historical background of each of those societies, on the one hand, and the way their thinking men and women interpreted them in the light of social concerns of their own, on the other. In that respect, the six countries of ASEAN which we shall examine in this volume will reveal a variety of normative emphases of their own, reflecting their historical and cultural background, and also contemporary social concerns. So while an increasingly higher standard of living for their people is a common concern of all of them, the goals of broader social

1

development are cast within the framework of their different social concerns. Their goals, and the targets within them, are expressed and defined with reference to their evolving conception of what they think is normatively desirable.

Different social segments within each of these societies have a differing notion of what they think is most likely to serve them as groups. Such notions coexist within the broader conception of what they think is normatively desirable for their society as a whole. Leaders with vision, persuasion and the understanding of effective means to realise them, are often able to gain a wider acceptance of what they consider to be in the broader interests of all the segments within society.

The leaders and decision-makers are also required to strike a balance between what is normatively desirable and what is economically and politically possible. There are possible pitfalls for them in both respects: either becoming too steeped in their normative commitments and losing sight of what can be realised in actual practice; or becoming unhinged from their normative anchor and starting to practise cynical politics. In the six countries that we shall examine in this volume, there is a variety of normative–pragamatic balances as well as imbalances. And despite their spectacular development successes during the decades of the 1970s and 1980s, the ASEAN countries continued to have their internal as well as external critics on both sides of the normative–pragamatic divide.

The terms 'normative' and 'pragmatic' need explanation, as does the notion of 'balance' which reflects a reasoned and effective situation of trade-offs between them. While these terms are, relatively speaking, more easily explainable with reference to *individual's* perception, assessment and reason for action, similar explanations of groups and/or collectivities, indicating development choices, should be attempted. In the development process nations, like individuals, are inspired by normative commitments and are then driven to explore how many of such commitments *can* be realised and by what means. Again, both can either overdo their normative commitments and bring to bear a utopian vision which sounds morally, intellectually and even aesthetically attractive and worthwhile, and yet falls short of realisable potential. At the other extreme, one could have a situation where normative principles and goals become materially realisable targets and nothing else, thereby making development merely a matter of affluence and standard of living instead of what can also lead to a higher quality of individual and public life.

In 1984, we had looked at the problems of learning the dos and don'ts, for individuals both in and out of power, in those developing countries which were trying to introduce liberal political institutions, ideals and practices. The focus of that work was to ask why such institutions remain fragile and what ought the people who implement them to do in order to sustain them. That discussion was contained in A. H. Somjee's *Political Society in Developing Countries*.

In that connection religion, ideology and personal morality were identified as the main sources which shape one's normative structure, which in turn influences one's predisposition to public action. Different individuals and segments of society will then be exposed to variations in normative influences.

At the other extreme, an individual may bring to bear the moral implications of his/her normative commitments to public causes that are espoused or opposed. And depending on the clarity of individual vision and the need to realise those commitments, one may make a judgment on the priority or the proportionality of what one emphasises. But some may even decide to separate temporarily or permanently the moral considerations from one's power or political drives and, instead of seeking a normative–pragamatic adjustment, feel free to pursue one's goals without any regard to their moral consequences on oneself or on the public at large. Arguably, at the pragmatic level there are the bounds of legality, propriety and morality within which such an action takes place; nevertheless, in politics individuals as well as nations, may subscribe to them formally but in actual practice dodge them.

We shall go into the nuances of normative and pragmatic considerations in the development process of the six ASEAN countries and examine a variety of their attempts at balancing such considerations, with what they regard as their core development issues. During this process they often had to move the goalposts – and the targets – in search of an effective mix of what they thought was normatively desirable and politically and economically possible.

They acquired either tentative or clear perceptions of goals – given the differing degree of discussion among their leaders, representatives of the people, people of distinction, achievement, experience, and leaders with vision – then formulated strategies, constantly evaluated and revised them whenever necessary, and showed remarkable sensitivity to what worked and what did not. Neither goals nor targets by themselves produced results. Effective strategies did. So the more they showed sensitivity to the effectiveness of their strategies, and the need to adjust them constantly, the more they produced results. And the more they produced results, the more they understood the complex interplay of norms and targets, on the one hand, and effective strategies to realise them, given their peculiar situations and problems, on the other.

II. SPECIFIC NATURE OF NORMATIVE–PRAGMATIC BALANCE IN ASEAN COUNTRIES

Singapore

i. Micro dimensions and the pragmatism of size
One of the core issues for Singapore has been its micro dimensions, which has forced it to be dynamic and continually on the look-out for alternatives in order to get the maximum out of its policies. To achieve this it has set the best available brains to formulate its policies and then implement them firmly. Its limited size also allowed it to experiment with a wider range of policy choices and then choose the most effective ones for implementation. It has thus often transformed its micro dimensions into macro opportunities. It could not afford the luxury of orthodoxy, ideology and power bloc affiliations.

ii. Pragmatic skill
The goal was always to provide its people with new skills and then use them to offer services to a rapidly changing international economic scene. Over the years it moved from being an entrepôt economy, to a branch plant economy, then to regional manufacturing, and finally went global to become the financial, high-tech, shipping, telecommunication and computer centre not only for the region but wherever such services were needed.

iii. Highly pragmatised normative considerations
While practical or pragmatic considerations often have a vital influence on normative commitments, in the case of Singapore they were almost allowed to take charge of the prescription of such commitments. What began as the compulsion of a micro state to become super pragmatic became, as it were, the sole definer of what Singapore should or should

not do. Up to a point that was understandable. But when such considerations superceded other concerns, then the very *raison d'être* for being pragmatic began to be less defensible.

iv. Continuing restriction on liberalising the political regime
It was precisely such considerations which prevented Singapore under Lee Kuan Yew from even considering the broadening of citizens' participation. He viewed it with alarm. Singapore, he thought, was not ready for it. He therefore sacrificed one of the most vital areas of human growth, namely, self-development through self-involvement. Lee Kuan Yew consiered that as long as the best brains gave the best results, any liberal ideal or value should not be allowed to get in its way. His successor, Goh Chok Tong, promised a more 'consultative' approach, but he, by and large, had been deeply influenced by policies and philosophies that had been put in place by his predecessor.

v. The core issue for development
The central issue for Singapore then is the acceptance of the limitations of its size and subsequent transformation into a superpragmatic, superefficient state. This could be done by means of meritocracy, discipline, and mobilisation.

Singapore has already attained a very high standard of living, second only to Japan in Asia. How then would it be characterised by contemporary observers and historians? Its own ideal is Switzerland, minus her direct democracy. But while Switzerland produced many efficient economic organisations and a stable political system, in terms of its distinctive achievement it is perhaps best known for the production of clocks and cuckoo clock. Similarly, Singapore may be judged as a country which did not utilise the opportunity provided by its very high standard of living to go beyond it to create conditions for the enjoyment of human freedom and creativity.

Malaysia

The ethnic divisions in Malaysia permeate all its political institutions, economic policies and social goals. This also affects its search for a normative–pragmatic balance. At the core of its continuing search for such a balance, there is the heightened awareness of its ethnic tangle.

i. Group based normative commitments

Like most divided societies, the various ethnic groups in the unreconciled plural society of Malaysia also derive their normative ideals from different sources. Not only that, their relative isolation from one another often results in a predisposition to finding practical solutions to their problems in isolated ways.

Historically speaking, the Malays have been exposed to different cultural influences such as Animism, Hinduism, Buddhism, Islam, and so on, and they tend to derive their normative standards from all these sources. As the Malays did not consciously work at syncretising the cultural influences to which they were exposed, there are often fragments of parallel normative systems to which they subscribe. Only in recent years has there been a religious and linguistic expression of Malay ethnic identity which tends to emphasise the Islamic normative system, on the one hand, and *adat* (customs), on the other.

The Chinese, however, tend to overemphasise practicalism. They are constantly reminded that as outsiders in the Peninsula, they will have to achieve success in all their economic undertakings and be several steps ahead of others. The way to do this is by hard work, discipline and cohesiveness. Since they are outsiders, socially and politically they may not be able to go far, but materially they can and should therefore concentrate on this goal.

Indians in Malaysia are a very diverse group. Since they place great emphasis on education, some seek upward economic mobility through professions and the learning of skills. In addition, there are the business castes and regional groups who concentrate on trade and commerce, but the bulk of them work as plantation labourers.

At a normative level the Indians tend not to take their material life too seriously, although this is only true of those who do not do well materially. This places at a disadvantage precisely those among them who should be taking their material concerns more seriously.

ii. Shifting pragmatic policies

The problem for Malay policy-makers has been how to manage the diversity of the two main groups – the Malays and the Chinese – with reference to their moderate and extraordinary economic acumen respectively. Earlier on, many solutions were suggested to this dilemma. One was to make the Malays as economically aggressive as the Chinese, another was to let the Chinese look after trade and the Malays to look after politics. The bulk of the Malays, however, have been pressing for increased privileges of affirmative action and benefits for themselves. This has resulted in the New Economic Policy of *bumiputeraism* whereby only one of the economically backward groups is singled out for additional help.

In the implementation of the New Economic Policy, Dr Mahathir, the Prime Minister, tried to be as aware of its results as the social justice it was supposed to dispense. First of all, he tried to assuage the fears of the Chinese that nothing would be done to place them at a disadvantage. After that all the *Ali Baba* style undertakings, whereby the Malay was only a front man for a Chinese undertaking, were carefully scrutinised. Finally, when a Malay senior executive did not give a good account of himself, as in the case of Proton Saga, he even replaced him.

iii. Core issue: remedying economic disparities
Mahathir thus tried to establish his normative–pragmatic balance for the remedying of economic disparities, which also coincided with ethnic divisions. At the same time, however, when the effects of his affirmative action policy detracted from economic growth he relaxed it.

With a lot of agonising both in and out of power, Mahathir is now veering round to a kind of development compromise. He cannot by himself or by means of state policy accelerate the economic rise of the Malays or make them succeed in the various opportunities that he can create for them. For this he and his successors may have to wait for a new generation of young Malays to come on the scene. In the meanwhile, he cannot afford to neglect or discourage the Chinese from making their own economic contribution.

Indonesia

One of the major political societies examined in this volume is Indonesia. With a population of more than 180 million Indonesia is also the world's largest Muslim, but not Islamic, country. Despite several attempts made by its various social components, in the main the *santris*, Indonesia refused to give up its earlier cultural heritage which resulted from its exposure to the belief systems of Animism, Hinduism, Buddhism, coastal coexistential Islam, which came through Arab traders via Gujarat in western India, and Christianity. An exposure to a variety of cultural influences, and a deep attachment to most of them, has helped the Indonesians to develop some of the most intricate cultural and intellectual eclectic systems. These historical legacies also helped them evolve a genius for sophisticated intellectual and aesthetic systems as well as practical adjustments for day to day problems. Such a background, given their core development issues – which ranged from the archipelagic character of the country, a huge rural population, cultural diversity, unrelenting resurgent Islam pressing for religious purity, and a utopian and chaotic beginning under Sukarno – helped the Indonesians to find their own specific normative–pragmatic balance.

i. Eclectic normative system
What is remarkable in the case of Indonesia is its highly evolved and challenge-tested capability for absorbing new influences within the framework of its cultural and intellectual matrix. It developed neither a dismissive nor a mindlessly imitative dispostion to such influences. The new influence was always intellectually reworked to fit into the existing framework of either the belief system or as an aesthetic resource.

ii. Social pragmatism
So great has been its eclecticising capability that with particular regard to Indonesia any attempt at rigidly demarcating specific religion or aesthetic system does not make sense. What can be relatively identifiable elsewhere becomes hopelessly intermeshed in the continuum of religions, cultures and norms derived from Animism, Hinduism, Buddhism, Islam and Christianity. And yet even in their bafflingly alloyed form they exercise influence on the conduct of individuals and groups. There are not many social organisations in the world where the absorptive and assimilative tendencies have been so severly tested, and remained triumphant, as in the case of Indonesia. Simultaneously, the same capacity becomes very useful in finding practical solutions to problems which call for sensitivity to mutual differences, understanding of nuances, and compromise resolutions.

iii. Development before politics
The normative–pragmatic balance her leaders tried to reach, and persuaded her people to accept, was characterised as 'development before politics'. Unlike India, where the freedom movement, spread over nearly one hundred years, was all about democratic self-government,

the Indonesians turned away from the liberal political ideals of the West partly because of the nature of Dutch colonial rule and the absence of leaders and lawyers emphasizing them. The post-independence experience in Indonesia, especially under Sukarno's leadership, registered much less enthusiasm for liberal political institutions. His successor, Suharto, was therefore able to sell the idea of 'development before politics' to his people without much difficulty. And as Indonesia prospered economically under his leadership, this slogan was not effectively challenged except within academic circles. Consequently, as of now the Suharto variety of pragmatism has placed liberal ideals and political institutions as matters of secondary importance to the nation.

iv. Balanced economic growth
Apart from its social and political pragmatism, which we have touched upon in this section, Indonesia has also registered a fairly diversified economic growth. Historically speaking, there had always been criticism of Indonesia as being too Java-centric. Such an approach was not very helpful to the cause of its national integration. Given the archipelagic nature of the country, it needed to spread its development efforts evenly in various regions. During the last three decades it has highlighted balanced regional development as one of its economic goals.

Moreover, it has also aimed at balanced economic growth which is not just confined to the development of agriculture and mining. It is now also addressing the problems of industrialisation and building up a skilled workforce which can attract more international investment. And in this respect Indonesia has rightly earned the respect of its fellow ASEAN countries for having formulated effective policies and produced the intended results .

Thailand

i. Normative influence of Theravada Buddhism
Thailand was exposed to the normative influence of Theravada Buddhism, on the one hand, and the pragmatic influence of Confucianism, through the Sino-Thai component of her population, on the other. But Theravada Bhuddism itself developed some very practical approaches to the concept of merit, whereby it not only influenced the cycles of births and deaths implicit in *karma* but was also a means of making progress in the material world. Such an interpretation of merit persuaded

the Thais to pay more attention to their own economic advancement. It also made them far more receptive and imitative of the economic organisation and thrust of the Sino-Thais who were the economic models to emulate. For the Sino-Thais themselves European traders and, later on, American and Japanese multinationals were the role models. Thailand thus surprised the countries both within and outside the region by registering rapid economic growth by means of receptiveness to groups and organizations which were doing very well materially. Despite such a drive towards economic growth, the bulk of the Thai population remained firmly anchored in the normative base of Theravada Bhuddism. Their normative commitments, strong cultural roots and receptivity to pragmatic approaches to improve their material well-being at once made them normatively and pragmatically the most balanced people in the region.

ii. Moral regeneration through short-term bhikku *status*
Theravada Buddhism in Thailand, unlike Hinduism in India, did not draw a strict line between religion and worldly concerns. In Thailand one can become a *bhikku* for a short time to recharge one's moral batteries, whereas in India a *sanyasi* has to give up worldly ties forever. For the latter there is no going back to the material world, but it is the other way round for the Thai. For a Thai the post-*bhikku* stage is very important because it is then that which can make a difference by bringing the teachings of Buddhism to bear in the real world.

iii. Spiritual–material continuum
For the spiritual–material continuum, Theravada Buddhism is closely organised. In Thailand, either in rural communities or in urban centres, you are rarely away from its various branches and facilities. And its appeal cuts across the rural–urban, class, region and generation divide. The royal household, too, has the responsibility for facilitating its operations.

The spiritual–material continuum of Thailand is also reflected in its extraordinarily large number of non-governmental organisations (NGOs). They work in a wide area of social concerns and bring to bear the idealism of the young regarding the various problems that Thailand is faced with in its extraordinary rapid rate of social change. They also exhibit a Buddhist conscience and heightened awareness of suffering among the population. Some of the members of NGOs are highly educated and they sacrifice their careers and comforts for that which they think would make a difference.

iv. *Canonisation of economic virtues*
Apart from the concept of merit-making in Theravada Buddhism, what has also been responsible for the growth of Thai pragmatism is the implications for one's involvement in the material world. You could now take charge of your educational and economic destiny. Despite the disadvantages of previous *karma*, you have another opportunity of which you must avail yourself. What is then enjoined in such an interpretation of merit is that you must first prepare yourself and then become a doer to make a difference to your own material life. You do not have to shun material life but can flourish within it, bearing in mind that others may not be as fortunate. To paraphrase R. H. Tawney, in his introduction to Max Weber's *Protestant Ethic and the Spirit of Capitalism*, Theravada Buddhism, with the help of the interpretation of the concept of merit, canonised the pursuit of material goals as something that was worthwhile.

The Philippines

i. *Morally devastating experiences*
Within the ASEAN family of nations, the performance of the Philippines in attaining a normative–pragmatic balance was about the poorest. The reasons for this, as we shall see in this volume, were not simply the presence of cynical characters like Marcos and his associates, but also the failure to apply the influence of her own normative commitments to the nature and implementation of public policy. Nor could she build a leadership with a minimum level of integrity to support such policies and pull her out of the series of setbacks foisted on her by historical, international, national and natural forces.

The Philippines had the misfortune of being subjected to two colonial administrations, the Spanish and the American. Apart from the exploitation and humiliation imposed by these on the Filipinos, they also devastated them in human terms. Time after time her people tried to pull themselves together but on each occasion they were unable to trust their own sense of direction or those who were supposed to help them. As the Filipino scholars themselves have pointed out, there is more self-denigration in the Philippines than in most other developing countries.

ii. A dual normative system
A worse factor was that the Spanish and American colonialisms, and the policies adopted during that period, weakened the Asian cultural roots of Filipino society. The people were consistently made to believe that the Philippines represented the Westernised variety of Asianism which would eventually earn the respect of others. Unlike various other Asian countries where Christian influence has been powerful, Christian faith in the Philippines existed side by side with the pre-Christian cultural systems and values. Consequently, the politically liberalizing aspects of Christianity, as in Europe, did not have much impact. Moreover, the Christian friars during Spanish rule used it to make the Filipinos docile to the colonial regime. They even discouraged higher learning and a questioning attitude in general.

The elite of the Philippines are aware of the need to develop a culture which has indigenous roots, pride in its Asianness, and at the same time able to combine the humanistic aspects of Christianity exemplified by Jesuits and clerics in their educational, medical and social organisations. Of equal relevance are the implications for social equality and social justice, embedded in Christian principles, for a very unequal Filipino society. This poses the question: how can you make this into a principle of social and political policy?

While the normative aspects of Christianity, barring the educational and medical field, were confined to religious spheres only, the deeper and stronger layers of the normative system in indigenous beliefs and practices remained integral parts of the smaller social units of families and extended families. Such values even had an impact on Filipino Catholicism and made it into what Filipino scholars have called 'folk Catholicism'. Pre-Christian values of 'honour' and 'obligation' have also survived, but since these have remained below the surface they have not been philosophised and made intellectually respectable.

The point to be made here is that, for historical reasons, the Filipinos did not find support against political oppression within their own indigenous tradition. And the Christianising of a part of their normative values emphasised religious affairs rather than political issues of deep social and human concern. The people able to emphasise the latter were the Jesuit educators, members of the religious and non-religious NGOs, and the agonising and soul searching intellectuals. The Philippine democracy, in times of crisis, thus could not fall back upon a clear-cut indigenous tradition to involve the bulk of the people.

iii. Unattained normative–pragmatic balance

Thus in many compartments of life the Philippines has been unable to strike a balance between normative commitments and the quality of public life in general. Being a democracy, problems of corruption, lack of accountability and apathy of the middle class, as in the case of India, become more compounded. As in all democracies the price to pay will be in terms of massive involvement on the part of her citizens to see that people in public office remain accountable for the way in which they exercise public authority. In no form of government, and least of all in a democracy, can the exercise of public authority and the use of social resources be left to the claims of integrity and probity of public officials, elected or appointed. They have to be made to live up to those claims under the scrutiny of the citizens, the media and political parties. Unfortunately, the Philippines is no way near generating such an interest in the different segments and institutions of society. In its absence the normative commitments of the various segments of her society are able to make very little difference to the quality of public life.

Brunei

As an affluent country, with highly developed social services and a paternalistic form of government, its core development problems are diversification of the economy, fairer treatment of the non-Brunei Malay population, and participatory public policy-making. As of now its high standard of living has put all these problems on a back burner.

III. SOME GENERAL OBSERVATIONS

The variety of normative–pragmatic balances that the countries of Asia Pacific were required to strike were, as we shall see in the following pages, deeply influenced by their own specific social and cultural background, on the one hand, and a clear understanding of the nature of their problems and the strategies they thought would help resolve them, on the other. Countries like Singapore and Thailand were even able to derive assistance from their normative background in order to help them improve their lives materially, and also to exert its influence, especially in the case of Thailand, on the quality of social and political life. The segmented nature of Malaysia's normative base did not provide similar help, but forced it to find a practical resolution to its problem. Indonesia used its cultural background to bring about a highly pragmatic solution to its diverse cultural heritage. The cultural background of the Philippines has not so far been used to resolve the large number of economic problems. The point to be made here is that most of these countries, in their development process, have, along with their other public policies, made use of their social and cultural backgrounds.

In their public policies – economic, religious, social and educational – they have shown much less dogmatism than is often attributed to emerging countries. Singapore, Malaysia, Thailand and Indonesia were constantly engaged in reviewing the results of their policies, followed by bold course corrections. Neither ideologies, nor trendy economic models, nor indeed religious considerations were allowed to shape their policies. The specific nature of their policies often cut across diverse ideologies, economic theories and development briefs. Simultaneously, most of these countries also trained and then put to work their own high-quality technocrats, who were not only result-oriented in their outlook but also bold, experimental and given to course corrections.

With the exception of the Philippines, all these countries were blessed with political leadership featuring great intelligence, integrity and the ability to work as a team with highly successful people drawn from the professions, industry, banking, academia, and international development agencies. They thus employed their own highly experienced and skilled human resources. The Philippines too has similar resources but in the name of democracy, as with India, individuals of inadequate background and experience are put in charge of policy-making.

Development success in Asia Pacific is also based on a lot of indigenous policies which utilised new opportunities which came their way as a result of multinational corporations (MNCs) looking for cheap labour, assembly facilities and regional markets. Undoubtedly that is how it all began in the 1960s. But since then most of the countries in this region have passed the reactive phase and are bursting with initiatives, baffling their investors with extraordinarily high quality background preparations. Such a process therefore deserves to be looked at against its own broader historical, social and human background along with the economic and political.

The general argument, which can be formulated on the basis of this study, may now be stated as follows.

1. In the development process the countries which use their own historical and cultural backgrounds effectively are thus able to exceed those which do not. Earlie, Japan used its cultural practice of associated living to contain adversarial relations between labour and management. Similarly, Singapore, Indonesia and Thailand have made use of their respective backgrounds in their own special ways.

2. A deeper and more realistic understanding of the specific problems, beyond ideologies, academic training, trendy economic models and international development briefs, is more likely to result in effective development policies. And countries of Asia Pacific, given their variety of background, were able to develop their own clearer understanding of their specific problems and then boldly formulate and implement their own policies. Most of their strategies for development success were homegrown. While knowledge is universal, in its development application to specific problems, trained indigenous human resources have a special role to play.

3. Apart from the quality and vision of the top leadership, development success largely depends on its ability to put to effective use country's own human resources with skill and experience. Of the countries of ASEAN, which put to maximum use such resources, and with maximum results, was Singapore. Most developing countries now have such resources but their top leadership is either too limited in its understanding, or in integrity, or is unable to work with bright and experienced people.

4. The quality of development success in Asia Pacific can be judged with reference to what the countries in the region thought was normatively desirable, and then went in search of effective pragmatic strategies to realise them. Such a judgment will have to take into account the argument relating to phases, sequences and instalments. But our overall judgment on their performance will be with reference to what emerged in their wider discussions, preceding the formulation of policies, as to what was normatively desirable and, in practical terms, what was possible.

1 Singapore: A Super Pragmatic Society

Among the developing countries, Singapore was one of the earliest to register stunning economic growth. It has since kept up that pace without interruption and become an object of interest and admiration worldwide. Scholars, reporters, statesmen, tourists, and others, come to its shores in order to understand the nature of its policies and the way they have been implemented. Their subsequent questions concern how evenly its development has been spread in different segments of the population, and also in the different compartments of its life. Above all they ask about the price Singapore had to pay to achieve and maintain such a high rate of development. We shall examine these and other questions in the following pages. And within them we shall also look for its normative commitments and the way it has tried to balance them with its pragmatic strategies, and compromises, so as to strike a balance of its own.

Our presentation will be divided into the following subsections: i. social organisation; ii. dynamic political economy; iii. the vision of the founding fathers and political institutions; iv. normative–pragmatic balance in a meritocratic society; v. some general observations. We shall now consider each of them in some detail.

I. SOCIAL ORGANISATION

i. Blurred State–Society Distinctions

In a span of less than three decades, society in Singapore had changed beyond recognition. It changed from 'a colony of traders and labourers'[1] to one which had the highest standard of living in Asia, next only to Japan, one of the highest proportions of ownership of dwellings in the world, a high rate of literacy, highly efficient social services, and some of the highest environmental standards. In inducing such a rapid social change, the vision and quality of its leadership, the nature of public policy, the firmness in implementing it and, above all, the responses

17

from its multi-ethnic community, consisting of workers, shopkeepers, traders, bankers, industrialists, professionals, students, and just about everyone helped it translate its good intentions into a living social reality.

However, a price was paid for such a rapid social transformation in terms of the nature of its political society, which very nearly excluded from participation all except those in charge of making public policy. Formal ways were devised to elicit public reactions and suggestions to proposed policies, but it was also known from the very start what the intent and the thrust of the policy makers were and how they would benefit everyone. So then leave policy making to those who were actually in charge of it. Not only that, even public scrutiny of the results of previous policy did not find much favour. Under the circumstances the very distinction between state and society became blurred.

Singapore brought into the field of policy-making the best available brains and experience within its society. Decision-makers were brought in from the corporate world, industry, commerce, academia, the professions, and so on, and persuaded to work in the highest offices in the land, and later moved on to create a place for the new generation of men and women who had achieved distinction in their respective fields. Singapore was thus able to draw upon new skills and experiences almost as soon as they were available. As a state-managed society it did not have to wait till old hands in offices could be eased out. In short Singapore created what Professor Ezra Vogel called a 'meritocracy' in the field of public decision-making. This 'meritocracy' was then placed solely in charge of policy-making and implementing it with little or no input from others, not even at the level of impact or the way it was received. Reflecting on the nature of Singapore's political society, one of its distinguished political scientists, Chan Heng Chee, expressed the view that for the foreseeable future it will be governed by a 'political elite'.

The two of the major areas which had made a difference to the nature of its society were the policy relating to housing and the use of the English language. In fact both these brought its ethnically divided society closer in physical proximity and communication. It was not possible to own an apartment in an area other than that which one was given, with a few alternative choices within the price range. This helped Singapore to breakdown, gradually, the ethnic ghettos that were there since before independence. While the policy was common for everyone it affected the minorities – the Malays and the Indians – more. Later on we shall examine the views of scholars who maintained that the housing policy also changed the very nature of family life in Singapore.

The economic component of society was changed radically through a series of efforts on the part of its leadership to find out what all it could do to develop its seaport and commercial facilities which had existed since before independence. In other words, it wanted to capitalise on its position as 'a centre of entrepôt trade'[3] and then go beyond it. But in so doing it did not want to lose political control of expanded economic activity. Apart from the political imperatives of a micro state, which could not afford political instability resulting from a premature introduction of liberal institutions and practices, its most senior rulers genuinely believed in a disciplined way of building the economy. Internationally, powerful multinationals, and behind them their equally powerful states and their activities, needed to be watched and even monitored in advance. For Singapore an understanding of the commercial strategies and movements of the multinationals was essential, in order to benefit from an advance awareness and preparation. It was a game of high stakes in which what ultimately paid off was the clarity of vision and purpose, the highly competent preparation of project proposals – often excelling in quality the proposals which came from the best brains of the multinationals themselves – indigenous trained manpower to implement them, and willingness to provide facilities and concessions to multinationals to get projects off the ground in the shortest possible time. Such detailed preparations were made to serve one ultimate goal and that is the economic growth of Singapore. Its well-known political scientist, Lau Teik Soon, said that 'international relations must serve the goals of national development with particular emphasis on economic growth'.[4]

To that end, the establishment of various boards and statutory bodies was most helpful. Through them it could not only furnish periodic initiatives, shifts in policy, and prepare proposals for offshore investors, but could also control a wide range of increasingly complex economic activity.

The other coordinate of such supervised and monitored economic activity was labour. There, too, the party in power, namely the PAP (People's Action Party), with its close relationship with trade union organisation, was able to make labour organisations realise that the party, the boards, statutory bodies and the union had a stake in making the economic policies bear fruits, and they must therefore work together.

In all these diverse undertakings what helped the most was the quality of top civil servants and the ministers in charge. There was an instinctive respect for their intelligence and integrity among the people. As Singapore began producing more and more social and economic results for its public, the respect for these men and women increased. These were no imitators of foreign models and solutions. They had a good grasp of the peculiar problems and potentials of Singapore's economy, and were cautiously improving and innovating their approaches to get maximum results all the time.

Such then were the compulsions of a micro state and its state managed society. Consequently, when we look at the broader issue of the diversity of the development process, we ought not to neglect the fact that Singapore's responses to development undertakings were shaped by its own built-in constraints as a small state, on the one hand, and the way these could be overcome by a skilful use of policy proposals and human resources, on the other. Unlike macro states such as China, India, the USA and Russia, it could not afford to be inward looking and had to prepare itself to go out and compete with others for the scarce investment dollar, not only in the ASEAN region but wherever it was available.

ii. The Chinese

Singapore is often mentioned as the fourth Chinese state after China, Taiwan and Hong Kong. Its ethnic composition in 1980 was as follows: Chinese 76.9 per cent; Malays 14.6 per cent; Indians 6.4 per cent; others 2.1 per cent. The Chinese concentration in Singapore had existed since before the colonial administration was established. Within the Chinese community, as among most Asian communities in the region, the family occupies a central place not only in social organisation but also in economic growth and the nature of the development process in general. In the following pages, therefore, we shall examine some of the insights into the Chinese family as generated by various anthropological studies. Simultaneously, we shall also look at the part played by the Chinese family as a block against the efforts of political authorities to restructure society to serve their broader social and economic goals.

One of the interesting aspects of this problem is the controversy among scholars who seem to put the blame on the Chinese family for everything that happened, or did not happen, in Chinese migratory societies. This controversy is significant from the point of view of what happened in Singapore because there, too, the Chinese had established a fragment of their own society, with their peculiar differences, which had implications for its social and ecconomic development. In this connection one of the arguments was that since the Chinese did not depersonalise their economic ventures, wherever they happen to emigrate, the family remained a vital unit of Chinese immigrant society.

One of the major works in the field is Maurice Freedman's *Chinese Family and Marriage in Singapore* (1970). Freedman had used the Singapore Chinese family to gain an insight into the Chinese family in China, where, for obvious reasons, this kind of research was not very easy to undertake until a few years ago. In adopting such an approach, Freedman may have underestimated the factor of adaptation in migrant communities. The other side of the argument was that since the Chinese immigrants to Singapore were also the founders, along with others, of that independent kingdom, their adaptations could have been more in the economic and political field than in social and cultural matters.

As far as Freedman was concerned his concentration was centred mainly on the kinship organisation of the overseas Chinese in a colonial society. Within the kinship itself, the family is the central unit. European observers often tend to describe it in negative terms as giving rise to ancestor worship, filial piety, large joint families, polygamy, etc.[5] The question for Freedman was whether the family was recreated in the same way by the Chinese who went overseas. Did such a family help or hinder the necessary adjustment to new economic and political conditions? What was the impact on the Chinese emigrés of the forces of Westernisation, Christianity and colonialism?

The bulk of Singapore Chinese are the descendants of Nan-yang Chinese who were traders or their subordinates. They came in search of trade, work, fortune and political refuge from secret societies. Whilst initially they were inclined to recreate their own kinship organisation, they were also forced to respond to the fact of colonial administration, a Western style legal system together with trade and industry, English education, and contact with the non-Chinese.[6] To begin with the Singaporeans became 'a branch' of the Chinese left behind in China and refused to 'depersonalise' their economic activity, but certain changes resulting from the impact of forces present in a different environment began to register themselves. Soon their marriage, adoption, *mui tsai* (adoption of sons-in-law) etc., began to have a character of their own. Moreover, they were also exposed to the cultural practices of the Chinese from different parts of China now coexisting with them in Singapore. In Singapore itself, there was the flourishing community of the Malayised and Westernised *babas* who sought a kind of 'retro-assimilation' with the Chinese after Singapore became independent. Other practices such as ancestor worship and filial piety no doubt continued, giving social stability to an immigrant community in a strange land.[7]

If the above practices were viewed as stabilising factors, then the question in reverse was what led to the phenomenon of chronic instability in Chinese society in the nineteenth century? One of the explanations for this is provided in Lee Poh Ping's *Chinese Society in Nineteenth Century Singapore* (1978). In this he argued that the British policy of free trade created a new Chinese society which then impinged upon 'an older Chinese society then existing in Singapore, based on gambier and pepper agriculture'. And social convulsions resulting from this situation stopped when the British themselves moved from free trade to colonialism.[8] A succession of economic changes in the way in which the Chinese made their living in Singapore directly or indirectly affected, though did not totally determine, their social organisation in a country to which they had emigrated. Over the years, Singapore's economy moved from pre-colonial free trade, to colonial control, to entrepôt economy, to manufacturing and service economy, to an international manufacturing and assembly economy. These successive phases in its economy evoked corresponding responses from the Chinese since they were the principal players in it.

Historically speaking, British traders shaped the British policy regarding commercial agriculture, and that in turn shaped the economic movement of the Nan-yang Chinese. As traders they were put in the middle position i.e. between the Malays and the Indians, on the one hand, and the British traders, on the other. Chinese traders were even encouraged to retain their cultural identity and middle level economic position, which differed from their position in other parts of Southeast Asia. Over the years, with the export of rubber and tin, the dependence of the European traders on the Chinese increased. The Chinese were moving into economic areas, or levels of economic activity, which were either being abandoned by the Europeans or not effectively handled by them. The Malacca Chinese, for instance, were entering into the fields of shipping and banking.[9] Simultaneously, they were suitably reshaping their own social organisation and cultural identity. After independence, several questions became important for the Chinese, one of which was how far to carry the re-sinification process, given the fact that Westernisation also had its own economic pay-off. Britain had already made Singapore a 'hub' of considerable commercial activity with which the Chinese were closely associated. So to follow the re-sinification route too far would have meant losing some of those international economic advantages. Singapore, therefore, followed the economic option, but allowed some degree of discussion on 'how much Westernisation' as encouragement. Moreover, an overly re-sinicised Singapore would have also created an ethnic problem of its own.

Apart from various pre-independence economic phases which had influence on its social organisation, the policies of independent Singapore not only in the fields of labour training but also in housing reshaped its family and social organisation in general. Janet Salaff, in her *State and Family in Singapore: Restructuring a Developing Society* (1988), argued that in the countries of Asia Pacific governments, including that of Singapore, were creating a different kind of labour force[10] by restructuring the family to suit the requirements of the multinationals. According to the author this was done in the following way. Many families which had exemplified 'the profile of third world poverty', in 1974–6, had progressed by 'sloughing off social bonds' to be 'integrated into a single class system'[11] in the middle 1980s. Two factors were mainly responsible for this: (i) services offering job training and technical education, which affected the kinship network; and (ii) public housing, to rent or purchase, together with family planning services, which enhanced the nuclear family 'at the expense of bonds with neighbour and kin'.[12]

With the neighbourhood and extended family of reduced importance, the nuclear family found itself increasingly dependent upon the services which the state offered. Thus through the economy and job training services, together with housing, Singapore was in effect restructuring its society.

However, by building her thesis on the sinister role of the state involving itself in restructuring society, Salaff may have overstated her case that developments in social organisation were induced by economic changes.[13] After all, changes in family structure, suggested by her, also transformed other European societies as a result of the impact of certain state policies which were not explicitly designed to change the nature of the family.

ii. The Malays

During the colonial period, the Malays were encouraged to go into the uniformed services, namely the police and the army, which they did. The colonial administration, in its earlier phase in the region, was relatively more strict with the Chinese. Having been brought in as labourers by contractors, apart from the traders among them, the Chinese had a much stronger social cohesion, imposed upon them by contractors or secret societies, and a clear direction of what they could or could not do imposed by the administration. When they became relatively more free from the controlling hands of contractors, their sense of cohesion and togetherness continued. Contrary to this, the Malays did not have a group with which to conform. In the words of Tania Li: 'The Singapore Malay culture has developed out of the varied traditions of the migrants and out of conditions of life in Singapore . . . The features that positively characterized Singapore Malayness, therefore, were the new identity developed *in situ*, such as the Malay language and religion.'[14] Such new identity gradually led to the crystallisation of 'ethnic sentiment distinguishing Malays from Chinese, Indians, and other non-Southeast Asians'.[15]

While the other ethnic groups in Singapore have their own stereotypes of the Malays as lazy, non-materialistic and given to spiritual things, etc., the Malays themselves have an ambivalent attitude to Malaysia, which lies just across the Johor bridge. However, the Malays of Singapore are treated as a cut below by the Malays of Malaysia, although in contrast the former tend to place themselves in a higher category from having to compete with the Chinese without much help from the state. Traditionally, the Malays and the Javanese, and within them the *sentris*, were well known for their pursuit of trade and commerce, and some of them had continued in those occupations despite Chinese resistance. Even as a minority in Singapore, the Malays preferred to try out their economic destiny in a rapidly growing country like Singapore rather than in the relatively less rapidly growing Malaysia.

One of the intriguing questions has been whether the dynamic economy of Singapore, which over the years has changed the social organisation of the Chinese, has also changed the social organisation of the Malays in any significant way. There are no simple answers to this question. While one finds a large proportion of Malay girls in the workforce of Singapore, always trying to emulate the Chinese girls, they also experience certain obstacles to their economic mobility imposed by the traditional component of their ethnicity.

The early Malay social life in Singapore revolved round the *istana* (palace), the mosque and the market. Over the years only the native born Malays in Singapore were left behind in that situation. The vacated places were filled by Jawi Peranakan (Malay women and South Indian Muslim men). The entrepreneurial Malays moved to other locations. Earlier, during colonial rule, the Malays believed that they would go far, economically, if they remained loyal to the British. To put that on a firm footing, in 1920, the Malays had established what was called Kesatuan Melayu Singapura or KMS. By means of such an organisation they planned to put their educational and economic demands before the colonial administration.

In the field of education, in particular, the Malays tried too many experiments relating to both religious education and education in the Malay language. That in the long run gave them a setback *vis-à-vis* the Chinese. The job market invariably required familiarity with English or Mandarin. Decisions in both these fields were made by a Malay leadership which had no long-term understanding of the nature of the problems which the younger Malays were facing.

From the beginning of independence in Singapore, the Malays failed to throw up a strong leadership which could effectively protect their interests. Over the years, the early Malay leadership had changed hands from the Jawi Peranakas to Malay Arabs and then to English educated Malays, but an active overall effective political leadership, in a modern sense, was still lacking. When the ruling political party in Singapore, which was bent upon developing a multi-ethnic plural society in which the influence of religious leaders was restricted to religious issues, the Malay leadership felt very uneasy. It did not agree with such demarcations and wanted to control the social and political conduct of the Malays by appealing to religious teachings. It also felt that the indigenous people of Singapore were not allowed to practise what they thought was their right. But there was no relenting from the line laid down for everyone so far as the appeal to religion was concerned. Having neglected the development of secular leadership, the Malays were far more affected by such a policy than the Chinese or the Indians.

The Malays of Singapore continued to sustain a separate identity. They were locked in competition with one of the most dynamic people in the contemporary world, namely, the descendants of the Nan-yang Chinese. In business, office, factory, school and university, the Malay younger generation had begun to realise that it had a long way to go.

iii. The Indians

Singapore Indians have been written about by many observers. Most of the nineteenth-century accounts saw Singapore as 'A European City', with an Indian neighbourhood which was a 'crowded filthy native locality'.[16] The locality in question here, until the early 1990s, had the appearance of a flourishing small town in southern India. Its appearance also inspired the well-known title by Kevin Lynch, *What Time Is This Place?* (1972).

The Indians have had an influence on the Malaysian Peninsula dating back to sixth and seventh centuries BC. Indeed, India had trade and cultural links with many parts of the Peninsula. However, when the Portuguese gained the control of Malacca in 1511 and the British arrived in Penang in 1786, the Indian economic and political influence there ended. After that, until Indian immigration to Malaysia was encouraged by the British colonial rule, only the traders continued to keep up contact with the Peninsula.

In order to develop Penang, Malacca and Singapore, Britain imported convicts from India to build what was described as the three 'Sidneys of India'. These three convict stations were managed by the Old John Company, and later on placed under the then government of India. To build some of the cities of the Peninsula, including Singapore, immigration from India began in 1833. Initially, most of the migrants were from the Tanjore district in southern India. The British sub-collector of the district whose responsibilities, among other things, also included law and order, had complained that the emigration was nothing but 'a regularly organized system of kidnapping'.[17] The recruitment, ill treatment, and brutalising of the Indians in Singapore had even become an issue in the Indian national movement. As early as 1937, Nehru had visited Singapore to find out for himself the conditions of the Indians.

The other side of Indian immigration to Singapore was the presence of traders and money lenders. It is said that there were 800 firms of money lenders in Malaysia from southern India called the Chettiars.

These were then followed by traders from other communities in India, such as the Sindhis, Gujaratis and Parsis. As traders, and because of the lack of cohesion among them, they could not compete successfully with either the British or the Chinese.

Sir Stamford Raffels allocated specific residential areas to each of the migrant groups. The Indians consisted of people from Tamil Nadu, Andhra Pradesh, Kerala, Utter Pradesh and Punjab. In addition, there were a few Bengalis, Parsees and Gujaratis. They brought with them their own regional identities, languages, religions, castes and customs. Serangoon Road in Singapore, which came to be known as 'the Little India' because of its cultural and linguistic diversity, almost became a fragment of India. So far as the caste system was concerned, it was described as the 'India–Singapore Caste Continuum'.[18]

Earlier, Singapore was treated as a place for Indian convict labourers. And those convicts, in the words of Professor K. S. Sandhu, came from different ethnic groups in India: 'Almost every stratum of Indian society was represented amongst the convicts, including Benares *brahmanas*, Sikhs and Dogras, *kshatriyas*, Chettiar, Bengali and Parsi financiers and ryots and untouchables from the various parts of the Subcontinent.'[19] After their penal sentence in 1838 when they were allowed to return, 60 per cent of them returned back to Singapore.

Since there were very few women among the Indians in the early migration, some of them married Malay women and embraced Islam. In 1901, there were 171 Indian women to every 1000 Indian men, but this improved to 482 women in 1931. Subsequently, more and more Indians went back to India to bring their brides.

The Indians not only carried their language, culture and social practices to Singapore but they also retained close ties with the land of their origin. 'The Indian Community never was and is not now, a hermetically sealed Singapore-based entity. It is a community within a country but with intricate connection to the world beyond.'[20] Singapore–India linkages – stretching into India's families, castes, villages and districts – continued. The short distance between the two countries, and the increasing facility for air travel for the very travel minded Indians, reduced the distance between the two countries even further.

The persistence of Indian culture proved to be of great value. Since Singapore has yet to develop its own cultural identity, being truly multiethnic and not mindlessly imitative of Western styles, the Indians continue to regard their cultural roots as embedded in the classical civilisation of India. Since their classical dances and classical music excel what is available in Singapore, by way of a poor imitation of Western popular music, rock music and dancing, the Indians continue to look to the country of their origin with great pride.

Paradoxically, 'the regional bully' image, which Singapore's *Strait Times* projects of India, because of latter's military and naval build-up, is secretly enjoyed by the Indians in Singapore. The fact is that India does matter. And the American media, in order to continue a role for the USA in Asia, continues to feed that image. In addition, middle-class professional Indians, who have done extremely well in Western countries, also boost the morale of their compatriots in Singapore. When the Singapore newspapers mention how Indian children in Britain achieve better exam results even in English language than British children, it is treated as a matter of pride by the Indians.

Modern day Singapore housing authorities now have second thoughts about scattering the Indian community in Singapore and thereby losing one of the major tourist attractions in the city, namely, Serangoon. And even if the Indians of Serangoon are scattered in different parts of Singapore because of non-ghetto policies on the part of the Singapore authorities, there is no knowing how soon long-standing Indian cultural capacities might devise new ways of overcoming the distance in housing, in what is after all a limited living space in Singapore. Such distances have not materially altered Indian cultural affinities in urban USA, Canada, Britain and elsewhere. Moreover, Indians abroad, including in Singapore, have learned to be more cohesive than before. Their professional and trading classes have begun to forge new bonds of common economic concerns, to fight against racial intolerance, and even to play a new role in pushing India out of its economic morass.

Given the large proportion of the Chinese population, its unceasing economic dynamism, and the vision and quality of its leadership, Singapore continues to have the imprints of the values and practical approach of the Chinese component of its population. During the building of modern Singapore, while the leaders from all ethnic groups have played some part under the overall leadership provided by the Chinese, the economic and social values and goals of its Chinese leadership have themselves been undergoing constant change. Later on, we shall examine the attempts made by Singapore's Chinese leadership to put to practical use the modernised version of traditional Confucian values of social discipline, respect for authority, reciprocity and togetherness. Singapore's normative roots, therefore, are embedded in the revised version of such traditional values and its leadership has found an extraordinarily practical use for them. Despite an outwardly Westernised exterior in the lifestyle of the average Singaporean, what has been put to effective social and economic development are the values that were inherited from the past. More about it later.

II. DYNAMIC POLITICAL ECONOMY

i. Devising Growth Strategies

Despite the fact that Singapore's earlier political leadership was exposed to the social and economic ideals of British Fabianism, in the actual shaping of its public policies its leadership was guided by clear notions of what was normatively desirable and what was socially and economically possible, given its limitations as a small country. Equally clear was the thinking of its leadership in setting up targets and priorities and the strategies needed to secure them. In this respect the leadership did not have any ideological sacred cows or trendy economic models. What was emphasised, from day one, was a thorough and rational understanding of the targets and strategies needed, as suggested by some of the best minds, and how to implement them. Thus in building its economy and society, Singapore utilised to the full its professional and scholarly resources and administrative experience.

In earlier years, Singapore's policy had consisted of finding effective ways of helping the private sector, as well as government undertakings, to bring about an 'an export oriented development'. To do that it provided: (a) physical infrastructure; (b) industrial parks; (c) manpower; (d) creation of a legal and administrative framework for industrial promotion; and (e) fiscal incentives for export led industries. But what was interesting in all this was that 'the visible hand of government and the invisible hand of the market ... went hand in hand.'[21]

Singapore's development strategy had not zeroed in straight away on an effective way of attaining its targets. It went through an experimental route, at first, of increasing the role of the state in the economy. The period between 1965 and 1984 is characterised as a period of 'the rise of the administrative state' in Singapore. And the 'administrative state' itself was defined by Chan Heng Chee as consisting of the: '(1) depoliticization of the citizenry, and (2) an increase in the power and role of bureaucrats, accompanied by the development and expansion of the bureaucratic and administrative sector.'[22]

This led to a symbiotic relationship between politicians, labour and bureaucrats. Such a triangular relationship worked very well because politicians were people of great skill and integrity, administrators had great efficiency, and the workers were willing to see the positive side of the various economic undertakings. What such a network also did was to shrink the arena of citizens' participation and their role as watchdogs of the actions of those who make use of public power. It ended up by creating 'a petitionary political culture'.[23]

Lee Kuan Yew's successor, Goh Chok Tong, tried to assuage the fears of the citizens who felt excluded. He therefore promised to adopt a more 'consultative' style.

Singapore currently falls into the category of the Newly Industrialised Economies (NIEs) like Hong Kong, South Korea and Taiwan. Each of these economies is trying 'to develop comparative advantage in more capital, knowledge, skill, intensive activities, and take measures to cope with the less favourable trading environment in the United States and Europe'.[24]

The development process of the NIEs is intimately tied up with what happens to older industrialised countries and the direct and indirect pressures they bring to bear on the new ones. Such a problem also sends the NIEs in search of new development strategies and opportunities. In other words, apart from the development of stragtegies which they need to devise to suit their own particular problems, they also have to take into account the international dimension which tries to dampen their efforts to develop. In this respect Singapore is far more dependent on, and therefore more vulnerable to, changes in foreign investment and transfer of technologies than are the other NIEs. Such a situation causes Singapore to prepare its development strategies far more carefully, pragmatically, and in advance of the others.

Thus Singapore had to take into account the 'contradictions and coalitions' of economic forces which were global, regional, and national, and then find within them an effective strategy for its own development.[25] In all these efforts, Singapore did not adopt a neo-classical position in its entirety, but like Japan brought into play a highly effective role for the state in devising development strategies. At the other extreme, it had to take into account the distrust of the state on the part of its trading community. B. G. Yeo, its Minister of State for Finance and Foreign Affairs, remarked that Nan-yang traders did not trust the government.[26]

Apart from stable government and geographic location, Singapore also possessed the 'ingredients' whereby business could flourish. These were: (i) a developed infrastructure; (ii) an industrious, disciplined and well-trained workforce; (iii) well-established international trading links; and (iv) relatively cheap labour. But these factors by themselves were not going to produce results, they had to be put to effective development use. And Singapore did precisely that.

Very early in its development strategy, it moved away from the short-sighted industrialisation which went with import substitution. Instead it aimed at export led growth and threw open its economy to various multinationals for investment. This no doubt increased its dependence both on foreign capital as well as on the transfer of technology. But as long as these could produce results, the external interest in developing Singapore's economy continued. In 1979, it entered another phase of development to 'supplant' labour-intensive, low skill, low value added economic activities, with capital intensive high technology and high value added ventures. This meant that its manpower had to be constantly retrained,[27] and 'brain services' constantly launched and updated. Added to this were its efforts to become a centre of finance, travel, and of all the high-tech developments in the region.[28] Thus what Singapore's development efforts indicated was a constant effort on its part to be ahead of others in launching new approaches and producing results all the time, and not resting but continually moving forward.

ii. Economic Growth and National Security

Given its micro dimensions, Singapore could not ignore the question of its national security as an aspect of its development process. While attending to the concerns of social and economic development, and the effective strategies needed to attain various targets within its development goals, Singapore was also required to pay attention to the problem of using its geopolitical location; to the newly developed facilities for international trade, banking, communication, technology and trained manpower; and above all to its growing capacity to act as a middleman between countries and concerns with limited direct access to one another. For Singapore, paying attention to these, with considerable development opportunities for itself, was a matter of self-survival. So the first thing it was forced to do was to act as a trader, investment client and subcontractor to investors overseas, no matter how very distasteful these roles and the countries involved in them were. It had to deal with them as trading partners or clients and thus could not afford to align itself with any one nation or bloc. It might be necessary to buy and sell goods and offer services to any nation including the former Soviet Union and China. Simultaneously, Western countries and their multinationals had to be kept interested in Singapore and its security. Thus there was trade with China, the servicing of Soviet vessels, and the attracting of multinationals to invest in Singapore and use its various manufacturing, assembling, and value adding facilities for exporting goods all over the world, including Western countries. Singapore has, over the years, turned this multitrading role, with its enormous pay-off, into a fine art. From the start, its model for this was another highly successful micro state, namely, Switzerland.

At the height of the cold war, Singapore would not allow America's phobia of China and Russia to restrict its style, persuading the Americans of the supreme value of knowing more about the non-belligerent aspects of the enemy. Such a tradesmanlike stance, which is the other side of the coin, was fully appreciated by the Americans, although they took their own time to do so. When Singapore did not denounce China at the time when the American-sponsored resolution was presented to the United Nations, some time ago, the Americans fully understood the underlying strategy. Singapore learned from Switzerland that a trader's neutrality will be respected and appreciated by both sides in the long run.

Its approach in the region and beyond has been to support emerging countries as well as declining countries in their trade with Singapore. Whether they grow more important or less significant in the years to come they still will have to trade. While trading belligerent instincts are kept in check and the moment comes when the time and reason for belligerence is past. So the need for guns can be abrogated by building manufacturing units and shopping malls, and with orders for buying and selling. Singapore has carried that message to all its trading partners and has, in the process, also transformed itself economically and thereby reduced the risk to its national security.

For a long time China regarded Singapore with suspicion because of its pro-Western sympathies. However, since China needed the overseas markets, which both Singapore and Hong Kong could provide, its denunciation of Singapore as a stooge of the big powers in the past was purely rhetorical, and Singapore realised this. While the denunciatory rhetoric took its time to die down, trade between the two countries expanded phenomenally. And in late 1992 Lee Kuan Yew denounced the governor of Hong Kong for wanting to introduce 'democracy' after nearly one hundred years of colonial rule, which would create problems for China. Instead, his advice was to learn to trade with communist countries during their process of change, and to try to understand the ways of red bureaucrats. Then he turned around and exhorted his own countrymen to invest in China.[29]

A similar practical approach was adopted by Singapore towards Japan. Over the years, it overcame the anti-Japanese feeling resulting from the Second World War. The next question was how to view the future role of this economic superpower within the region. It was easy to share Western prejudice and fears of Japan, but that might not help Singapore. Moreover, the contribution of post-war Japan in building the economies of Southeast Asia, and in that process undoubtedly building future competitors for itself, could not be overlooked. And in this respect the top leadership provided a balanced perspective on Japan. Despite the Western media's reiteration of the fact that Japan's ascendency was cause for concern, Singapore did not forget that Japan was its largest trading partner and an example of what a nation can become even though it lacked many natural resources of its own. Thus Singapore did not accept the Western stereotype of Japan and its alleged designs in Asia.

For its own survival and economic growth Singapore has developed a dynamic and experimental disposition which is perhaps unequalled in the developing world or in the developed world of tigers and cubs. It has turned its dynamic for survival into developmental dynamism. It has also changed the constraints of its micro dimensions into a facility for experimentation and course corrections whenever necessary. Its limited population of 2.6 million people, living on an island with very limited resources, are constantly reminded to exercise development forethought and to undertake a careful examination of the available alternatives. In its development strategies, Singapore did not allow unquestioning acceptance of traditional wisdom, Western models or ideologies laying claim to social justice. Everything had to be discussed, thrashed out with the help of the best brains and available experience, and then implemented with unswerving efficiency bordering on ruthlessness. Once policy was agreed upon its implementation was absolute.

III. THE VISION OF THE FOUNDING FATHERS AND POLITICAL INSTITUTIONS

i. The Founding Fathers

In the building of Singapore, the vision of its leadership, and Lee Kuan Yew in particular, has played an important part. Lee, and the meritocratic team that he built round himself, made Singapore, in a span of three decades, the envy of the developing and developed world. Unlike some of the strong men in developing countries, Lee preferred to surround himself with some of the most talented, skilled and experienced people available and gave them plenty of scope to operate so that they could contribute their best to the building of Singapore. Some of the methods used by him, especially in the silencing of his critics, were not always above board and he therefore became a subject of both adoration and ridicule at the hands of his biographers. In this section we shall have a close look at his vision, development strategies and performance.

One of the biographers of Lee Kuan Yew has observed that 'he represents an Asian version of pragmatism and a set of socio-economic values adapted to suit the special conditions of a developing country; his place in history is solidly based on his achievements which have made Singapore's level of prosperity second only to that of Japan's'.[30]

Unlike most other Asian leaders of the post-war generation, Lee, in his earlier years, was not a populist leader but a power broker between organised political and economic forces. He succeeded in making himself indispensable and maintained that role until such time as he and his colleagues were in positions of power.

Since he did not rise by means of populist support, he developed a contempt for those who did. And because he did not interact politically with the common man, he never developed a sense of popular mandate, a repository of electoral trust with accountability attached to the use of public office. Furthermore, as his political party, the PAP, did well in election after election, and Singapore went from strength to strength, Lee did not have occasion to cultivate a sense of being a representative and therefore answerable to those who put him in office. On the contrary, each election was treated by Lee and his colleagues as an occasion merely to announce what they were going to do next. Throughout his political career Lee remained uncomfortable with situations of dialogue, mandate and accountability, and of the cumbersome process of evolving democratic decisions in which every participant felt that he/she was listened to and included. Repeatedly he felt that Singapore did not need all these trappings of liberal democracy. He had no conception that together with an improvement in the standard of living, people also needed to grow by means of their participatory involvement; that development was more than just attending to the standard of living, housing, education, medical services and pensions; that its ultimate test was growth and development *as* human beings. For Lee this was merely mushy political liberalism. Ultimately, what mattered for emerging countries was a good standard of living, education, housing, and social sevices for everyone. In providing these his contribution was second to none, not only in developing countries but also in those already developed. He wiped out poverty and even introduced a measure of distributive justice, but saw no need to deepen the normative commitment of his society and treat these achievements as a means to the enrichment of human social and cultural life in general. He balked at human enrichment, quality of intellectual life, creative cultural contribution, and the sense of freedom which all come through the involvement and participation of human beings themselves. He merely wanted them to be happy as a result of what he had done for them in the social and economic field.

On the cultural side of Singapore's development, Lee was worried about the fragmenting of its multicultural society if the three cultural groups, and in particular the Chinese, overemphasised their own cultural roots. His own ancestors came from the Hakkas of northern China, but added a mixture of Malay and Indonesian blood as they made headway into the Malaysian Peninsula in search of economic fortune. He therefore wanted to discourage too much emphasis on cultural roots. He repeatedly opposed the outright re-Sinonisation of the Chinese population in cultural terms, especially during such functions as the Chinese New Year. Moreover, beyond its own shores Singapore was surrounded by a sea of Malays.

Lee therefore deliberately introduced a move towards Westernisation whereby each ethnic group was supposed to find its own economic level which matched its economic acumen. The Westernisation of Singapore thus created an economic race where the government of the day, run largely by Chinese politicians, could not be accused of favouritism. It was possible to sink or swim economically, progressing to various levels of prosperity if one became educated, learned new skills, showed economic enterprise, and grabbed the development opportunities that came one's way.

In an economic race of this type, the Chinese, as could be expected, flourished the most in business and high-tech industries; Indians with professional backgrounds, especially those who came via Sri Lanka, did well in the professions and services; while the Malays did not always register as having done well in any specific economic category.

The net result of all this was that while Lee was accused of many things during his long political career, no one accused him of favouring one ethnic group over another. Chinese businessmen favoured their fellow Chinese, Tamils fraternised with fellow Tamils, and the Malays got together to improve their economic backwardness. But this was at the level of group effort and not as a result of the government's doing. Lee thus steered clear of the ethnic problem. Whenever he spoke to ethnic groups, his message was to 'forget separate identities; think of Singapore; cooperate with the government'.[31]

Lee had his own confrontations with the newspapers and journals of various countries. The papers which praised his pragmatism and performance also ran down his illiberal tendencies. In the early years of Singapore's independence, the *Daily Mirror*, 'likened Lee Kuan Yew to Goebbels'. The *Daily Express* implied that Lee had hijacked Singapore's freedom. 'To such men Britain entrusts independence. Greedily they seize their new freedom for themselves and deny it to the people for whom it was intended.'[32] Then there was the controversial victory, in 1989–90, over the *Far Eastern Economic Review* for libel in the courts of Singapore. And there were references to dynastic rule in Singapore, when Lee's son, B. G. Lee, was included in the cabinet of Lee's successor, Goh Chok Tong.

In the first ten years after independence the economy grew phenomenally. The production of goods and services doubled. Singapore became industrialised and emerged as a major centre of international trade and finance. Low cost housing sprung up, town planning took education and medical facilities into account and provided a world class service, and the people of a micro state experienced the euphoric feeling of boundless growth.

After that, Lee's ambitions became global. Instead of depending on regional prospects, which were fraught with jealousy and suspicion, he began, what he called 'plugging into the global market', with the help of the multinationals who wanted to trade and manufacture in Asian locations – provided they got facilities for finance, trained manpower, transport and communication. Lee made no secret of the fact that outside North America, Europe and Japan the facilities provided by Singapore, even in technology and electronics, were second to none. Through their vision, skill and daring, Lee and his men made Singapore, in the third decade after independence, a global city with manufacturing, banking, shipping, technology and communication facilities found only in the most developed Western countries. And in certain respects, in those fields, he even placed Singapore ahead of them.

The Western countries which benefited from Singapore's bold initiatives called it an Asian democracy performing economic miracles. Daniel Patrick Moynihan, the then US Ambassador to India, showed great enthusiasm over what a flexible and pragmatic Singapore was able to achieve which India, with all its talents, did not seem able to do. The comparison was restricted strictly to Singapore's GDP performance.

For Lee there were political costs to be paid in terms of the suppression of those elements which led to political instability. From his point of view, in a developing country, in the absence of traditions of liberal governance and the automatic acceptance of liberal dos and don'ts, economic growth cannot be achieved in a situation of political instability. While he did not mention India, his followers did – as an example of liberal democracy and limited economic growth. For Lee, therefore, politics had to take a backseat or, better still, be left to him and his men. Singapore thus gave to its would-be investors an assurance that they did not have anything to fear by way of instability, changes in government, politicians, ideologies and political philosophies. Singapore was as stable as a Western country and wedded to pragmatism in public policy so as to improve the economic life of its people.

Western statesmen, diplomats, envoys, investors and media people praised the principle of democracy, implying that it was for *them*, not for an Asian country, and then went on to shower favours and praise on a regime which had given stability for them to do business with.

Progressively, fewer and fewer Western statemen and media people spoke of the quality of political life as a necessary aspect of development. Everyone spoke about the cleanliness of the city, the high rise housing, the shopping malls, the transport system, the airport, and the incredible efficiency of the bureaucratic machinery.

In the meantime, Singapore's pragmatic approach to public policy was widely acknowledged and applauded – there were no sacred cows or traditions or ideological commitments. And as far as its pragmatism was concerned, only the people in power were the sole judges of that. It was a governmental pragmatism in which neither the professions, the media, the elites, academia or individuals had an independent voice. They had already been approached on a select basis when pragmatic public policies were drafted. Outside those circles there was no more pragmatism to be found. When some of those policies were abandoned, overnight, as in the case of the size of family, and the need for graduates to produce more children, equal claim to pragmatism was recognised in diametrically opposite positions. By definition then, whatever those in power did was pragmatic enough. There was no more pragmatism left to add, especially by those who were not a part of the power structure.

This made a lot of Singaporeans political disbelievers and cynics in their hushed outpourings. Right from the academics to the cabmen you heard a lot of reservations on too much success claimed and too much pragmatism paraded. For a country which had achieved so much, this could have been avoided. But then all this did not bother Lee. He even thought that it was a harmless way of letting off steam.

What we thus had in Lee was a leader who had not only shaped Singapore into a development miracle but in turn was also shaped by the limitations and strategies devised to ensure its survival. One could even see a kind of lasting generational imprints on him. When he came to power, there was criticism of the leaders of developing countries for being too soft on their own people. Gunnar Myrdal, in particular, with his concept of 'the soft state', explained the reason why developing countries were in a mess. Lee wanted a different kind of Singapore where policies were implemented and laws were obeyed, no matter what. He vowed that Singapore would not be another soft state – and it was not.

In building Singapore, Lee was supported by the deep commitment and unfailing assistance of his finance minister, Dr Goh Keng Swee, and foreign minister, S. Rajratnam. While Goh was the architect of various pragmatic policies and the constant changes within them, Rajratnam brought to bear his keen understanding of the limitations and opportunities for a micro state in national and international fields.

Highly respected for his 'monumental intellect', Goh Keng Swee earned the reputation of a 'problem solver'. As such he was moved from one problem situation to another, and to each of them he applied an intellectual-cum-pragmatic approach.[33]

Of the 'big three'[34] leaders, Rajratnam had had the greatest exposure to Fabian socialism while at the LSE, and therefore the distance he had to travel towards pragmatising, and putting into practice, Singapore's policies was about the boldest and the most difficult. In a span of three decades these three had put Singapore into the big league of Western industrialised countries, with a commensurate urban lifestyle and the constant acquisition of advanced skills for its people. And what is more it even imports unskilled labour from neighbouring countries to do the jobs its skilled population prefers not to do.

Nevertheless, Singapore does have a sense of rootlessness, resulting from a blind search for its own roots and ending up with a cheap imitative pseudo-Western identity which earns it no respect for culture either in the west or with its Asian neighbours who have now pumped a lot of life into their own classical performing arts. Indonesia, Thailand, Malaysia and even the Philippines have, to different degrees, revitalised their cultural roots and built on them. And Singapore, with its great resources and managerial efficiency, could have done wonders to its triple cultural heritage by experimenting and then projecting a new integrated Asian indentity. Its dimensions are ideally suited to any experiment it cared to launch. Moreover, it has the genius for it, the experience of it, and a pragmatic sense of getting results from it. In undertaking such a syncretic exercise it might have rivalled Asia's other nation with a genius for cultural syncretism, namely, Indonesia.

As neighbours become more industrialised, technologically more sophisticated, and more attractive to offshore investors, Singapore may find difficulty in staying at the top of the pile. Within the ASEAN family it remains important as long as its neighbours remain backward. However, not only ASEAN's but even Asia's larger picture is in the process of continuous change. And when countries like China and India come on stream technologically in the next century, with various smaller powers exercising influence through various regional bodies, Singapore may be left with an awkward colonial image of a Western cloned nation. With all this coming on top of its micro dimensions it may suffer a great setback. While Lee, who had been impeccably futuristic in all the things that he did, in Singapore itself he missed out on the fact that nations like people do not live by bread alone.

i. Reconstituted Political Process

Understanding the political development of Singapore confronts us with some peculiar problems. This is because there is a tendency to view it from the perspective of either dependency theory or deductive theory, i.e., deducing political development from economic growth, as in the case of Japan. According to the former, since in the economic growth of Singapore, the MNCs have played a major role in terms of investments, it is presumed that they must have twisted Singapore's arms to keep its opposition leaders, unions, and media in line.[35] And according to the latter, since Singapore, like Japan, has had an explosive economic growth, it must have done everything politically correct. And, therefore, why even bother to find out how very substantial has been the political development of Singapore and Japan. Should one merely ask questions relating to political development only in the case of those societies which are in trouble economically, and look the other way when their economic growth is in good shape.[36] Unfortunately, even those countries which swear by liberal democracy have maintained such standards in their evaluative judgments.

In this book we shall avoid these two extreme theoretical positions: of making political development dependent upon international economic interests or merely a deduction of economic growth. Instead we shall adopt an analytical approach when viewing specific events which shaped Singapore's political process over the years. The elections of 1968 and 1972 gave the ruling party a mandate to build 'a modern industrial state' and 'a global city', respectively. But with that also came a 'tight society'.[37] From then on political institutions were turned into instruments for implementing policies and the will of the ruling party. In print and the electronic media there was never much criticism of the policies which the government had decided to pursue. Occasionally, there were suitably cut and edited versions of comments on policies. Even in the readers' columns of newspapers, few letters appeared questioning indirectly the wisdom of some policies.

Unlike the Indian subcontinent, and especially India, which came through an historical experience of questioning British rule throughout, Singapore had no such experience. The Kuomingtang in Singapore, which was formed in 1912, and the Malay Communist Party, which had been active during the Japanese occupation, did not do much to build a questioning political culture. Nor did they emphasise political participation as a political goal. The PAP thus instilled an uninterrupted tradition of political compliance, nurturing a political culture in which submission rather than opposition was rewarded. In the words of Professor Chan Heng Chee again: 'The style of governance looks for the elimination of politics.'[38] Further, it 'disdains the need for conciliation and trusts in the expertise and the judgment of the leadership'.[39]

It all then boils down to the politically numbing effect of economic prosperity. The years of lean economic growth stimulated a greater emphasis on the scrutiny of policies. Surely Singapore would be well advised to launch an orderly increase in participation when economic conditions are good and the sense of public well-being unmistakable. In fact, in the winter of 1989, we requested Lee Kuan Yew to grant us an interview to discuss what we called 'participatory soft landing'. Unfortunately, that privilege was denied to us.

In spite of its obsession with economic prosperity and political stability, the PAP was not devoid of people with a socialist past and the ruboff effect it had had on its policy in general. While educated Singaporeans became involved in modernising the economy and improving its standard of living, those with socialist leanings became useful in making mass contact and in undertaking 'mass mobilisation'. Singapore did not have a feudal element in its society nor, mercifully, a bureaucracy which could have been obstructionist, negative and self-serving. Even the radical element within the PAP lost its *raison d'être* because the economy was going from strength to strength, with a good standard of living enjoyed by the population. It was therefore relatively easy to emphasise values which might look paternalistic and even folksy in other contexts, such as 'work hard, save and achieve, be socially disciplined, adapt to constant change, be pragmatic, avoid complacency . . . ensure that the social order and cohesiveness of the country' are not threatened.[40]

It was not politics but discipline and hard work that paid dividends – that was the message. In a short span Singapore became a rich country with a standard of living next only to that of Japan in Asia. It also became an international centre of finance, banking, shipping, technology, oil exploration, trained manpower, education and medical facilities, in short all those things which may be said to be the attributes of a highly developed nation. What is more, its urban environment, transport facilities, housing, safety in the streets, and absence of corruption would place it above almost any other Western country. In the words of its former foreign minister, S. Rajratnam, its new religion was 'money-theism', and the price tag was the 'depoliticisation of public life'.[41]

In order to sustain such a level of development, which was by no means an easy task, Singapore went in search ceaselessly of people of exceptional merit in the professions, banking, shipping, commerce, industry, academia, the construction industry, and so on.[42] These men and women had been trained in world's best universities. They were as much at home in public life as in the professions and academia, and they did not have to worry about politics which was handled by those who specialised in mobilisation. Singapore has thus become a 'technocratic society'[43] of a high calibre in Asia. In that sense it also subscribes to the view that 'technology holds all the answers to the important problems facing human civilization and that society is better off with rational application of scientific techniques'.[44] Singapore has thus become an 'administrative state'.[45]

iii. Mobilisation in a Closed Society

Lee may be said to be the real discoverer of the value of mobilisation in Asia Pacific. Apart from national movements, waged against colonial powers, and communist mobilisation before and after independence, most countries in the region took support for the regime for granted and therefore did not engage in mobilisation. Lee used mobilisation until the very end of his stay in office, and even in this respect his sensitivity for results was unrivalled. He therefore had no hesitation in dropping some mobilisation efforts halfway through and launching others instead.

In the winter of 1989, we were amazed to see posters, TV ads, and radio comments about the relinquishing of various Chinese dialects and the sole retention of Mandarin. No one could possibly dispute the value of adopting a common language and graduating from dialects to a more evolved language such as Mandarin. Normally, one would expect a quiet effort in that direction to be made in schools and universities. But not in Singapore, where the place for mobilisation, as in classical Athens, was always the market-place. Grocery stores, shopping malls, hawkers' stalls, wet markets, etc., all displayed enormous placards advertising the abandonment of dialects and the adoption of Mandarin. While that appeared to be a matter in which the state had followed a more aggressive and presumably quicker route to change the language, it only lasted a few days and then reverted back to the quiet work done in schools and universities.

More irksome to the citizens, however, was the propaganda, and the subsequent change in it, relating to how many children citizens should have. When the campaign was launched each couple was asked to produce two children. Then qualifications appeared saying that they could have more if they were graduates. Finally, the campaigning with regard to the size of the family was given up when Singaporeans started talking about the 'invasion' of their bedrooms, and external critics began making comparisons with Hitler-style eugenics. At such moments the Singaporeans realised that they would have killed the very idea had they been allowed to express their views. And all this was happening at a time when Singapore was experiencing shortages of manpower and giving work permits to people from neighbouring countries.

There was also a positive side to mobilisation. Like other 'new' countries formed by immigrants, Singapore had the problem of welding together various ethnic groups into a new nation. Different 'new' countries such as the USA, Canada, Australia, New Zealand, etc., have had different degree of success in attaining that goal. In the case of Singapore the problem was more complex. Singapore had literally been a meeting ground of the world's two most powerful, living, classical civilizations, namely, the Chinese and the Indian, both of whom are considered to have a very strong cultural appeal to their people. Then there are the Malays and Eurasians who, over the years, have developed their own distinctive lifestyle, and, in the case of the former, a living culture. Given such divisions, what Singapore needed was a mobilisation which could bring its diverse population together and give it a sense of belonging. For that purpose, the media, schools, party exhortations and all conceivable means of socializing have been used.

In addition to that, what was also cultivated was a sense of orderliness, cleanliness, courtesy, quick response in government offices, and social discipline in general. In a literal sense the Singaporeans have internalised social discipline. But social discipline, in particular, has unfortunately been utilised to facilitate obedience to authority. The average citizen, under the weight of social discipline, does not think that it is his right to question, criticise and replace his government. Whenever such thoughts arise he or she discusses them with close friends and not in the open. In liberal political terms the cost of keeping Singapore well ordered, clean, quick in official response and socially disciplined is limitation in political freedom.

The leadership of Lee in Singapore, and the way he shaped his country from its very inception, will be discussed by scholars for a long time to come. For one thing, there is not another developing country which even remotely approaches what Singapore has achieved. With all its mobilisation and control, Singapore is not a blatantly repressive society: it is a closed society where the will of the ruling group prevails. Dissidents are neither beaten up nor hounded: they are just made innocuous or involved in long and expensive litigation for infractions of the law. It is a closed society in which political power and influence are not accessible to those who are outside the PAP, and where the amazing economic performance and general prosperity of the people often make you wonder whether what you want to achieve by way of criticism and denunciation is worthwhile. The prospective critic is, therefore, often turned into a self-doubting isolationist. No one can predict which way the development process of Singapore will go: will it follow the direction of South Korea or Taiwan or just remain content with what it has materially and look for more?

IV. NORMATIVE–PRAGMATIC BALANCE IN A MERITOCRATIC SOCIETY

i. Normative Parallels of a Multi-ethnic Society

One of the difficult tasks is to identify the normative basis of Singapore's society apart from the official version of it. So far as its societal versions are concerned, cultural fragmentation and isolation have given rise to separate normative bases on ethnic lines. At the official level modernisation – industrial, technological, urban, educational, linguistic, social and political, in the sense of a law abiding socially disciplined society – is continually emphasised.

As a society, which is entirely urban, educated, affluent, disciplined and conscious of its achievement, it is constantly reminded that the route to follow is modernisation and even Westernisation. These have served its people well in the past and therefore there must not be any second thoughts concerning their usefulness. Simultaneously, Singapore also experimented with the possibility of using traditional Confucian values of respect for authority, family, social cohesiveness, reciprocity and social discipline, by giving them a modern interpretation and then popularising them through educational institutions. But that was given up for fear of the non-Chinese accusing the state of sinicising of their values. The net result of this was that the state and society came to have different normative bases, unrelated but linkable whenever the need arose.

Over the years, the Singapore Chinese had also changed. They were no longer only street smart Chinese traders who came from the Nanyang region to make a quick profit and then think of returning 'home'. After several years, Singapore was their 'home'. In the meantime trading contacts with Europeans, mainly the British, and later on Americans, also taught them that they could do better by organising their business on Western lines, and by concentrating on areas such as industry, banking, insurance, shipping, electronics, travel and hotels, and above all by joining hands with the European, Japanese and American multinationals. But that required the necessary education and skills. Until the 1980s the learning of such skills was possible only by going abroad. The ambitious families among them sent their young abroad, but soon the learning of all these skills became possible in Singapore itself. Nevertheless, the more ambitious continued to go abroad for higher training.

Chinese pragmatics during those years continued to show great success in adapting, innovating and securing the intended results. As they infiltrated modern Western style business and industry, they also made use of their family support and the cohesiveness of the extended group outside family. In that sense the modern Chinese of Singapore have put all their traditional attributes, such as family, hard work, social discipline and reciprocity, etc. to the greatest possible pragmatic use. In that sense also their development has been closer, on parallel, though not similar lines, to that of the Japanese.

Malay social values, in Singapore at least, continued as a process of reflection, argument and group controversy. This was because some Malays thought that historically Singapore belonged to Malaysia, while others felt that they could live there only as expatriates and not as first-class citizens. Therefore, it was necessary to observe traditional Malay values and at state level to remain law abiding, loyal citizens. Finally, if the situation became too difficult they could always go back to Malaysia.

Some of the Malays in Singapore adopted a more pronouced religious identity, often as a reflection of what was going on in Malaysia and in the Middle East, whilst others preferred their expatriate status with more social freedom and a modern urban environment, together with better education facilities for their children. Politically, they had no strong preferences beyond the recognition of their cultural contribution to Singapore as a whole and a few official positions for some of their number.

The case of the Indian minority group was different. The educated among them competed successfully with others in the professions and for employment in private firms. This, coupled with their pride in the classical civilisation of India, gave them an extraordinary amount of self-confidence to participate in discusssion on various social and economic issues and to give their own views on what the solutions ought to include. So far as the less educated were concerned, they merely accepted the values of their caste and religion as imparted by members of family and social and religious leaders.

Politically, the Indians were inclined to be more articulate even though their views were frowned upon by the authorities. The educated amongst them were deeply influenced by the Indian national movement and the continuous critical evaluation of colonial rule. They thought this was the right attitude to adopt even in Lee's Singapore, and frequently questioned decisions and made suggestions for governance in a society that was accustomed to listening only to those at the top. Invariably the top political leaders amongst them were in trouble with the PAP style administration.

Like the Malays some of them toyed with the idea of returning to India but eventually settled for their expatriate status. This minimised their effectiveness in a society in which they had made their home. There were also those among them who had overcome such problems and wanted to play a full part in Singapore's social and economic life – and in some cases had extraordinary success in doing so.

Unlike the Chinese, the Indians lacked cohesiveness – regional differences, language, religion and caste were some of the aspects that prevented unity. But they did come together when problems of the utmost importance occurred for the entire community.

ii. Normatitve Commitments of the Founding Fathers

The three founding fathers of modern Singapore are Lee Kuan Yew, S. Rajratnam and Goh Keng Swee. Some of their contributions, both normative and pragmatic, will conclude this chapter.

The social and political ideals to which Lee subscribed changed during his years in power. As a student at Cambridge, and later on as a nationalist leader, he had come under the influence of liberal political ideology tinged with British socialism. In office, however, these gave way to a constant exploration for solutions to practical problems in building the economy of Singapore and ensuring its continuous economic growth. To achieve this, right from the start, he went in search of those highly educated, gifted and experienced people who would help him to find solutions. When there was a shortage of people in specialised areas, Lee sent them for training and then used them in his team. He believed that a society which puts its talented people in charge also reaps the benefit of the quality of their mind, energy and character. Their services are not free and adequate financial compensation must be provided for what they contribute. By adopting such an approach he built a virtual meritocracy with little or no room for public scrutiny. Until the end of his stay in office in Singapore and beyond, Lee remained convinced that non-Western societies, given their social problems and economic backwardness, ought not to be burdened with the load of liberal democracy which exists in advanced Western societies.

Since society in developing countries has not advanced significantly, either as a result of colonial intrusion or the nature of their political regimes, unqualified introduction of liberal institutions, he thought, should be the last thing they should aim at. The two immediate goals should be to reform the administration and pursue economic growth. For both these he placed responsibility squarely on the shoulders of top executives. In his own words:

> research and analysis will probably show that success or failure was quite unconnected with the constitutional pattern of authority, but

more closely dependent upon the quality of leadership – *the first leader and the men immediately surrounding him.* If together they constitute a balanced team in which ability and intellect are matched with imagination and executive capacity, success is more likely.[46]

While Lee remained in charge of the overall formulation and implementation of public policy, Goh Keng Swee was the economic architect of Singapore's amazing achievements. His policies balanced the role of the privatised economy under the overall supervision of the state and its various statutory bodies, on the one hand, and served the broad social goal of keeping income disparities in check, on the other.

S. Rajratnam steered Singapore's external relations with extraordinary imagination and skill. His contribution was also unique in warding off the ideological attacks on Singapore which came especially from socialist quarters and by which all its founding fathers, at some stage, were influenced.

Rajratnam, along with Goh and Lee, agonised over the problem of what would work and what would not, given Singapore's peculiar problems. Their education in Britian, involvement in the anti-colonial movement and, above all, their close association with Barisan Socialis, had brought them close to the corpus of socialist ideas. But when they went into the business of building the economy of independent Singapore in 1965, they had the advantage over a country like India where its founders too were exposed to the similar ideological influence of Fabian socialism. In 1947, the founding father of the Indian Republic, Jawaharlal Nehru, and various economists who acted as his advisers, did not have the benefit of knowing what had happened to Fabian socialism in the country of its origin, namely, Great Britain. In that respect Singapore was more fortunate, for it witnessed nearly two decades of socialism in Britain which had not given a good account of itself. Consequently, by 1965 Singapore began to question its validity, and also its suitability. The three founding fathers thus brought with them a kind of socialist conscience, and although Singapore remained a market economy which was supervised and managed by the state, with a strong component of multinational interest, it, nevertheless, did not allow the disparity of income to get out of hand.

Lee, Goh and Rajratnam were also the architects of turning Singapore into 'a global city'. Given its micro dimensions, Singaporeans were exhorted to give up their inward-looking shopkeeper's mentality and go beyond their comfortable shopping malls, hawkers' stalls and wet markets. There were neighbours and industrial countries to trade with, but more than that, Singapore had to become an indispensable component of multinational manufacturing. Given the revolution in transport, whereby the cost of the transportation of goods had not kept pace with the cost of labour, multinationals were relocating themselves in countries where they could find cheap labour. Singapore, however, had to do better, by providing skilled labour for high-skilled, high-tech, high-paying manufacturing industries and assembly plants. Simultaneously, there had to be educational facilities for constantly updating skills, banking, shipping and research. The globalisation of Singapore also meant avoiding close association with any particular group of nations, ideology, regional perceptions and collective grievances. It could always get out of an awkward situation by saying that it was a micro state. In fact its micro state status and global city aspirations worked ideally together. Multinationals felt attracted to it because it was politically stable, business minded, full of facilities, and of dimensions which could easily be manipulated if problems arose. In turn, the presence of the multinationals helped Singapore to ride on their backs, plug into their markets, become an indispensable part of their overall strategy and planning away from its shores.

V. SOME GENERAL OBSERVATIONS

In all six ASEAN countries that we are examining in this volume, the economic dynamism of the Chinese, generated by their normative commitment and pragmatic approach, is of vital importance to their respective economic growth. But in Singapore, which is overwhelmingly Chinese, their social values and their methods of finding solutions are carried out in a businesslike manner. What therefore passes as a normative and/or pragmatic approach in Singapore is essentially what the Chinese component of its population has brought to bear on it.

The Chinese component, as we noted elsewhere, has its personal and social norms which are deeply rooted in the traditional values of Confucianism, together with individual and family experiences both in the place of their origin and in the Malay Peninsula. They also include their experiences in pre- and post-colonial Singapore. Combined with this is the common-sense wisdom of the unskilled workers, the shopkeepers and the traders who, in recent years, have learned the ways of Europeans and Americans in organising small and middle-sized businesses and manufacturing units. The three decades of the success story that is Singapore, based largely on the pragmatism of the educated, the skilled, the foreign trained, the cooperator and competitor with multinationals, the rational guesser of the various international moves of large corporations, and the late coming on stream of the various large and small countries of Asia, the networker with others in Asian countries, and, above all, the quick learner from experiences of any successful business, have together contributed to some of the components of Chinese pragmatism. There is no universal model for them, even among the Chinese of the ASEAN region. They have all faced the challenge of unique problems posed by regimes, other ethnic groups, their own early successes, and the reversals of war and foreign occupation. They surmounted all of these with their own unique responses.

What then are the common threads which run through such experiences in different regions? One of them is learning to surmount local disadvantages and problems by means of accommodation and adjustment at the social and political level, so that an increasingly free hand in economic activity is secured. Once an initial freedom to trade is obtained then the message should be put across so that everyone can gain by means of their economic experiences. Simultaneously, the fruits of economic success should be played down. Thousands of miles away from the country of their origin there may be Chinese traders and their families who might be undergoing similar experiences and disadvantages. They can strike mutually beneficial friendship. The overseas Chinese are thus forced to be more cohesive than in fact they were in their own country. This social cohesiveness then translates itself into the economic cohesiveness of excluding competitors from other ethnic groups.

When confronted with more advanced traders such as Europeans and Americans, one should work for them, learn from them, attempt to do what they can do, equip oneself with their skills and ability to organise, and learn their ways of business, manufacturing and marketing. In short, one should clone the economic ways of more advanced traders and manufacturers, and not just stopping there but surpassing them in cost, skill, efficiency, speed, standard and customer satisfaction. This replication is seen at its best in Singapore because the route by which it was attained was education and the learning of new skills in the best of the Western institutions.

Over a span of less than three decades, the Chinese could thus achieve by their own ability and enterprise, and with encouragement from a state like Singapore, what took the Europeans and Americans considerably longer to do. This also reflected their ability to learn, compete and excel in the shortest possible time. And while the learning of new skills, for which the state had made ample provision, paid the highest economic dividends, there was no apparent point in worrying about how illiberal some of its policies and their actual implementation had become.

2 Malaysia: Ethnic Disparities and the Search for a Normative–Pragmatic Balance

In order to understand the complexity of the development process in Malaysia, we need to take into account Malaysian history and its legacies; the ethnic composition of society, political institutions, public policy and the nature of the political bargaining process; economic growth; and the views of scholars and observers on the future of its political society. The chapter is divided into the following sections: i. background and legacies; ii. the ethnic mosaic and the matrix of the development process; iii. the tangled incorporation process; iv. economic and political disparities; and v. a troubled political society. We shall now examine each of these in some detail.

I. BACKGROUND AND LEGACIES

One of the major factors which has influenced Malaysia's public policy in the economic and social fields is the ethnic composition of its society. The census of 1980 had reported that the Malays had constituted 56.7 per cent, the Chinese 33.7 per cent, and the Indians 10.1 per cent of its population. That, however, was not the case in 1931. Much to the surprise of everyone, the census revealed that there were more Chinese in the then Malaya than the Malays themselves. The figures were: Malays 1 644 173; Chinese 1 709 392.[1] That indeed came as a shock to the Malays who regarded themselves as much older settlers in the Peninsular region. This particular realisation had always been present when the formation of the Malay Union was being discussed, or when Singapore separated, or when public policy concerning educational facilities and economic opportunities for various ethnic groups were discussed. Then there were the tribals or *Orang Asli*, especially in the regions of Sabah and Sarawak. Their lack of full assimilation and international investments and interests in those two regions evoked sterner measures from the capital, Kuala Lumpur, to keep them in line. But despite the diversity of the ethnic groups and their tenacity in holding on to their own cultures, in relative terms Malaysia had much less ethnic violence than elsewhere in Asia.

Like most of the countries in this region, Malaysia has also been culturally a multilayered society. Initially, it was exposed to the cultural influences of Hinduism. Then came 'the coastal Islam', which differed in its predisposition to other religions from the Islam which came through the land route in the countries of South Asia. Within the former type of Islam there also came a strand which was known as Sufism which almost verged on religious 'heterodoxy'.[2] By the time the Portuguese, the Dutch and the British landed in Malaya, it had deeply assimilated 'the coastal Islam' into its existing cultures and customs, and was left with very little receptivity to Christianity, except among the unassimilated *Orang Asli*. Its response was the same to Buddhism and Taoism brought in by the Chinese, and the more ritualistic and detailed form of Hinduism introduced by the Tamil immigrants in the nineteenth and twentieth centuries. As in Indonesia, there was also a segment in Malay Islamic society which continually looked for a purer version of Islam over and above the syncretised version which had become a part of its mainstream Muslim society.

The British kept clear of the social and cultural life of the people. Land tenure, however, was another matter. The British recognised the ownership of land which it registered, and offered considerable room for letting in groups and interests that it supported. This resulted in the 'restructuring of local society by regulating relations among groups of people and reorganizing of resources for the greater aim of economic progress'.[3] Towards such a goal the British built railways and communication systems, created a suitable legal and administrative machinery, brought in immigrant labour – both Chinese and Indian – injected European capital, provided protection for estates and facilities for banks, encouraged well-known trading companies such as Gutheries, Sime & Darby, and Harrisons, etc., to come to Malaya, and experimented with the possibility of using and exporting rubber and palm oil.

Then began the search for cheap labour for exploiting the natural resources of what is now Malaysia. As its hold on the territory consolidated, and competition with the Dutch and the French in Southeast Asia eased, Britain started launching ambitious schemes for exploiting the vast metal, mineral and agricultural resources of the newly acquired territory.

In importing and employing cheap and often destitute labour, Britain followed its own judgment on what kind of immigrant labour would be suitable for what purpose. The Malays, for example, were good enough only for subordinate level office work, the police and the army. There again, special attention had to be paid to the displaced Malay elites who had to be provided with senior administrative positions. Consequently, for that purpose, the Raffles Institute was established in Singapore in 1823 to influence and shape 'the sons of the higher order of the natives'.[4]

By this time, Britain had learned to depend on the Jaffna Tamils from what was formerly known as Ceylon. Britain had depended heavily on the Tamils of Madras to administer the then Madras Presidency. In Malaya, however, Britain had given special encouragement to the Jaffna Tamils. Not only were they preferred for the administration in Ceylon but were also offered better paid jobs in Malaya, if they decided to emigrate. Later on Indians, Eurasians and Chinese were also given access to some positions in the civil service.

The arrival of English language schools created its own reaction among the orthodox Malays, and they therefore sought permission to start their own schools. One of the greatest impacts of British rule on Malayan educational systems was the development of the Latin script or *Rumi* for the widely spoken Malay language. In 1903, an inspector of schools by the name of Wilkinson introduced Latin script for writing Malay words. This had a far-reaching impact: educated Chinese and Indians could now write in it. The orthodox Malays, however, felt that they should have gone back to the Arabic script. In a sense, along with the English language, the Malay language in Latin script also united many people and laid the foundation of a national movement.

Initially, Britain had hoped to get by with a policy of shaping the Malays to work within the administrative structure and let the other ethnic groups work out their own economic destiny. But before long the Chinese and their enormous economic dynamism demanded the rulers' attention. Although brought into the workforce at first to work in mines and service-related jobs, the rapid movement of the Chinese labourer continually defied their job descriptions. By 1930, nearly 70 per cent of the Chinese had graduated from mining to agriculture and commercial agriculture, and the rest were moving more and more into commercial enterprises. By 1947, only 42 per cent of the Chinese remained in agriculture. Their unaided and self-directed economic diversification spoke volumes for their dynamism.

So far as the Indians were concerned, they were considered to be more suitable for rubber estate work. As rubber estate workers they no doubt made a little more money than they had done in India, nevertheless, the very nature of their work had insulated them from the mainstream economic life and left them with no alternatives to look for. Even the educational facilities for their children were either non-existent or just deplorable. Consequently, the younger generation of Indians had to pull themselves by their bootstraps to go to the nearby cities and start corner coffee shops or grocery stores.

The Malay national movement, because of ethnic divisions, took longer to get off the ground. And for the colonial administration, the presence of ethnic diversity, duly slotted into specific economic divisions, was helpful in delaying a joint demand for self-government. Colonial policy had successfully fractured society. In Malaysia, therefore, an internal bargaining by the elites had to precede any effective demand for self-government.

The greatest single factor which helped the Malay national movement – apart from the electrifying effect of Indian independence, and the towering personality of Jawaharlal Nehru who spoke on behalf of colonial people – was the defeat of the British at the hands of the Japanese. While the Malays, the Chinese and the Indians did not like the Japanese occupation, they nevertheless welcomed the defeat of the seemingly invincible British at the hands of an Asian power. Consequently, after the war the perception of the people of Malaya towards those in the colonial administration had changed considerably. They were now dealing with a people who were on their way out.

As in India, when Britain decided to quit, everything was done with much grace and benevolence before power was handed over. The political organisations of the three major communities, i.e. UMNO (United Malays National Organisation) representing the Malays, MCA (Malay Chinese Association) representing the Chinese, and MIC (Malay Indian Congress) representing the Indians, after considerable horsetrading presented a united front to the British. For the three ethnic communities, as it always happens in national movements, it was easier to unite against an alien rule than in co-existing, co-building and in co-prospering undertakings. Since Malaysia has prospered continually since independence, it was spared any economic strain on its fragile unity. Its stunning economic performance and increase in exports from agricultural products to manufactured goods, earning it the name of an NIC (Newly Industrialised Country), reduced its ethnic tensions to manageable proportions. Moreover, its pragmatic policies, and an increasing realisation on the part of the major ethnic communities that what it had achieved had to be consolidated and improved upon rather than thrown away in the heat of ethnic strife, also helped it pull back from the brink again and again.

II. THE ETHNIC MOSAIC AND THE MATRIX OF THE DEVELOPMENT PROCESS

Let us now look briefly at the ethnic diversity of Malaysia and see how it has shaped the general framework of its development process. In this connection we shall examine the background and evolution of its four major ethnic groups: the Malays, the Chinese, the Indians, and the *Orang Asli* or the tribals. While one can use generic terms such as 'the Indians', 'the *Orang Asli*' and so forth, they themselves are by no means homogenous groups. Their internal differences become more pronounced when we look at them *as* groups. For our purpose here, however, what is more significant is the way in which their ethnic diversity influences their development process, on the one hand, and Malaysia's emerging political society, on the other.

In this connection we have advisedly used the term 'mosaic' to describe the ethnic situation in Malaysia. This is because not only are there ethnic groups in Malaysia with separate cultural identities of their own – reinforced and compounded by economic and political forces – but also within each of them there is the diversity of cultural influences to which they were exposed. There is something for us to learn here from 'the mosaic tradition'[5] in anthropological works, especially when an ethnic background, as in Malaysia, simultaneously creates situations of coexistence, accommodation, syncretic penetration, tension and conflict within its mainstream development process.

i. The Malays

The ethnic identity of various groups in Malaysia, and in particular of the Malays themselves, rests on a different set of criteria. Moreover, because of certain provisions in the constitution, land tenure policy which is governed by certain customary practices which is collectively known as *adat,* and conscious attempts made through education and the New Economic Policy to help the Malays overcome their relative backwardness *vis-à-vis* the Chinese, all these in different ways contribute to the ongoing redefinition of the Malays as a people. On top of that come efforts at reviving ancestral linkages, religious fundamentalism in certain provinces wanting to make the Malays conform to the unalloyed principles of Islam, together with the search for specific identities of adjoining islands, all making the problem of the identity of the Malay as a people very complex indeed.

The four ethnic groups, namely, the Malays, the Chinese, the Indians and the *Orang Asli,* call for different sets of criteria for determining their identities. The Malay identity has, for instance, the more pronounced 'host' characteristics, which are expressed through religion, language and economic concern at being left out of the great many economic opportunities which the development process has introduced. The Chinese, with a changing affinity to the land of their ancestors, racial characteristics, minimum emphasis on religion but greater emphasis on custom, social cohesion, and given to bartering away certain political advantages in return for economic security and advancement, call for a different kind of criteria than do the Malays to determine their ethnic identity. Then the Indians, who are a highly fractured group in terms of religion, caste and region – with estate workers emphasising religious customs, and middle-class groups emphasising economic opportunities – require yet another set of criteria to identify the characteristics of their composite identity. Finally, the *Orang Asli,* or the Tribals, express their identity in terms of their littoral affinities with the tribals of neighbouring islands, and end up having, what Edmund Leach called, the 'oscillating identities'. In recent years with educational development, new economic opportunities, modern lifestyle, and increasing Christianisation, their identity requires yet another set of criteria.

Let us take the definition of 'Malay', as a citizen, as given in the constitution of independent Malaysia. According to the definition of Malay in the Federal Constitution, 'a Malay is a person who professes the Muslim religion, habitually speaks Malay language, conforms to Malay *adat* (custom) and is a Malaysian citizen'.[6] This also means that the constitution has extended some of the characteristics of 'Malay' as an ethnic category to 'Malay' as a citizen. In other words, formally speaking, the characteristics of religion, language and custom have been added on to the normal requirements of birth or residence in citizenship. From time to time there have also been instances when other ethnic groups in Malaysia have expressed their reservations on such qualifications. This then brings us to the central problem of Malay self-definition as an ethnic group. Indeed, this has been an ongoing process whereby different segments of the Malays have tried to distance themselves, in different degrees, from the earlier historical and cultural influences, on the one hand, and the modernising Western influences, on the other. Invariably in such dynamics there are moves which bring a segment closer to the purer or Arabic form of Islam, and then there are counter moves, on the part of others, to disassociate themselves from such a proximity, and they begin to search again for the essential differences in their cultural identity.

Malaysian society is unique in respect of being a Muslim majority society, with more than 40 per cent of the population subscribing to other religions. It also subscribes to liberal political institutions though not to unrestricted civil rights. Such a background also provides freedom within the Malay ethnic group itself to reflect and express views on its cultural perceptions, on the one hand, and differing cultural aspirations, on the other. Unlike in most other Muslim countries, it is possible to witness an open discussion on views, in university seminars and elsewhere, on social movements which want to make the Malay Muslims conform to the Saudi Arabian style of 'pure' or *Wahabi* Islam, and those who oppose them and point out the greatness of the tolerant and coexistential Malaysian variety of Islam.

Historically speaking the Malays of the Malaysian Peninsula had come under the influence of Hinduism and Buddhism. Consequently, the foundation of Malay society was essentially Hindu. The subsequent Islamisation of Malay society did not eradicate a number of values, gods and operating principles to which the Malays had become accustomed. While the gods and the demons of the *Ramayana* and *Mahabharatha* became Islamised, the stories of good and evil implicit in them continued. Similarly, while there was an outward switch towards one god instead of the earlier Hindu polytheism, the polytheistic tolerance of others' gods and principles of worship continued.

At the level of values, some of the Hindu terms were reworked to suit the practices and emphases of the people in society. One of those terms which occupies a central position in the Malay system of values is *budi,* which is derived from the Sanskrit word *buddhi,* a composite term for both intelligence and wisdom. *Buddhi* was thus reworked to include the capacity to control emotions, to show consideration for others' feelings and to build a moral cum intellectual personality which then reflects human consideration in one's outward behaviour. So what we have in *budi* is a term of Hindu individual intelligence converted into an imperative of social obligation governing individual social behaviour. Such a change, in other words, brought in the social or community reference which was missing in its earlier form.

Certain aspects of the normative base, which was heavily influenced by Hinduism and which has still survived despite admonitions from the orthodox Islamic clerics to the contrary, are spread in various fields, including customs, belief in spirits, limited gender distances, and so on. A number of day-to-day customs which the Malays observe still have a strong Hindu flavour. Then there are different spirits whose protection is sought for different undertakings, including health, which are the relics of early Hindu influences. And then so far as gender distances are concerned, the women have much greater visibility, proximity to men and strangers, and importance in family management than the orthodox clerics, who bring in the standards from Arabian countries for Malay women, can put up with.

At a deeper level, there is still greater evidence of the survival of the Hindu notion of 'time', 'death', and a predispostion to other religions. Had some of these values, in particular those of religious coexistence, not been there, Malaysian ethnic problems would have been further compounded by religious intolerance and violence that we often see in South Asian societies and in the Middle East.

Among the surviving but constantly modifying values are what Malaysia's well-known anthropolgist, H. M. Dahlan, calls 'the *budi* complex', which influences the entire range of social relations.[7] To Dahlan, the idea of *budi* is embodied in the distinction between the superiority of *rasa* (intuitive inner feeling) over purely rational understanding. So with *budi* you go beyond simple rational understanding to evaluating what you understand. To the Malays, therefore, *budi* opens up the door for something beyond Cartesian rationalism where only intellectual comprehension is involved.

Other Malay scholars, such as Halim Ali, have identified the influence of *budi* beyond understanding, intuitive feeling for the situation, and feel of the deficiencies, to cover kindness to others.

The Malays thus went on reworking the concept of *budi* to mean many things instead of devising new concepts. One of the reasons for this could have been that the scholars were identifying usages of the term in communications and social relations rather than turning to concept-making enterprises. Even in a rigidly supervised language such as Sanskrit, terms such as *dharma* and *sanskar* came to have a large range of meanings.

The point to be made here is that *budi* had to remain an interpretative vehicle for many things in adapted cultural conditions where scholars were following the trail of usages and adaptations of terms. In a situation of cultural deposits of various ages, and cultural heterogeneity introduced by various ethnic groups which made Malaysia their home, the scholars were overwhelmed by the richness of meanings and diversity of usages of certain terms. But above every thing else these cultural deposits were very much there despite an emphasis on making society conform to puristic dictates of any particular belief system. The Malays were thus heirs to rich living cultural influences and deposits which were pre-Islamic, and which they did not want to give up despite periodic efforts at religious and cultural purity. The Malays have thus retained both the pre-Islamic values and values that have developed in their interaction with Islam. Such a societal base of values deprived the religious clerics of coming up with a narrow interpretation of Islamic values which would then have excluded all that existed before. That did not happen. While the Malays showed preferences for their broad cultural heritage, their encounter in social and economic fields with other ethnic groups often persuaded them to go in search of a clear-cut exclusivist Islamic identity. But so far they have hesitated in taking that course. Again and again they counter such moves by claiming that Malay values, as they have developed through a long period of evolution of customs and practices, have a lot of historical and cultural desposits within them, and are ideally suited for building a society which makes not only coexistence but integration and assimilation of those values the test of Malaysian tolerance.

While the Malay intellectuals wage an indirect struggle against the narrow interpretation of Malay cultural identity, primarily based on religion, they, according to some observers, do not offer effective opposition to the orthodox elements in society which want to push the Malays to a greater and greater expression of their Malay identity in pure religious terms. They leave that job to politicians. In the words of Sharon Siddique:

One of the consequences of the lack of Malay intellectual leadership is the relative absence of respected religious authority amongst the Malay community which may be able to solve 'problems of' a changing Malay society, within the Islamic context. This is reflected in a demonstrated hostility towards religious leadership, a lack of faith in their religious guidance, and a repeated recommendation for a search for an 'enlightened' leadership.[8]

Talking of 'modernisation', the Malay intellectuals also have certain reservations against the 'corporate culture' which is essentially a part of Western style modernisation and industrialisation. They feel that such a culture, which is an undiluted American import, may not be altogether suitable for Malaysia. This is because Malay executives, apart from the outward adoption of marketing and packaging techniques, have to rely on human resources which cannot be divorced from their own cultural values and practices. The Malays, Dahlan argues, cannot become as forthright, precise and aggressive in their human relations as do American executives. Apart from certain indigenous adaptations of certain values, such as *budi,* which influence the social relations of the Malays, and therefore becomes a factor in the expression of their cultural identity, there is the vital role played by Malay *adat* (custom, religious law) in regulating social and economic relationships, including land tenure. Land tenure in Malaysia is governed by an 'amalgam' of three vital components which are: the basic land tenure system; *adat,* religious law governing family relationships among the Muslims; and an 'overlaying judicial, legislative, executive system founded in colonial English law'.[9]

The development of a common Malay identity for all its citizens has a special problem. Judith Nagata, making use of the concept of 'oscillating identity', as developed by Edmund Leach, argued that there was the case of 'switching' from one kind of identity to another on the part of the Malays for the 'purposes of avoiding tensions due to inconsistencies of role expectation in any given set of circumstances'. Such a 'situational selection' of ethnic identity created problems for themselves when the question of 'Who is a Malay?' came up.[10]

ii. The Chinese

The Chinese of Malaysia, as could be expected, came in different waves and at different times. Each wave of Chinese immigrants interacted culturally and economically with the idigenous population. Some of their interactions resulted in marriage, in the preservation of Chinese culture and identity, or in protecting and advancing Chinese economic interests.

Apart from the early but limited immigration and settlement of the Chinese in the Malaysian Peninsula, the bulk of them were brought into the colony of Malaya during British colonial rule. Britain needed additional labour to work in the tin and gold mines. It also needed labour to work in the rubber plantations.

The imported Chinese labour created its own social problems. Apart from the fact that they had the features of a 'slave trade', there was a disproportion of men and women among them. In 1901, there were ten Chinese women for every 1000 Chinese males. The Chinese thus lacked the characteristics of a stable community.[11]

The early groups of Chinese immigrants who came with the ostensible intention of making a good living and, after some saving, returning to China, soon realised that the prospects of returning were not too attractive. Some of them married Malay women and the children of such 'out marriages' were called *babas,* in the case of males, and *noniyas,* in the case of females. More of such marriages took place in areas surrounding Penang, Malacca and Singapore.

But the interesting thing about such marriages, and the children born to them, was that the culture of the Chinese father rather than that of the Malay mother often proved to be more attractive. The *babas* were thus unwilling to give up the cultural identity on the father's side, and settled for a few features of the Malay society on the mother's side.

The rootless *babas* of the Singapore area, in particular, retained a separate identity of their own for a long time. They took English education and some of them also embraced Christianity. During British rule both these proved to be of great advantage. In the pre-independence period, therefore, they emerged as the Westernised elite of Malayan society. Their importance, however, began to dwindle when others too took English education and competed with them in professions, government jobs, and for government favours in general.

Over the years such marriages have declined. Even marriage between Muslims and non-Muslims have some specific conditions attached to them. One of these requires the spouse to embrace Islam and raise children in Islamic faith.

Over the years, the Chinese population – of the former Malaya, under the British, and after independence and separation of Singapore – has done very well. During British rule and since the Chinese moved wherever and whenever economic opportunities were attractive. After their initial stint in mining and other related fields, they were left by the colonial administration to their economic resources and initiatives. In the economic field the Chinese went wherever European interests and organisations went. They were, in other words, the quickest economic learners as opposed to the other ethnic groups in the country.

During the colonial period, the Chinese were not favoured with administrative positions. To most of them it did not matter as long as they could make more money through their commercial enterprises. The law and order established by colonial rule boosted their economic activity tremendously. For a long time they were allowed only minor participation in various councils. By the 1930s, the unrestricted Chinese immigration to Malaya came to an end, and instead a quota system was introduced. The Chinese became heavily concentrated in specific areas of the Peninsula.

After the Second World War, the negotiations with the colonial administration for independence also revolved round the question of citizenship for the Chinese. While these transactions centred round the official position of the colonial administration, implying a 'broad based citizenship', 'without discrimination of race or creed', in actual practice the fears of the Malays concerning a large number of outsiders in their homeland had to be assuaged. Finally, there was agreement on the clause governing a 'common citizenship', based on residence or length of stay, which was highly reassuring to the Chinese. By 1947, 60 per cent of the Chinese population was Malay born.

The proportion of Chinese women (some of them born to Malay mothers) to men, also greatly improved, indicating an end to the previous 'commuter' attitude on the part of the Chinese. The Chinese also went to great lengths to establish Chinese schools to ensure that their culture was not lost to their children in their new homeland.[12]

The Chinese of Malaysia, apart from their effectively expressed cultural identity and tightly knit social organisation, also have their own wide-ranging educational and economic associations to speak on their behalf and protect their interests. The major one among these is known as the Chinese Guilds and Associations (CGA), which is a coalition of different bodies seeking to bring to the notice of the decision-makers their grievances in various fields. At the same time, it also seeks to oversee the cultural, educational and social needs of the Chinese. The CGA is thus an amalgam of various local, state and national level associations for the protection of Chinese interests and welfare. From time to time it has made efforts to influence decisions on vital issues such as citizenship, language, and the effect of NEP (New Economic Policy) on the Chinese economic interests in general. As far as possible, it tries to avoid a confrontational attitude.

The CGA has displayed a shrewd pragmatic sense in its demands, knowing full well that there is an ethnic problem in Malaysia concerning which, so far, the Chinese have the most to gain. So it does not like to rock the boat too much. After an initial experiment, therefore, it has desisted from joining political opposition parties – the Chinese in Malaysia wanting to avoid the posture of an opposition group. They try to cooperate in a number of ways, but at the same time keep pushing their own demands in a more sophisticated and inoffensive manner. In recent years, the role of the CGA has become more significant, because of the increasing marginalisation of their party organisation, namely, the MCA, and the unchecked drift towards the favouring of the Malays under the NEP. It is therefore required to play the game of protecting Chinese interests with great delicacy and finesse, and does not want the continuing economic prosperity of the Chinese to be hurt in any way.

The CGA is often required to handle complex issues delicately, and frequently behind the scenes. For instance, when the Malays make a demand, it is always couched in the name of either 'the poor' or 'the people'. The background of their demand is always characterised by claims regarding 'national interest'. Whereas, whenever the Chinese make a demand, it is deemed in the interest of people who have already done too well or are viewed as hostile to 'national' interests. Consequently, in the days of open Malay demands for a great volume of affirmative action under the NEP, the negotiating skill of the CGA was stretched to its limits.

One of the enduring and frustrating features of mainstream Malaysian society for the Chinese is that they, as well as the Indians, are perceived, and will be perceived for the foreseeable future, as *outsiders*. Only the considerate and enlightened Malays see them as parts, though not yet essential parts, of Malay society. The NEP affirmative actions which are purely on ethnic rather than economic lines further reinforce their view that no matter how hard they have tried to identify themselves with the country they have made their home, they and their children will always be looked at *as* outsiders. This engenders various reactions. The Chinese, in particular, sometimes argue that the original settlers of the land are the *Orang Asli* and not the Malays.

Within all the ethnic groups, however, there is a growing realisation that while the other group is having more than its fair share, either in terms of the benefits of a special policy or greater economic opportunities, they have all flourished in Malaysia. Consequently, they all have a stake not only in Malaysia but also in each segment doing what it has been doing for the economic growth and the general development of the country. While there is envy for what the Chinese have achieved in the field of commerce and industry, there is also a realisation that they have brought a great many benefits to Malaysia. Similarly, the Indians have slogged away in plantation economy with very poor returns but they have remained the backbone of the operational success of such an economy. Finally, the Malays, despite their unhappiness with the rate of their economic development, are considered to be a gentle and reasonable people, and fair-minded administrators, who would not go to extreme lengths to make life difficult for the other two ethnic groups. Thus they have all benefited by one another's presence and economic and cultural contribution.

In a recent 'political' seminar, arranged by the Chinese, a volume entitled, *The Future of Malaysian Chinese* (1988), was prepared with statements from the founding father (*bapa mardeka* or the father of independence) of Malaysia, namely, Tunku Abdul Rahman:

> We must look at the nation as a multiracial community as a whole . . . and not only strive and struggle for the betterment of Malays and Muslims.

> We cannot and must not forget that we achieved independence from the British not by ourselves but with the help of other races as well.[13]

> . . . national unity is the natural aspiration of all peace-loving moderate and tolerant Malaysian citizens. But despite this, racial polarisation still rears its ugly head threating the peace and stability of the Malaysian nation.[14]

Over the years there could be a general shift on both sides. This is because, apart from the realisation of the contribution of each, there are also forces at work which bring different people together and forge new bonds. These are the forces of education, the growth of professional elites and their ability to do business across the ethnic divide, greater understanding of each other which then chips away at the negative stereotypes and sees the common human side in the other.

iii. The Indians

The Indians of Malaysia, because of their number and the fractured nature of their society, have not been able to play an effective role in the economic development and political process of the country to which they emigrated. Imported into Malaysia by the colonial adminstration, largely to work as estate and plantation workers, the Indians also suffered as a result of the nature of estate economy, insulation from urban centres where there were greater educational and economic opportunities, and, above all, the nature of their political leadership which was more keen on making political deals than on emphasising the need to help them out of their economic backwardness.

The Indians were imported into Malaysia because Britain could not raise sufficient labour to work on the estates and plantations from among the Malays and the Chinese. There was the problem of clearing land for plantation, periodic weeding, collection of rubber and maintenance of the rubber plants, and a number of other activities related to agriculture and agriculture products for which additional labour was needed. Britain brought Tamils from India to do the basic road and railway construction work, and from there they were absorbed into the estates and plantations for which European investments became increasingly available. For supervisory work on the estates, the colonial authority had imported Malayalis and Jaffna Tamils from Sri Lanka. The Jaffna Tamils never forgot the fact that they had come for work which was superior to that for which the Indian Tamils were brought.

In a sense the Jaffna Tamils, or their children, were being moved around for a second time within the British colonies. Having tried them out in Sri Lanka, British plantation owners were inclined to trust them as experienced hands who could also be given supervisory functions. Started at a relatively higher level of work assignment than the Indian Tamils, the Jaffna Tamils and their children put more emphasis on education and progress, particularly in moving out of plantations to towns. In relative terms also they had greater success. Twice removed, tougher, better prepared, relatively more educated, the Sri Lankan Tamils also preserved a sense of separateness from the Tamils of India. Their spoken Tamil language was purer and preserved within it the nineteenth-century imprints of stricter linguisitic standards. Not only did they develop a sense of separateness from the other Tamils, they even felt that they had a different cultural identity.[15] Jaffna Tamils were not the only ones who came with more defined assignments; there were also Sikhs, Bengalis, Biharis, Uttar Pradesh (northern India) Muslims, Parsees etc., who came under one job description or another and all registered different levels of economic success.

Most of those who came to work on the plantations came under what was known as the 'indentured system'. Then there was the 'kangani system', under which labour was also imported. The latter was confined to South India and, because of protests, the officials agreed to look into their conditions and report back. As a result of protests in India concerning the deplorable conditions, the Indian emigration to Malaysia started dwindling. In 1931, Indians comprised 15.1 per cent, but by 1947 it had declined to 10.8 per cent of immigrants, not including Singapore. As late as 1992, one could still come across incredible stories of inhuman conditions in which the Tamils of Indian origin lived on plantations in rural Malaysia.

Given their divisions, the Indians had to consolidate themselves both as a distinct ethnic group, internally, and then bargain for concessions with the Malay authority, outside their group. In the beginning that proved to be a formidable task. Political leaders with a short-term interest sprung up everywhere and started speaking on behalf of the entire group. The negotiations between Indians and Malays acquired a seriousness on occasions when the latter needed their support *vis-à-vis* the Chinese. When that was obtained their interests in the Indians often waned.

Politically, the Indians were cast in a different mould. This is because there were several national and international factors which had conditioned their orientation to political participation in Malaysia. For instance, Nehru's visit to Malaysia had galvanised the Indians. Then, during the Japanese occupation of Malaysia, they offered their cooperation as a measure of their help to the enemy of colonial administration in India. But that had only short-lived repurcussions in Malaysia. Finally, being a smaller group in the ethnic equation, they were not always very sure of the political direction except to say, ineffectively, that they too needed economic help.[16]

iv. The Orang Aslis

Malaysia, like most countries in this region, has a substantial percentage of tribal population or what are locally called the *Orang Aslis,* the original people of the land. Such a term used to be resented by the Malays since they claimed to be the *bumiputera* or the sons of the soil, also implying that they, more than others, were there before the immigrants such as the Chinese and the Indians arrived. The bulk of the *Orang Asli* are concentrated in the provinces of Sabah and Sarawak. Because of the recent accelerated economic growth of Sabah, in particular, the assertion of *Orang Asli* identity of the tribals has created a problem of political accommodation.

Like all other newly independent countries, Malaysia had to go through, and is still going through, a trying period of welding its different ethnic groups into a nation. In its case, especially, the challenge has been all the greater because the colonial power had deposited on its territory two of the most difficult people to integrate, namely, the Chinese and the Indians, who brought with them their own religion, culture and links with the countries of their origin. Equally great has been the challenge of incorporating into a wider sociopolitical system the sizable population of *Orang Aslis.*

While the economically and educationally more developed segments of its population – the Malays, the Chinese and the Indians – were entering into a broader incorporation process, by making their own demands and simultaneously shaping the process of coexistence and direction of public policy, in a similar process where the *Orang Aslis* were involved, this process had to go through economic and religious intermediaries. The economic intermediaries were sometimes overseas organizations or Chinese who were working closely with those interests, and also religious intermediaries who were either Christian missionaries or the Christianised *Orang Aslis* with a growing subcultural identity of their own. Scholars have estimated that nearly one-third of the *Orang Aslis* may have embraced the Christian faith in their own polytheistic and often flexible ways.

Among the tribals the non-Muslims are Ibans or Sea Dayaks, Bidayus or Land Dayaks, Kayans, Kenyahs and Kelabits. The Muslims are Kedayans, Bisayas and a good proportion of Melanaus. In Sabah a proportion of Maruts and Kadazans (formerly Dusmus) are also Muslims. Then there are Bajuns, the Bruneis, the Sulus, the Illanus and Kedayans who are culturally and physically akin to Peninsular Muslims.

The line between Muslims and non-Muslims in the tribal situation is not always sharply drawn in cultural terms. Even when they embraced Islam, they did not always give up their previous cultural practices. On top of such a complex situation came the proselytisation by Christian missionaries. This latter cultural addition became significant when mines, minerals and timber attracted European colonial interests and, later on, the renewed attention of Western multinationals.

Let us now have a closer look at Sabah with a view to having a glimpse of the nature of social change which has affected that province and its overwhelmingly tribal population. From 1951 to 1970, the population of Sabah nearly doubled, registering a population growth rate of 3.7 per cent. Its rapid industrialisation and urbanisation attracted the tribal population from the interior.

Sabah has three major towns: Kota Kinabalu, Sandakan and Tawau. In all these there was a heavy concentration of tribal workers from the interior. Sabah's population is divided into eight major groups: Kadazan (also known as Dusun) and Kwijau; Murut; Bajau (Bajau and Illanum); Malay; Indonesians; Other Indigenous Groups; Chinese (Hakka; Cantonese; Hokkien; Teochev; Hainanese; others); Others (Natives of Sarawak; Filipino; European; Eurasians; Indians; Coco Islanders).

With a population of less than 1 million (1978), Sabah is richly endowed with vast natural resources, agricultural land, fisheries, and mineral wealth including petroleum. It exports timber, palm oil, rubber, and now petroleum. Kota Kinabalu, its capital, formerly known as Jesselton has been rapidly expanding and often referred to as a boom town. Its growth rate in real terms since the 1970s has been in the vicinity of 9 per cent. It was estimated in 1978 that its per capita growth rate was 23 per cent higher than Malaysia's national average.[17]

The rate of urbanisation of Sabah, attracting the tribal population from the interior, began to worry the planners in Malaysia. The Malaysian Fifth Five-year Plan in 1990, expressed a note of concern over its urbanisation being the cause of social and economic problems for its people. Sabah's resource rich economy opened up at precisely the same time as the Malaysian programme of privatisation went into top gear. What then began to cause anxiety was the fact that Sabah's economy had weak links with the rest of the country. Its import and export, under the multinationals, were carried on more with the outside world than with the Malaysian Peninsula. On top of that there were the growing disparities between the urban and rural development of Sabah. None of these issues were of concern to the multinationals.[18]

For a long time, the colonial administration did not think that educating the people of Sabah was its responsibility, and it was left predominantly to the Christian missionaries, mainly the Roman Catholics. They had been in the field since 1881 and the kind of education they gave was similar to that in other parts of the British colonies. The tribals of the then underdeveloped Sabah were oriented towards Western values, lifestyle, and a more receptive attitude to foreign rule. When the colonial administration also began to share the responsibility for education, it worked within the framework that was already established by the missionaries. Even in the 1990s, in the shopping areas of Kota Kinabalu, one was amazed to hear the English language spoken by tribals who made their living by doing odd jobs in the town. Such an education of the urban tribals did not, however, result in political consciousness and a questioning attitude, questioning their domination by people from outside.

The colonial administration had used Sabah province to serve its own overseas interests. Things began to change, but only just, when Sabah became a part of independent Malaysia in 1963. This was partly due to the ethnic differences between the people of Sabah and those of the Peninsula – a wedge that was further widened by the nature of Sabah's economy.

The historical, educational and economic policies of the past had their own 'dislocative' impact on tribal society.[19] The tribals came to the town from the interior in an increasing number to sell their labour. Their familial and social dislocation was temporarily covered by an apparent look of higher standard of living than they previously enjoyed. Such an impact was not only confined to urban centres but had also spread to rural communities. For one thing, the development of the infrastructure to feed towns with raw materials from the distant interior resulted in an increasing number of rural settlements by the roadside. The tribals who used to make an independent living by means of fishing and agriculture now began to depend on an emerging propertied class. The dislocative process thus converted the very nature of villagers as farmer-producers into a subservient unit in another kind of economy, which was designed to help them but where they had to fit in at the lowest level. Instead of a closely knit rural community of mutual help and cooperation, new and artificial roadside communities were born. These then came under the influence of religious leaders, both Christian and Muslim, wanting their political support for issues in which the roadside migrants were not directly involved. Thus the poor and the not-so-poor peasants, mostly tribals, were caught in the 'negative side of the change' where the effects of 'the dislocative change' were about the worst.[20] The cost of development was economically and socially paid for by the community in Malaysia which was least able to afford it. Judged by any standard, such a community was more in need of affirmative programme assistance than the *bumiputeras* themselves. Their neglect by the Malaysian government, as we shall see later on, came to haunt it in the 1990s, when frustrated politicians together with outside economic interests began encouraging a mood for disassociation from the Malaysian Federation itself.

In 1992, Dr Mahathir wanted Sabah to fall in line with other provinces in Malaysia and thereby agree to abort the special status given to it when the Malaysian Federation was constituted in 1963. Sabah's Chief Minister, Joseph Pairin Kitingan, belonging to PBS (Parti Bersatu Sabah), saw it as a threat to Sabah's special identity within the Federation.[21]

In 1959, Sabah and Sarawak had their first taste of democratic politics. The then Governor of North Borneo warned that 'It is . . . essential that party politics should not cause further divisions in our community.'[22] British North Borneo, which comprised Sabah and Sarawak, was multi-ethnic in composition, with a history of paternalistic autocracy at the hands of 'the White Rajah' and the British North Borneo Company which ruled Sabah and Sarawak, respectively, for nearly seventy years. In the election, as was to be expected, the various political parties had acquired a racial character.

Naturally, this was a cause of worry for Kuala Lumpur. These two states with their social and economic backgrounds were becoming 'fringe' provinces inhabited by people who had not become integral parts of the plural society of Malaysia.[23] The various political parties which had appealed to the racial background of the voters in 1959 were increasingly coming round to the idea of building their support structure based on cross-cutting ethnic ties. That was easier said than done. For one thing, the old attitude, whereby the tribals were looked down upon as people with scant respect for their social and cultural practices, at best evoked a paternalistic attitude towards them. Moreover, additional attention was paid to them only when there were elections or when political discontent was brewing. Consequently, new political parties emerged in Sabah, once more on ethnic lines, but this time representing the *Orang Asli* as a separate group in Malaysia's plural society.

In 1961, the United National Kadazan Organisation (UNKO) was started, with emphasis on Kadazan language, culture and economic problems. Its leader was Donald Stephens, a timber magnate who was also editor of the *North Borneo News* and *Sabah Times*. Stephen's mother was a Kadazan and his father was an Australian. The British had encouraged him and had coopted him into the legislature. It was he who successfully campaigned for the change of name from North Borneo to Sabah and vigorously supported the protection of Kadazan economic interests and identity. The bulk of his Kadazan followers practised the Christian religion mixed with Kadazan animistic beliefs. The average Kadazan found the Malay Muslims in Sabah culturally too intolerant.

The Malay Muslims in Sabah formed their own party in 1961 and called it the United Sabah National Organisation (USNO). Its leader was called Mustapha. The party wanted a Malayification of Sabah in a cultural sense. They thought that after independence, there was not much point in keeping one's earlier identities. But they wanted the *Orang Aslis* to renounce their pre-Christian and Christian identities as the price for integration.

The Chinese, who had penetrated deeply into the timber and mineral resources of Sabah, did not welcome the prospective fight between the two groups. To them the Malays represented the interests of the Peninsular Malaysia rather than those of the locals. Away from the Malaysian mainland, the Kota Kinabalu Chinese looked to Singapore for their ethnic linkages, and Sandakan (another town in Sabah) Chinese looked to Hong Kong.

Stephens and Mustapha dominated the political scene of Sabah for a long time. In the end it was Mustapha, with the backing of the Peninsular Malaysia won out. He even succeeded in incorporating some Kadazans into his party. The Chinese too stopped looking outside, especially when Singapore separated from Malaysia. Stephens rose to a high position as a federal minister, and then suffered a decline.

Sabah and its people thus illustrate yet another problem for Malaysia's ethnically diverse society. While some workable economic and political arrangement seems to have been made, and is renewed from time to time among the three major ethnic groups, i.e. the Malays, the

Chinese and the Indians, a similar arrangement with the *Orang Aslis* is not in prospect. This is because national and international economic and political interests have assumed the kind of position which the *Orang Aslis* think should be theirs in the economy and political society of Malaysia.

III. THE TANGLED INCORPORATION PROCESS

Unlike most other developing countries, Malaysia, as far as its society was concerned, had to start afresh when the colonial administration ended. It was also left with some marked disadvantages and challenges of far-reaching significance, for while its society was technically designated a 'plural society', it was in fact more complex than that. It was a fractured society with mutual suspicion on the part of its various ethnic components who would run to the state with complaints, and demand concessions and favours against other groups. Malaysia would not have been able to hold itself together had it not been for accommodating measures on the part of its rulers, and a commonsensical and practical disposition of give and take on the part of its seemingly unreconcilable ethnic components. With these advantages it was able to rebuild its resource-blessed economy and then transform it into a manufacturing economy. Such an economic base then acted as a cushion for the setbacks resulting from the continued wrangling for concessions and favours on the part of the various ethnic groups. While these groups showed a spirit of give and take in a lot of areas, in others they remained either doggedly culture-bound or impervious to the plight of those who were economically less fortunate. The net result of all this was that the process of building a post-independence political society had become hopelessly bogged down with jealousies, suspicions, pigheadedness and indifference to the plight of others.

The incorporation process, of building a broader political society – leaving behind ascriptive group concerns and cohesions to the ethnic groups themselves, and concentrating on building a legal and political system to pursue effective economic, educational and social goals – did not get off the ground smoothly. The process got mired in the expression of group identity in religious terms, in sustaining and advancing economic advantages, in remaining indifferent to the political process, and in not being able to put one's claim to social and economic benefits for being the most disadvantaged in society.

At the time of independence, the Malays, the host community, had two grave concerns: first, their own cultural identity and that of the country; and second, the wide economic disparities between themselves and the Chinese. Within the second concern there was little or no anxiety as to how the Indians and the *Orang Aslis* were faring economically. It was, as it were, each group for itself. In search of their own cultural identity, the Malays, unlike the Indonesians, became increasingly Islamic. And the more they emphasised their indentity in purely religious terms, the more they were seen as wanting to put others at a disadvantage.

The narrow definition of their own identity, almost disowning their own cultural past, did not stop there. It was allowed to enter into the definition of 'Malayness' and, finally, into that of citizenship. As could be expected, there were reactions to such an emphasis on the part of other ethnic groups. The well-known political scientist of Malaysia, K. J. Ratnam, expressed his views as follows. 'They [Indians and Chinese] are willing to become Malay, politically; culturally, however, they are determined to remain Chinese and Indians'. While 'cultural pluralism' in plural society was being talked about, the Indians and Chinese argued that 'what is required of them is not affiliation to a Malayan culture but a surrender to Malayan culture; and this is automatically repugnant to them, since they consider their own cultures to be superior to that of the Malays'.[24]

This was then further compounded when the policy of helping the *bumiputeras* economically to catch up with the Chinese was proposed. The proposal for affirmative action for the economically disadvantaged, including the Malays, could have been couched in simple class terms, but this was not done. The concern for the *bhumiputera* (sons of the soil) stopped at the Malays. It did not extend to the *adiputeras* (the ancient inhabitants of the land, namely, *Orang Aslis* or tribals). Concern was shown for their conditions in the various five-year plans and policies, but it was not of the same quality or urgency. The suspicion therefore continued, implying that Malaysia would be increasingly for the Malays.

At the other extreme, the Chinese social incorporation process in the colonial period, namely, *babaism*, also got itself reversed when the male *babas*, following the departure of the British who had favoured them, increasingly started identifying themselves with their Chinese fathers and, in some cases, becoming rootless Westernised Chinese.

Initially, the Westernised *baba* Chinese enjoyed the advantages of Western education, professional occupations, and select places in commerce and industry. For some time they had considered themselves to be some what above the unmixed Chinese. But after the departure of the British such an identity made less and less sense and was not very advantageous economically. They therefore returned to their Chinese origin.

Through its various phases, Chinese identity was rarely defined in terms of religion. In their case it was always race, culture, social cohesion and economic muscle. They nevertheless remained highly receptive to any brokered deal and compromise that the Malay elites brought to them. Their emphasis was always on building a secular political society which suited their position as a demographically shrinking second group in Malaysia. It was this Chinese posturing which facilitated several accommodating deals and processes in Malaysia's tangled political society. Such a response also suited the component of the non-Islamic Malay political, administrative, professional and bureaucratic elites. Time and time again they brokered deals with the Chinese and overcame crises of coexistence.

The Indians were far too divided internally to pose any threat to the Malays. Moreover, their number was not great, but sufficient to tip the balance in the ethnic seesaw of Malaysian politics, usually in favour of the Malays. Their numerical support was important to the Malays before the separation of Singapore, which is predominantly Chinese. After that they were of much less significance in ethnic arithmetic.

The Indians did not have a powerful Westernised *baba* style component to give them any economic advantages during the colonial period. Their leadership came primarily from the Jaffna Tamils. In Singapore any such component sided with the ruling Chinese, whereas they almost always sided with the Malays in Malaysia and took the rest of the Indians along with them. They, however, failed to turn their political support into an economic advantage for themselves.

The Indian incorporation process had two sides to it: the internal and the broader Malay process of integration. Not all the Indian segments were concerned with the continuing plight of the estate workers. Even the Tamils of Tamil Nadu did not think it was any of their business to worry about what was happening to their fellow Tamilians on the estates. But when it came to presenting demands on behalf of all Indians, practically all the Indian subsegments came together.

Finally, the *Orang Aslis* presented yet another dimension of the halting and tangled incorporation process of building a political society in Malaysia. Apart from various divisions within them, the tribals were forced to change the source of their livelihood from agriculture and fishing to urban wage earning as the nature of the economy changed. Their leadership came from outside the group and did not always work in their interests. The educated amongst them fell under external influences to such an extent that they did not think it worth their while to work for the improvement of conditions of their fellow tribals. So what we saw was politicians treating them as wards. In order to change their status from fringe people, who had also become wards, to integral parts of Malaysian society, they will have to wait until their own leadership develops and is able to put across their demands effectiveby.

The incorporation process of Malaysia as a part of its broader development process, is thus a highly diverse process. Sometimes reinforcing incorporation, and at other times contradicting and dismantling it; constantly throwing up new, and even baffling challenges to the affiliation of the Malaysian people to their own political society.

Incorporation process in any society is about the basic welding together of people and the minimising of their differences so that they can live within a common set of institutions and shape policies which are in the interests of all of them. It is a process which ensures increasing efforts to evolve together on the part of a people who have differences among themselves, but who do not want to separate because of those differences. Behind that you have individuals' conviction that someday they will be listened to, and their grievances and problems will be attended to. In the meanwhile they must learn the political skill of acting in concert with others so as to secure response to their demands. And those who live through that process also have a conviction in the fairness and accessibility of various public institutions where their voices can be heard. Of course there are gains and losses in each round of attempts, but you also develop a sense of normative–pragmatic balance in your demands, and then hang on to some and give up the others.

But while such a normative–pragmatic balance is being learnt or acquired, what helps the building of political society, through the ongoing incorporation process, is that regardless of major-minor ethnic groups, you remain a part of that process which sements the political society as a whole.

So while in the arena of political society it is advantageous to subordinate ethnic and primary group matters to the wider secular concerns of society. Then at a secondary level of lesser importance, group concerns can be pursued, bearing in mind that the achieving of wider objectives, which are in the interests of everyone regardless of the individual ethnic group, are not harmed in the process. Such a dualist sense of concern – emphasising the broader goals of political society, and within that, at a subordinate level, emphasising group matters – did not strike root fully in Malaysia. Problems of a broader political society continued to be plagued by secondary level group concerns. Despite such setbacks, the process of building a political society was continued through education and media discussions, the exhortation of leaders, the vision and perception of the elite, and a commonsense belief by the average citizen that what he or she had was worth preserving and improving.

IV. ECONOMIC AND POLITICAL DISPARITIES

i. The Transformation of the Economy

We will now examine the principal features of Malaysia's political economy and the persistent disparities within it. Malaysia, like Thailand, surprised the industrial world and became the envy of emerging countries when it reported that its exports for 1992 consisted of a relatively higher proportion of manufactured goods than raw materials. This shattered the stereotype image of Malaysia as a merely resource-based economy with rubber, tin, oil palm and, in recent years, petroleum, and nothing else. What was brought home to the world, instead, was that it had not only established a network of industries to process those resources, but had also persuaded various offshore investors to invest in its newly established industries and then export manufactured goods. This had rightly earned it the title of a NIC (Newly Industrialising Country), and a newly arrived cub on the Asian scene.

Even Malaysia's growth rate had registered an impressive performance. Among the Asian countries its relative position can be seen in Table 2.1. Furthermore, 'After four successive years of average real growth of 8.9 per cent, Malaysia's gross domestic product expanded in the first quarter (of 1992) by a startling 9.2 per cent.' This invoked the

Table 2.1   (percentages)[25]

	1980–8	1989–91
Thailand	6.0	9.8
Malaysia	4.6	9.0
Indonesia	5.1	6.7
The Philippines	0.1	3.8
Singapore	5.7	7.9
South Korea	9.9	7.4
Taiwan	8.1	5.7
Hong Kong	7.3	2.7

comment from a visiting US diplomat that, 'Malaysia's challenge now is to manage its success.'[26]

Various explanations have been provided for Malaysia's achievement. Among others there was the keen receptivity to new ideas, policy suggestions, willingness to experiment, and above all readiness to learn and profit from the experiences of the 'Four Tigers', namely, Taiwan, Hong Kong, South Korea and Singapore. Singapore, in particular, loomed very large in the consciousness of Malaysian policy-makers. Until the early 1960s it was a part of Malaya and whatever happened there was keenly watched and compared with its own performance. Singapore had become Malaysia's reference group for comparison and unacknowledged envy and emulation. But emulation was possible only up to a point because, unlike Singapore, Malaysia had a huge big load of agricultural population which took to change very gradually. However, Malaysia learned from Singapore that it was always helpful to engage in constant course correction of policy when the outcome did not match the anticipated results. In other words, Singapore had a pragmatising influence on Malaysia. Particularly influential was the practice which Singapore had adopted of selecting the best available people in society for handling ministerial portfolios. The best brains were culled from the big corporations, banking, shipping, the oil industry, manufacturing, academia, medicine and the media, and were given a free hand and asked to produce results – which they did. Since Malaysia was a little more liberal than Singapore, with more pronounced ethnic divisions within its ranks, it was restricted in its choice, nevertheless, it did increasingly succeed in putting the best brains and the most experienced individuals to work in public positions. What Malaysia could not do, however, was to establish a circuit for moving around the most meritorious in society from commerce to industry, to government, to academia and back again, simultaneously scouting for new talent all the time.

There was an increase in Malay economic initiatives under the benevolent policy of favouring the *bumiputeras*. Their numbers in manufacturing jobs, managerial positions, and share of institutional credit improved steadily. 'And Malay ownership of all capital stood at 8 per cent rather than 2.4 per cent of 1970.'[27]

Yet there was a worrying side to all this. Invariably the increasing Malay participation in the economy had an *ali-baba* side to it, in that Malays were in charge in name only because the economic unit was operated by the Chinese. And Prime Minister Mahathir had repeatedly denounced it as something that was not acceptable to him under the NEP.

Malaysia also realised that in the game of economic growth emerging countries cannot afford to have 'sacred cows' in the field of public policy. Every policy should be continuously questioned in the light of its results, and in this respect the greatest of its resolves was its fledgling car industry. Malaysia built cars with the help of Mitsubishi of Japan and manufactured the *Proton Saga* with a view to export. Initially, under the policy of *bhumiputeraism*, the government had insisted on appointing a Malay to be in charge of the plant. When things did not work out as expected, Dr Mahathir had the good sense and courage to tell the Japanese to take over and produce results, which they did. Apart from supplying a quality car for the Malaysians themselves for about US$ 10 000, in 1990 Malaysia exported 20 000 *Proton Sagas* to Britain, its former ruling country which in the past had exported cars to Malaysia.[28]

During Mahathir's years in power, Malaysia's economic policy has changed constantly. In the words of R. S. Milne, 'Dr Mahathir's policies may be divided into six categories: "Look East" Policy; "Malaysia Inc."; privatization; the policy to emphasize heavy industry; a shift in population policy; and the New Agricultural Policy.'[29] Further, any revision of the NEP must take account of the overriding requirement of growth.[30]

The growing pragmatism in Malaysian society was also reflected in its Fifth Five-Year Plan for 1986–90. At the social level, its 'declaration' referred to 'creating a just society in which the wealth of the nation shall be equitably shared'. It also ensured 'a liberal approach to her rich and diverse cultural traditions; to building a progressive society which shall be oriented to modern science and technology'.[31] The document calls for 'a greater unity of all its peoples', and 'poverty alleviation'. It also exhorts the private sector to progress from property development and estates to 'manufacturing for exports'. In its policy objectives it stated: 'Malaysians need to keep their racial and religious differences to a minimum, and instead stress on the common elements which link all the communities. Values of moderation, tolerance, and appreciation of the sensitivities of each other will be crucial ingredients in the building of a united, just, stable, and progressive nation.'[32]

Its Sixth Five-Year Plan, for 1991–5, referred to the challenge of 'managing success' and 'making Malaysia a developed nation by the year 2020'.[33] But the concern for poverty still remained. The Fifth Five-Year Plan had reported that nearly 18 per cent of people were still below the poverty line. This was then brought down to 17 per cent in 1990. Malaysia was thus experiencing the simultaneous presence of impressive economic growth and undiminishing, or only gradually reducing, poverty.[34]

At the local level, some NEP programmes often provided benefits to those who least deserved them. In an intensive study of a rural community, Shamsul, in his *From British to Bumiputera Rule* (1990), concluded that funds allocated to 'eradicating poverty' often went to rich Malay contractors, with Chinese partners, for construction jobs. Outwardly those Malay contractors were eligible for 'fulfilling the 30 per cent quota of *bumiputera* ownership in business and management, as outlined in the NEP'.[35]

ii. Ethnicity and Economic Growth

Despite such an impressive economic performance Malaysia's basic problem of the 'dual economy' reappeared and this time worked 'within ethnic demarcations'.[36] In other words, the pluralism of society squared with the dualism of the economy. Such squaring off then supplied the matrix within which its subsequent development process was cast. Such a structured approach, needless to say, ignored the social and economic dynamics whereby, under encouragement from the state, some of the *bumiputeras* were graduating from agriculture to commerce to new industries. Conversely, not all the Chinese economic activity was directly or indirectly devoted to the export of whatever they were dealing in.

A perceptive scholar of Malaysian economic growth, namely, K. S. Jomo has argued that it needs to be understood against the background of global economic trends as well as the changing character of Malaysian economy itself. By the 1980s, according to him, the economy had been transformed from a 'pre-colonial peasant economy' to an economy that had a capacity for producing goods which could be exported. For him, therefore, it was fallacious to argue that the economy had remained unchanged since colonial days or had continued its 'dualistic' character.[37]

Furthermore, Prime Minister Mahathir had South Korea as his model. Ever since he took over, he has emphasised the need to 'look East', and emulate its 'labour discipline', 'work ethic', 'increased productivity', and so on.[38] But while economic prosperity in South Korea and elsewhere in East Asia may have presented new social problems, in Malaysia they further deteriorated its already tangled ethnic situation. Such a situation undermined the class differences which were at the root of the problem. What Jomo, therefore, wanted was a 'transethnic popular alternative to the *status quo*.' However, the ethnic elites have stood in the way, giving the impression to their followers that 'they are effectively protecting, if not actually advancing the interests of the rest of their community'.[39]

For Jomo mere democratisation may not solve the problem because the political parties themselves are firmly anchored in ethnic cleavages of Malaysia. While Malaysia's economy has turned around, its politics had not, and in that respect none of the Southeast Asian countries, not even South Korea, can be a role model for Malaysia. Whatever may be the case, Malaysia's current economic prosperity has given it a leeway, and a cushion, to experiment with solutions and minimise the ethnic divide which has plagued it since birth.

Another perceptive scholar of the problem of ethnicity in Malaysia is James Jesudason. He believes that in the economic growth of Malaysia 'key economic actors, such as multinationals, state enterprises, and private local capital' have all played a vital role. Then there are the 'state elites' which play a mediating role between their competing demands – demands which often have specific ethnic references and interests. So what we have then in Malaysia are economically manipulated ethnic demands which create a role for the 'state elites' to sort out. It is a peculiar situation where 'neither dependency nor world-system approaches, with their focus on external determinants, had much to offer as an explanation'.[40]

Jesudason feels that not only have ethnic studies become 'a growth industry', but they have also cast their discussion in a narrow mould of the characteristics of successful ethnic groups. What they have ignored, however, are the 'macro-economic consequences of ethnic divisions' in society.[41] Such studies should also be able to take into account the problem of economic policies and choices. Concluding his argument, he maintains that Malaysia's response to its basic ethnic problem lies in building 'a new Malay business and managerial class'. That in turn would curtail the freedom of the state elites to play with ethnic interests. The new economic and managerial elite would have the wider interests of the whole society before it.[42]

In terms of economic growth itself, Jesudason has reached the conclusion that 'the lack of cooperation' between the state and the Chinese has resulted in the failure of the Malaysian economy to develop a strong manufacturing sector. This has forced the state to compensate with either its own resources or bringing in the multinationals to do the job.[43] This could have been avoided had the ethnic situation evolved on more accommodationist lines, that is to say, beyond an uneasy coexistence to an active participation by all segments to advancing the economic growth of Malaysia.

Alasdair Bowie has argued that 'there has been a change in state industrial strategy, from a market led approach with very limited state involvement . . . to mixed market-led/state-regulatory strategy during the 1970s, and finally to a state-led strategy beginning in 1980'.[44]

iii. Political Costs of Ethnic Cleavages

'Everything political or economic in Malaysia is dominated, and must be dominated, by considerations of "racial arithmatic" '.[45] That was the view of Milne and Mauzy who have watched the Malaysian political scene for nearly three decades. Malaysia, despite its impressive economic performance since independence, has had a troubled political evolution because of ethnic cleavages in society. The presence of large groups of people brought in from outside did not present too many problems as long as Malaysia was under foreign domination. After independence the newly independent Malaysians were forced to enter into complex negotiations and accommodations for which they had little or no experience.

The expression of ethnic differences, moreover, was further accentuated by the presence of ethnically based political parties for the three groups, the Malays, the Chinese and the Indians. And while they had their 'Alliance' to contest elections and then divide the electoral gains, such an understanding did not go much beyond the elections. In post-election periods what dominated the political scene was the expression of grievances on the part of organised ethnic groups and demands for state attention and support. The three major groups, in course of time, had also grown used to their own group approaches and devices. The Malays, being the host community, and economically not as prosperous as the Chinese, looked to the state for continuing policies in their favour. The Chinese, by and large, relied on their own economic resources, initiatives, venturesome risks, ethnic linkages, and collective pressure to win responses from the state. The very divided ethnic group comprising the Indians sometimes pressured the state and at others reverted to the typical Indian emphasis of taking more education and building oneself individually to compete successfully in various service and professional opportunities.

Such ethnic divergences, isolations, and working at cross-purposes did not help the growth of the broader Malaysian political society. The only times when individuals came together was when there was something to gain from the state by way of collective pressure. They, the ethnic groups, thus alternated between individual economic initiatives and group pressure, often at cross-purposes with other groups. The role of the politicians in the various political parties was one of countering and balancing the demands of the rival groups. Similar also was the function of the bureaucratic elites who were supposed to execute the policies of the state in a non-partisan fashion.

In the early years of the relatively balanced ethnic composition of Malaysia, there was a strong incentive for give and take. In the words of K. J. Ratnam, 'poltical power is largely with the Malays and economic power with the Chinese. This feature, together with the fact that no community is numerically dominant, has helped to make communal bargaining a very prominent feature of Malayan politics'.[46]

Since then what has changed significantly, however, is the relative decline in 'communal bargaining' process. Instead of entering into mutual accommodations, the ethnic groups invariably try and get the attention of the policy makers to favour them with new policies or a favourable application of the existing policy.

On the positive side, apart from the resource-blessed economy of Malaysia, great success has also been registered in industrialisation, foreign investments, privatisation and, to some extent, the playing down of the religious issue in politics. The nature of economic growth in Malaysia, particularly in the 1980s, also brought in changes in its elite structure. For one thing it became 'functionally more diversified', relegating the ethnic leaders to secondary issues. That once again gave a new lease on life to the bargaining process which was now on a more informed and professional level.[47]

V. A TROUBLED POLITICAL SOCIETY

Like most other emerging societies, Malaysian society too is elite-oriented. What the elites do is considered right, proper, useful and therefore worthy of emulation. But such societies which came under colonial influence were deprived, as it were, of the full measure of influence of their own people. The indigenous elite and their values, during that period, had to compete with those values introduced through Western education of the colonial variety. Until nationalist movements in each of the colonies, which invariably went in search of their national past and their own heroes and elites, the intruding colonial values prevailed.

In the case of Malaysian history, as seen by indigenous scholars, there were additional issues. After the exposure to Western values and achievements, some of the indigenous elites wanted a rational and individualistic approach to religion, together with what they called 'capitalistic Islam'. They saw value in capitalism but wanted to Islamise it.[48] They also wanted the gentle Malays to become more aggressive and competitive in spirit, because it was precisely these qualities, they thought, that had helped the Europeans to get where they were. But when the Chinese and, to some extent, the Indians displayed such qualities, the Malay elites did not see them as worthy of emulation.

The earliest leading elite of Malaysia, since before independence – who sought to persuade the Malays to think in broader terms in which different ethnic groups could live together in the kind of political society in which all of them could prosper – was Tunku Abdul Rahman. He wanted to find a solution to the ethnic problem in Malaysia within the traditional Malay gentleness and predisposition for coexistence. For Tunku, given the Malay situation, there was no other way out. Exhorting

Malays to be as aggressive as the Chinese, or giving them the protection of specifically designed public policy, would in the long run divide people rather than bring them together. He also wanted Western liberal political institutions, which were introduced during the colonial administration and were struggling to strike roots, to continue. For him the logic of the situation required the country to follow such a course. In his words: 'My experience tells me that everybody wants to continue to live the life they have been living.'[49] He did not share the uneasiness of the Malay elite towards the Chinese. 'Chinese have no intention of taking over the country . . . their ambition is to do business . . . [they] are happy to leave politics and the administation of the country to the Malays.'[50]

The political institutions which Tunku built, with a gradual evolution of the political capacity of its citizens, did not experience too many problems during his time. He combined within himself the background of a royal household, the aura of the father of freedom, and the powers of a modern day prime minister. His successors, however, had to face the growing interest of the average Malay citizen in politics, together with the concerted efforts on the part of various ethnic groups to gain concessions and protection for themselves as groups. It made the weaker ethnic groups more and more dependent on the state. Simultaneously, it gave a setback to the growth of a normal political society whereby, through your own participatory involvement, you grow in your political capacity and secure public response towards what is rightfully yours.

Neither the pre-independent emphasis, of making the Malays as aggressive as was needed, nor Tunku Abdul Rahman's solution of letting the situation evolve the way it would – with the Chinese in charge of economic development, and the Malays in charge of administration and public policy – survived for long. Dr Mahathir, before he came to power, argued that since the Malays were a soft people they did not have a chance *vis-à-vis* the Chinese, and consequently needed what he called 'constructive protection'.[51] Such views had a far-reaching influence on Malay politics. And to that we now turn.

Dr Mahathir, before he became Prime Minister of Malaysia, wrote a book entitled *The Malay Dilemma* (1970). In this book, he took a position that because of the factors of heredity and environment, the Malays were no match for the Chinese in economic and social field. Close marriages among the Malays, according to him, gave them a setback as a people. In addition to this, the fertile conditions of the land of Malaysia made them a soft people. Contrary to this, the Chinese had survived very tough conditions in their own country, which gave them a distinct edge in terms of hardiness, survivability and acquisitiveness.[52] Then as immigrants in Malaysia, the Chinese prospered during the colonial administration.

To Mahathir, therefore, the only way out for Malaysia was to pay attention to the antecedent inequality existing between the two since before colonial days and its impact on the morale of the Malays. In his words:

[T]he Malays seem to be teetering between the desire to assert their rights and arrogate to themselves what they consider to be theirs, and the overwhelming desire to be polite, courteous and thoughtful of the rights and demands of others. Deep within them there is a conviction that no matter what they decide or do, things will continue to slip from their control; that slowly but surely they are becoming the dispossessed in their own land. This is the Malay Dilemma.[53]

Mahathir's various policies and directions, while in power, have been to some extent influenced by his views which had crystallised when he was in the political wilderness in Alor Satar, and the above statement is an example of it. In power, however, Mahathir acquired a more balanced perspective. Given the enormous economic contribution of the Chinese, his criticism of their business activities moderated considerably. He nevertheless increased his exhortations to the Malays not to depend too much on the state to bale them out.

The unreconciled plural nature of Malaysian society throws up not only normative emphases on segmented lines, but also the various forms of pragmatism and attempted balances within those segments. The Malays largely derive their notion of normative emphases from the various cultural influences which they have been heir to, right from Animism, Hinduism, Buddhism and then Islam, on the one hand, and the evolving *adat* (customary laws) shaping social relationships and practices, on the other. Malay expressions of pragmatism are rather limited. This is because they remain overly concerned with the need to be polite, tolerant and act according to *budi*, and in such a process personal interests sometimes get the least attention. Reflection on *bumiputera* policies, after obtaining concessions in limited areas, may induce a coming to terms with practical limitations regarding what they can demand from the state as a majority group. It may also reflect the fact that all affirmative provisions are good only as a starting point for equal opportunity – after that one has to compete on one's own.

The Chinese are the other way round. Their pragmatic considerations often remain paramount. They are constantly reminded of the fact that they are outsiders with not much of support to fall back upon. That only their fellow Chinese can be of assistance to them. Cohesiveness, discipline, hardwork and respect for the leaders of the community are the normative virtues which will help them in the long run. They therefore must stand behind the leaders who negotiate on their behalf. The Chinese carry their cohesiveness from the social to the economic field, and then to the political.

The Indians, over and above their own fragmentation, add their own individualism to it. Their fragmentation is sustained by their caste and region, and individualism by the nature of Hindu religious philosophies. And within these, they find their normative principles of individual and social action. But they know that numerically they are not so strong so as to continue to play the game of tipping the ethnic balance. As a way out their emphasis, therefore, often falls on self-improvement and development through education and contacts, but only as individuals. Consequently, among them some of the individuals have done extremely well as advisors and professionals. This is then rarely translated into a group advantage

Nationally, the Malaysian may be seen as more given to coexistence, tolerance, mildness, and trust the Chinese to find pragmatic solutions in business competition between the Malays as a people and the overseas interests. Unlike the Indonesians, the Malays do not score well in social pragmatism but in keeping their differences within the civilized limits in the hope that prolonged coexistence will forge new bonds.

3 Indonesia: Cultural Eclecticism and Pragmatic Applications

Let us now briefly examine the historical and social background of the largest country within the ASEAN community, namely, Indonesia to be able to evaluate the nature of its development process and a variety of attempted normative–pragmatic balances in its various compartments of life. The population of Indonesia (180m. in 1980) is spread over its 13 600 islands, with a strong tendency to remain self-contained. Its geographical isolation is further reinforced by the diversity of its ethnic groups and their social systems. Moreover, its economy is still predominantly agricultural with different degree of resistance to change. Such constraints meant that it had to take much longer to implement, uniformally, its new policies or carry out course corrections. Added to these were the major political upheavals and structural changes of the 1960s. Despite such disadvantages, the Indonesian development process virtually kept pace with the growth rates and qualitative changes that were being introduced in the economies and societies of most other ASEAN countries. We shall examine those and other related aspects of its development under the following subheadings: i. historical background; ii. the nature of social organisation; iii. political process; iv. changing attitudes; and, v. indigenous perceptions. We shall now examine each of these in some detail.

I. HISTORICAL BACKGROUND

While the Indonesians, like most other Asians, did not pay attention to the need to write historical chronicles and opted either for oral versions of history or literary compositons mixed with mythologies, or even sculptured monuments to immortalise their deities and significant events, the colonial administrators took upon themselves the task of writing histories of people who came under their rule. And if some of the colonised people had the misfortune to be governed by two or more alien rulers, then they had to contend with two or more competing versions of their colonial history. That is what happened to the Indonesians, first under British rule and then under the Dutch.

Thomas Stanford Raffles produced his monumental work entitled, *The History of Java*, to record how very benevolent was the British rule as opposed to the Dutch.[1] Raffles's work was the product of a number of discussions with surveyors, geologists and botanists who wanted to put a seal of their own name on the works of scientific value which were relatively less known to other Western scholars. In his introduction to Raffles's volume, John Bastin tried to identify the reason behind this massive work at the hands of a person who was supposed to be busy consolidating colonial administration in the region. According to Bastin, the motivation behind such an undertaking was 'to contrast the benevolence of his [Raffles's] own measures with the "tyrannical and rapacious" [nature] of the Dutch colonial regime'.[2]

But neither Dutch scholars nor the Dutch colonial administrators were in agreement with Raffles. They, however, were at a disadvantage in trying to substantiate a claim to equal benevolence. Only a third party without colonial interests could have done that. To the delight of the Dutch, an American historian appeared on the scene, namely, Clive Day, who in his *The Policy and Administration* of *The Dutch Java* maintained that the Dutch took some time to understand 'the native institutions', the ignorance of which initially caused many problems.[3] As could be expected he became very popular in the Netherlands.

At the end of the day, none of the finer above-mentioned distinctions were acknowledged, recalled or even discussed by the Indonesians. For them there was little to choose between one colonial master and another. The sequence of self-serving colonial administrations, the defeat of the Dutch at the hands of the Japanese during the Second World War, and the reluctant and messy Dutch withdrawal from the former colony after the war left very little goodwill for the former colonial rulers.

What is most surprising in all these claims is that the Indonesians – who would go down in Asian history as the great eclectics who most successfully combined diverse, complex and even incompatible cultural forces – largely turned away from the British and Dutch influences of colonial days. Barring some legal institutions, administrative practices and, of course, historical buildings, one could almost assume that neither the Portuguese, the British, nor indeed the Dutch had had any significant influence upon them. This was indeed in sharp contrast with India where social and political life was deeply influenced by Anglo-Saxon legal and political philosphies and public institutions, as a result of British rule there. This was also in sharp contrast with some of the other countries in the ASEAN region. Both Singapore and Malaysia had assimilated the influences of British rule, as did India, in the field of the rule of law, governmental institutions, bureaucracy, the judiciary, education, and select portions of liberal political ideals. These countries had also started off as Fabian states and then diverged into state-directed and supervised free market economies by way of their own pragmatic course corrections. Thailand – which is one of the two Asian countries which was never colonised, the other being Japan – even felt that it had 'missed out' on colonial exposure and therefore approached Britain to help it build a civil service and governmental structure similar to that which Britain had built in India and Burma. The Thai royal household even actively tried to emulate the social and legal ideals of Britain, France, and later on of America. This was also true of Brunei.

Indonesia, moreover, shook off Dutch and British colonial influence and opened itself up to select American influence through a generation of US trained technocrats and academics. Among the Indonesian elites of the older generation, in particular, there is a deep sense of gratitude to the US for having rendered timely help when they were rebuilding their economy after the chaotic days of the Sukarno administration, preceded by the ravages of war and Dutch rule. This is now being substituted by Japanese influence. The social and political life of Indonesia does not bear many traces of these latter day influences. Indonesia still continues to live on its extraordinary skill in assimilating and perfecting cultural eclecticism.

Still on the question of historical encounter between the Western countries and Indonesia, we find a number of differences between the views of scholars on the Dutch contribution and influence on Indonesian society in general. One of these differences centres round the cultural and physical (geographical) history of the city of Jakarta itself. While Indonesian scholars go to the Hindu–Javanese and Muslim cultural roots of the urban centre of Jakarta, all of them pre-Dutch, an earlier generation of Dutch scholars spoke of Batavia (the Dutch gave that name to Jakarta but it reverted back to its old name after independence) as *their* creation after the conquest by the East India Company in

1619. Thus Batavia was for the Dutch entirely their creation and they even dubbed it 'the Queen of the East'.[4]

Jakarta had gone through several cultural reincarnations. For a long time it was a flourishing centre of Hindu–Javanese civilisation and one of its earlier names was 'Sunda Kalpa'. But that was not all. There is also a vast body of archaeological evidence of human settlement there stretching back to prehistoric times. The first Europeans to invade Sunda Kalpa were the Portuguese, and they were turned back. The residents of Sunda Kalpa, in order to celebrate their victory, renamed their town Jayakarta. *Jaya*, in Sanskrit, means victory, is a popular term in Indonesia, and even today city centres, monuments and hotels use that term to commemorate an emotional or historical event.

When the Dutch conquered Jayakarta, there were more than 10 000 residents there. But in order to make it resemble a Dutch town, they tried to construct six canals and built houses the architecture of which resembled what they had at home. They also reintroduced slavery and brought in the Chinese in a big way to open up the hinterland.

However, just as the Dutch tried to erase the earlier traces of Indonesian culture, so also the Indonesians, after independence, paid them back in their own coin by obliterating their memory. Barring some buildings, there is nothing corresponding to the British layer of culture in New Delhi in Jakarta. The point to be made here is that there was very little impact of Western social and political ideals on Indonesia resulting from prolonged Dutch colonialism stretching over three centuries. Such an exposure came through the Americans. *Vis-à-vis* the Dutch, the Indonesians remained very selectively eclectic.

On the eve of independence, the reaction of the Indonesians to Dutch colonial rule took off in different directions. One of the earliest, which then developed into a massive movement, was by Serekat Islam, a Muslim organisation, which was deeply resentful of the Westernisation of the Indonesians at the hands of the Dutch. Then there was the Communist Party of Indonesia (PKI) which concentrated its attack on the economic exploitation by the Dutch. Both these played a vital role in the anti-colonial movement. Finally, there was the nationalist movement launched by Sukarno and his associates which was inclined to take a much broader perspective on what Indonesia should do after independence. Such a vision crystallised during the Japanese occupation, the post-occupation liberation struggle, and in the early days of independence round the doctrine of *pancshilla*.

Within the ASEAN countries there was always a variety of ideological strands present in their nationalist movements. But none of them has come out with as bold a statement as did Indonesia in its pronouncement of *pancshilla*. Despite all its vagueness it did turn the nation in a more non-religious, and subsequently, pragmatic direction.

As in the case of India, the heritage of nationalist movement against colonial rule in Indonesia was something that was deeply embedded in its national psyche. It set a standard for what had to be done in society and how men in public life should carry themselves. There was nothing comparable to that within the ASEAN countries. Although the Filipinos did wage a long struggle against the Spaniards, their attitude to the second colonial regime, established by the Americans, remained ambivalent. Some of them even wanted the Americans to give direction and shape to their political institutions.

The freedom movement in the case of Indonesia did not become the basis for continuing public participation during the post-independence period. It only helped the nationalist leaders to review the performance of the colonial rulers critically and reflect on the kind of public policy needed to rebuild the nation. The continuing and groping participatory consequences of the nationalist movement were unfortunately curbed by the military takeover.

While the Indonesian elite actually involved in the national movement could not reflect on the broader issues concerning the modernisation of Indonesia, within the framework of the inherited rich culture, those who were forced to stay outside did. One of them was Soetan Sjahrir who was considered to be moderate, pro-Western and even 'Hollandophil'. He was the product of his time and circumstances. In his well-known work, *Out of Exile* (1949), he gave expression to the dilemma in which his generation of elites found themselves. 'We intellectuals here [presumably abroad] are much closer to Europe or America than we are to Boroboedeor or Mahabharata or the primitive Islamic culture of Java and Sumatra. Which is our basis: the West, or the rudiments of feudal culture that are still to be found in our Eastern society?'[5]

Although he had languished in a Dutch prison for some time, he had tried to view the Western contribution to human civilisation in a wider context, and had therefore emphasised the need for his country to widen its normative horizons, especially during its formative years, by assimilating the best that the West had to offer. In his words again: 'the West is now teaching the East to regard life as a struggle and a striving, as an active movement to which the concept of tranquillity must be subordinated . . . The concept of striving is not, however, necessarily connected with destruction and plunder as we now find it.'[6]

Sjahrir's remarks represented the thinking of the post-independence elites in Asia, which was trapped in the dichotomy of the greedy, arrogant, exploitative, but materially and scientifically active and productive, West, on the one hand, and the tranquil, virtually non-materialistic East, on the other. This dichotomy was turned upside down towards the end of this century. For it was now the turn of these 'tranquil' societies of the East to become incredibly active, and by means of their searching pragmatic approaches to extract more out of the technological developments that Western societies had launched. By contrast, Western societies were made to look more leisure–pleasure minded, always wanting to avoid hard work or do things half-heartedly and unwillingly.

In this topsy-turvy comparative picture, each of the ASEAN societies has produced – though not uniformly – complex normative–pragmatic balances and solutions which are increasingly home-grown and rooted in their own social and historical experiences. What we may be witnessing in that part of the world are economic and political solutions which are adapted to indigenous ways of doing things. Earlier, it was precisely such an advantage, of a highly developed indigenous ways of doing things, which had furnished the Western world with an incomparable advantage in embarking upon a career of bringing distant lands under its economic and political control.

Although the European powers, after prolonged colonial rule, had only a limited influence on the Indonesians, the encounter furnished Indonesia with an invaluable opportunity for social and economic development. The national movement had the same effect on the social and political psyche of its people as did the French Revolution on the thinking of the French. Apart from the fact that the Indonesian national movement stood in a cause–effect relationship with national independence, it also taught them the importance of fighting for a political goal, consolidating it by means of internal solidarity, and then engaging in a correction of policies, and replacement of personnel – even top personnel – when they did not produce intended or promised results. We shall see later on that the shift from Sukarno to Suharto, although painful in its early years, was subsequently seen as a necessary exercise in course correction.

Japan had tried to ingratiate itself not only with the Indonesians but with Asians in general by playing its Asian card with three 'A's, that is, Japan as the leader of Asia, protector of Asia, and the light of Asia.[7] Despite some of the excesses committed by Japan during its occupation, its help in the struggle for freedom and subsequently in investments enabled it to occupy a place of honour in Indonesian minds. This was then reinforced by Japan's amazing economic performance in the post-war years. The Indonesian goal was now to learn not only about Japanese technology but also about its human resource development.

While the Americans, for their own geopolitical reasons, had succeeded in preventing a large Asian country from moving too close to communist China, they also earned the goodwill of the elites and the army in Indonesia. Subsequently, the American trained economists, popularly dubbed 'the Berkeley Mafia', not only established a number of economic reforms but their own connections with their counterparts in the World Bank and International Monetary Fund also helped Indonesia to get timely help at favourable terms. Along with the Japanese approach to rebuilding their economy, the Indonesian elites now also had the American model to reinforce it. Thus within the ASEAN group Indonesia was perhaps the country which had the longest exposure to European colonial influence and yet was the least affected by it. What then are the normative results or influences on the goals and policies of Indonesia deriving from the triple exposure to the Dutch, the Japanese and the Americans? We shall consider this, together with the influences of culture, religion and efforts at economic advancement and political management, at a later stage.

II. THE NATURE OF SOCIAL ORGANISATION

Let us now briefly examine the religious system and social divisions within Indonesian society. A closer examination of its social organisation will reveal a remarkable tendency towards various forms of eclecticism, coexistentialism and combinationism on the part of its different social segments. Despite some lapses its various social segments have continued to live together with minimal friction. In working towards this, the Indonesians have achieved the rare distinction of not allowing their religious and social problems to impinge upon their broader social and economic development. In its eclectic and accommodationist approaches, it has built what we would like to call the religiosity of the practical, the likes of which are rarely to be seen in emerging countries.

Later on, we shall examine the contention that in achieving such a rare religious solution various segments of society have made their own contribution. The *prijajis*, who are at the top of the social ladder, contributed their highly sophisticated aesthetic and philosophical eclecticism; the *santris*, and within them the *umadiyas*, did not go too far towards building of an exclusive Muslim *ummat* (community) among the Indonesians and settled for a rare form of coexistential Islam; finally, the *abangans*, at the base, built their own combination of belief systems with fragments of Animism, Hinduism, Islam, Christianity and secular and practical modern-day values. In this section we shall examine the normative bases of each of these segments of Indonesian society, identify peculiarities of their dynamics, and the manner in which these have affected the broader development process in Indonesia.

Whilst a number of religious and literary influences on Indonesian society came from the neighbouring state of India, the Indonesians themselves built their own distinctive cultural and belief systems, works of art, and literature, which bore a uniqueness of their own. In the words of a perceptive scholar: the Hindu–Buddhist kingdoms of Java attained great cultural heights.

> For a millennium or so, Javanese aristocrats, courtiers, literati, and men of religion had been studying and adapting the fruits of Indian civilization. They created a culture which was truly their own: much inspired by Indian culture but nonetheless Javanese as well. They produced a great body of classical literature in Old Javanese, and a political tradition which sustained a series of major states of great sophistication.[8]

The classical Javanese civilisation thus skimmed and adapted the best in Indian civilisation, added to it and changed it, and built something highly original on its own. In so doing it also discounted hierarchy, bigotry, intolerance, disregard for the here and now implicit in the doctrine of *Maya*, excessively deductivistic reasoning, and impractical disposition, which all existed at the source of what was borrowed. Above all it kept the way clear for building new cultural systems to solve its indigenous problems. Moreover, its own borrowings and adaptations were further classicised without losing either sophistication or scope for solving problems of day-to-day living. Over the centuries, the Javanese thus became the refiners and innovators of what was borrowed without turning their backs on the practical and the here and now. Their observation of the practical sometimes acted as a constraint on what was exclusively the preserve of the human mind and spirit.

The more the Javanese were exposed to a variety of cultural influences coming from Hinduism and Buddhism, the more they perfected the indigenous eclectic capability of accommodating contending cultural systems. The real test of their accommodationist genius came when Islam, a monotheistic and comprehensive belief system, injected itself into their carefully worked out cultural system. Once again Javanese eclecticism triumphed in finding a place for Islam which did not jettison the deeply entrenched Hindu and Buddhist elements, yet absorbed the best into its normative sources.

In such a performance Java clearly excelled India in building accommodationist cultural systems, whereby the masses, and not only the intellectuals, subscribed to them. What Java thus did was to build bridges of tolerance between the diverse and the incompatible, and to leave those bridges in place to inspire efforts at intellectual rationale whenever and wherever they were needed.

Islam was brought to Indonesia in various waves by traders who came via India. The version of Islam which struck roots in its soil arrived from Cambay, Gujarat, India in the fourteenth century, and was itself very diluted. It was also used to coexisting with other belief systems and was not only accommodationist but also incorporative, incorporating pre-Islamic beliefs and practices.

What was still more impressive was the involvement of Javanese philosophers and literati in providing rationales for a variety of cultural accommodations that were continually made over the centuries, and are still being made. Thus unlike in India, where eclectic efforts were largely confined to a very high level of philosophical systems, what Java saw was the ever renewed contribution of activist-cum-accommodationist philosphers, poets and performers. In a sense the Javanese could be compared with the Japanese who also reproduced throughout their history various cultural influences, including Western science and technology, which they absorbed within their own cultural framework.

The Indonesians are thus heirs to civilisations whose people did not give up their past cultures but almost always found a place for the new. Normative considerations were operative in preserving what had already been there and, simultaneously, pragmatic considerations dictated in accommodating what was let in. Once in, the new was woven into the cultural fabric of a people whose intellectual sophistication brought into line what initially appeared to be contentious and extraneous.

Surprisingly enough, the Indonesians – descendants of perhaps the greatest eclectic sophisticates among the living Asian civilisations – do not want to talk about what they could also have eclectised from the Dutch. Explanations for this can be found in colonial brutality and the complex feelings of hurt and humiliation of a culturally very proud people. Even today, Westernized Indonesian intellectuals would rather talk about Japanese, American, and even Australian influences but not the Dutch.

While Indonesia's neighbour, namely, India assimilated what was considered the best in British achievements – including liberal legal and political institutions, the rule of law, the independence of the judiciary, responsible government, political ideals, the welfare state, bureaucracy, literature, education, and so forth – the Indonesians, particularly at the level of normative influences, remained disparaging and dismissive of everything Dutch. The assimilation of the best in the British civilization by the Indians, at the other extreme, was so impressive that V. S. Pritchett is supposed to have said that the only English left in the world are the Indians!

The point to be made here is that apart from a non-receptive view of the Dutch contribution, the Indonesians did not consider that they enriched the normative base of their social existence, even at the level of liberal values. Unlike the British in India, where there was a continuous acrimonious dialogue on liberal political values which the British claimed they had and the Indians did not (in their past political systems), thereby forcing the Indians to take the British normative background seriously, the Dutch did not make such claims or enter into dialogues of that nature in their relationship with the Indonesians. The Dutch did not feel the need to explain to the Indonesians how they evolved their superior system of law and government, with the result that the Indonesians did not think that the Dutch had anything worth taking seriously while they were on Indonesian soil or beyond. Indonesia thus remained immune to the best in European civilisation, namely, the liberal, legal and political values and institutions, despite the Dutch presence stretching for nearly three centuries. There is no knowing what that would have done to Indonesia's power of eclectic accommodation had those values been injected.

Indonesia – the largest Muslim country in the world, with nearly 85 per cent of its 180 million population subscribing to that religion – presents an incredibly complex picture of the practice of its special variety of Islam. While the bulk of the population officially subscribes to the Muslim religion, the actual faith that they practise is heavily influenced by the pre- and post-Islamic belief systems. In the case of Indonesian society, with its strong proclivity towards combining the new with the old – even if what is combined may be unmalleable or incompatible – the nature of its variety of Islam becomes far too amalgamative. This is also true of the entire region of Southeast Asia wherever Islam has a following. To understand 'Islam in Southeast Asia one must begin with data from the area rather than with some middle-Eastern theological formulation of Islam. This, however, is not to deny that Islam is universalistic theology originating in the Arabic Middle East.'[9]

Given the eclectic disposition of the people of Indonesia, they variously sought to 'translate' the teachings of Islam to fit the frameworks of their pre-existing belief systems. Consequently, not only did the different social segments of society take different aspects of Islam seriously, they also varied in the degree of emphasis on what they finally chose. Such a variety of Islamism often led to debates, claims and counterclaims as to who were really true Muslims. This debate continues on two fronts – among the different segments of society, and with public policy-makers who, without using the term 'secularism', want to keep religion out of law and politics. Thus in the world's largest Muslim country, not only has Islam been confined to the religious field proper, but has also been combined with a 'baffling complexity'[10] of heterogeneity and amalgam of belief systems.

The influence of Islam in transforming social life had been greater on the Malaysian Peninsula and Sumatra, historically speaking, than on the highly eclectic and culturally vibrant island of Java. In Malacca, especially, as far back as the fifteenth century, Muslim rulers had sought to codify Malay Law combining within it the Islamic as well as the pre-Islamic Malay Law.[11]

Since before independence attempts were made by devout Muslim leaders to push Indonesia further towards being an Islamic state from the heterogenous Muslim society it had been for centuries. At the other extreme, there was also a continuing anxiety on the part of the syncretic elites to keep on providing intellectually respectable statements to continue the amalgam and coexistence of belief systems which had survived the test of time. The best of these was in Sukarno's statement on *pancshilla*. Since that statement came during the crucial days of the post-independence constitution, there was not much scrutiny of it. On the contrary, it became associated with independence itself and is much revered even half a century after its formal adoption. So great has been the emotional appeal of this statement that even today children are named *pancshilla*.

In his fight against the Dutch, Sukarno had to depend on Islamic political movements which were largely critical of Western modernisation. However, he could not share their goal of bringing Indonesian society under Koranic laws. He had deep respect for Javanese culture and the contribution made to it by various historical and cultural forces, including Hinduism. 'The fact that Sukarno's mother was said to have been Balinese reinforced the association'.[12] It was that classical culture of Java that he wanted to revive and combine with modernistic elements.

The course of religious syncretism in Indonesia, as we shall see in the following pages, was not at all simple. It was full of compromises, give and take and gradual maturations, all these guided by a quiet realisation that what Indonesia had achieved in terms of religious tolerance had no parallel in the developing world. It must therefore be protected at all costs.

One of the remarkable things about the Javanese or Indonesian society as a whole is that it has been able to derive the norms of its social behaviour and guidance, and the meaning of individual and social life in general, from highly diverse sources such as Animism, Hinduism, Buddhism and Islam. At every stage when Islam in Indonesia sought to play that role exclusively, it did not get very far. While Islam never relinquished the effort, it also agreed to live within the framework of norms and laws which other belief systems and the state provided. It accepted all this as long as, within its fold, it was able to practise what its faithful adherents wanted.

In his much acclaimed work entitled *The Religion of Java* (1960), Clifford Geertz has argued that Javanese belief systems are a complex mix of Animistic rituals with Hindu and Islamic elements. Depending on one's social background and vocation in life, religious needs will be met by different proportions of such a mix.

For Geertz, there are three main groups in society. First, there are the peasants who live in villages and make a living out of agriculture. They belong to the broad category of *abangans*. Their belief system is a combinational mix of Animism, Hinduism and the kind of Islam which has evolved over the years within the framework of 'the island's true folk tradition'.[13] Secondly, there are the rich peasants, some of whom had migrated to the towns and had undertaken commercial ventures. As traders they came into contact with other traders on the shores of Java who happened to be Islamic. Over the years the immigrant and indigenous traders interpenetrated each others belief systems: Islamising the indigenous and syncretizing the extraneous. Within such a group of people, who are called the *santris*, there are those who can live with the wide-ranging syncretic Islam of Indonesia and those who want to keep trying to achieve an unalloyed variety of Islam.

Then there is the third segment of Indonesian society, namely, the *prijajis*. They consist of the descendants of the old aristocracy who joined the middle-class professions, the bureaucracy and the courts, and served as elites in society. Such an elite, with 'its ultimate roots in Hindu–Javanese courts of pre-colonial times, conserved and cultivated a highly refined court etiquette, a very complex art of dance, drama, music, poetry, and a Hindu–Buddhist mysticism. They stressed neither the animistic element in the overall Javanese syncretism as did the *abangans*, nor the Islamic as did the *santris*, but the Hinduistic.'[14] It was the *prijaji* who acquired Western education, developed a secular approach to politics, and increasingly manned administrative and technocratic positions in society. With the modernistic element, it did not give up its cultural heritage, refinement and the continuing syncretic capabilities, and remained a model for the educated within society.

None of these groups is as rigidly identifiable as people across the religious divide. Moreover, each of them shares a varying degree of Islamic faith which is then mixed with elements of other belief systems. In relative terms, the least diluted Islamic faith is that of the *santris*, but there again within their own confines there are variations of extraneous faiths, practices and willingness to coexist with those whose Islamic faith is more diluted. Within the *santris* themselves, there are several degrees of ascending Islamism. The more one is committed to religious orthodoxy, the purer and therefore higher is one's claim as a Muslim.

As opposed to the *santris*, the *abangans* have no socio-religious organisation, and much less prescribed codes of behaviour. The *abangans* thus enjoy much greater freedom to combine and pursue their own individual combination of different belief systems. As long as there is conformity to some of the rituals and social practices of the *abangans*, there is freedom to add or subtract a few gods and spirits from the pantheon.

Still greater freedom of worship is enjoyed by the *prijajis*. While all *prijajis* remain Islamic, formally speaking, like the *abangans* they nevertheless enjoy far greater freedom in sycretising their own combination of Hinduism, Buddhism and Islam. Like the other two, the *prijajis* as a group have their own intervariations which range widely as a result of their individual interests in faiths, aesthetics, literature, philosophy, performing arts, professions and pursuits.

With all the possible combinations, the *prijajis* do not abandon the notion of purity of ultimate values. God is characterised by *alus* (purity), and like the Hindus and Greeks their ultimate normative standards are derived from truth (*satyam*), beauty (*sundaram*) and goodness (*shivam*). These in turn are formulated by means of reflection and rational analysis of human experiences. One should order one's outer life in such a manner that one's inner life is set free to pursue one's depth of experience. One's aesthetic standards thus have a far-reaching significance for the pursuit of the inner life.[15]

With the *prijajis* there were many norms which came through the classical Javanese tradition of continuously reflecting and theorising on what the ultimate goals of life should be. In combining aesthetic with intellectual dimensions, as did the Hindus, the *prijajis* also introduced some degree of individualism. This was in marked contrast with the group considerations of the *abangans*, and the goal of building an Islamic community, an *ummat*, on the part of the *santris*, to practise Islamic laws.

The *prijajis*, the *santris*, and the *abangans*, in the ultimate analysis, all remain essentially Javanese, and bear deep imprints not only of cultural eclecticism but also a continuing ability to combine the seemingly incompatibles. Regardless of which group they belong to, they all possess the unmistakable characteristic of letting others pursue their own gods through their own belief system, by an amalgam of philosophical, mystical and ritualistic practices. Such a situation has allowed the *prijajis* to be highly eclectic, the *santris* to be coexistential, and *abangans* to be combinational.

To date, because of the diverse dynamics of various social groups, as we shall see in the following sections, even the purists among the *santris* have accepted an accommodationist coexistential position. They have in a sense followed the pragmatic advice of the great Muslim scholar, namely, Ibn Khaldun that the power of the state may remain an autonomous power, not necessarily geared to realising, in law and practice, the dictates of religion.[16] Thus even the *santris* have become more pragmatic, coexistential, and recognise the legal supremacy of non-Islamic laws and political authority. While they could accept such a position for the present, given the distaste of the army and the indifference of the technocrats to any revived Islamic thrust, they may continue to keep trying as they have done elsewhere, whenever the opportunity permits.

Indonesia takes pride in being a Muslim but not an Islamic state. It prides itself in not giving up its cultural heritage, which is overwhelmingly non-Islamic, for the sake of letting the *ummat* take over, and practise exclusively, the laws and customs which have come from an extraneous source. In a way, Indonesia has organised its own brand of Muslim society and restricted the involvement of religious movements in politics, and has sought to preclude the Wahaby Islam of Saudi Arabia from defining, in absolute terms, what a Muslim society ought to be.

Behind such an adjustment what one notices is a rare, normative–pragmatic balance even in religion, brought about by different segments of Indonesian society, segmentally at first and then collectively, earning it a distinction in its developmental achievement which is so rare within emerging societies.

The political and economic relationship between these groups, and also with the economically most powerful group, namely, the Chinese, did not always remain the same. The *prijajis*, the elites, who mostly moved into administration and the professions, were most dependent upon the economic opportunities provided by the state or state-related institutions. The elites within the *santris*, with a commercial background, became more competitive with the Chinese wherever they could advance further either on their economic resources or with the help of bureaucrats. The rest of the *santris* had much less success in their upward economic mobility. The *abangans* made a few gains in agriculture and service-related sectors in urban centres. As a rule they looked to the *prijajis* rather than the *santris* as their role models and also as guides to economic advancement.[17]

As these three broad social groups became involved in the process of social and economic change, together with the opportunities provided for their upward mobility, their belief system too registered changes and variations. Further modifications were already noticeable in the highly varied syncretic, Islamic and Indic world views of the *prijajis*, the *santris* and the *abangans*, respectively. Indonesian society was thus moving from an earlier 'mosaic' of social groups to an ever shifting 'kaleidoscope' of social fragments as it constantly responded to the broader process of social and economic change within mainstream society.[18]

There were in addition other social groups, outside these three, which were responding differently to various changes in mainstream society. One of them consisted of the inhabitants of Bali. Bali had remained relatively insulated from outside influence. Its social organisation, including a caste system, is based on a 'revised version of Hinduism'. Unlike the Hinduism of India, however, its emphasis falls more on the ritual than on the philosophical aspects of the religion.[19]

We will now briefly consider the diverse dynamics of the different social groups in Indonesia. Clifford Greetz had made a rare attempt, albeit controversial, at the 'social mapping' of a complex society such as that of Indonesia. He attempted to look at it from the point of view of social groups and the variations in their eclecticism. This put the *santris* in the middle; the *abangans* at the base, grabbing and combining the new with the old in a more ritualistic and less enlightened fashion; and the *prijajis* at the top, developing eclecticism into the art of integrating the cultural, philosophical and aesthetic heritage – no matter how diverse and incompatible it might have been – into a living lifestyle of classical taste and intellectual sophistication.

In addition, we also need to look at what happened to the various components of society when they became involved in the vortex of rapid social change. Did each of them register a dynamics which was different from the other? Moreover, in what significant respects did those groups differ in such dynamics in the rural and urban centres? In the next few pages we shall attempt answers to some of these questions.

The urban centres of Indonesia reacted strongly to Western modernism, as initially introduced during the Dutch colonial rule, and later on as a drift towards imitative American mass culture. While the Hindu–Buddhist layer in the culture of urban intellectuals could not come up with critiques or alternatives, the Islamic groups did. Among the urban dwellers those who were swept along by such a reaction were a portion of the middle class with children at university. These latter began delving deeper into Islamic principles arising from Islamic practices and rituals. While some young women started putting scarfs (*hijab*) over their heads, the bulk of them demanded academic courses on the Islamic religion and philosphy at university level.

The intellectuals and academics sympathised with the reaction of the students but did not approve of any wholesale move towards Islamisation. At the other extreme, the army had made its distaste for Islamic movements, and particularly that which obstructed sustained economic development, very clear. For its part, the army merely reaffirmed its commitment and faith in Islamic principles but simultaneously made it clear that it would not tolerate any attempt to turn the country into an Islamic state. Such a strong reaction on the part of the governing force was welcomed by intellectuals, academics and the media.

However, that did not reduce the demand for opening up more mosques in urban centres. The top officials in the Ministry of Religion, or *agama*, have recounted that there is a continuously growing attendance of middle-class educated youths in mosques. There has also been a demand, though not quite so rapid, on the part of parents, to provide schools where their children can have traditional Islamic education. It is reported that nearly 10 to 15 per cent of the student body is enrolled (1980) in such schools, which, along with others, are administered by the Ministry of Religion.[20]

But even within those who demanded an Islamic education there arose a movement of moderate Muslims called the Muhammadiya movement. Founded in 1912 by Kyai Haji Ahmad Dahlan in Yogya, this movement sought to 'invigorate the teaching of Islam' by 'purify[ing] the faith of Muslims in Indonesia'.[21] To that end it had done a considerable amount of work in society. Although it sought to emphasise education and social welfare as the two basic components of Islam, it could not give up 'pursuing the goal of the establishment of an Islamic state within the framework of parliamentary democracy'.[22] It therefore built its own political organisation called the Masyumi Party. Sukarno, however, was suspicious of it and banned it.

After the military takeover, the army adopted the ideology of *dwi fungi* (the dual role) which happened to be military as well as civilian. Sheltering under this ideology, it penetrated the civil administration, elected bodies, business enterprises and even sports organisations. It subsequently provided stability and, in recent years, economic prosperity, its entire drift of policy being in a secular direction. In early 1980s, the Suharto regime also re-endorsed *pancshilla* as the sole legitimate ideology of the country, which caused a setback to any movement with religious intentions. Furthermore, it passed the New Marriage Law in 1974, giving minor concessions to the orthodox elements, but by and large bringing marriages within the framework of civil law. The final blow to the aspirations of the purists came at the hands of the Western trained technocrats and their ability to transform the economy of Indonesia in a span of twenty-five years.[23]

Throughout the chequered history of Islam in Indonesia, during which it tried to retrieve itself from the syncretic mould into which it was cast ever since its arrival, suspicions were aroused among those social groups which had deeper roots in the pre-Islamic, or even pre-Hindu, Animism of its archipelago. One of these groups, which constitutes a very large proportion of the Indonesian population, consists of *abangans*. And throughout its history, they remained fearful of the Islamisation of Indonesia on Middle Eastern lines. They therefore consistently supported those political groups opposed to such a move.

The other insecure group in the pre-independence period was that of the Hindus of Bali. Until the early post-independence years, only two religions were recognised: Islam and Christianity. And so far as Balinese Hinduism was concerned, it was even classed as a 'religion of ignorance'. In the early years after independence, Sukarno, with his strong emotional ties with Bali Hinduism, protected it.

This then brings us to the internal dynamics of Indonesia's most powerful social group, namely, the *prijajis*. Throughout their social history, the *prijajis* have been close to the royal courts, bureaucracy, the professions, seats of learning, the army and political parties, in short, anywhere where effective decisions were made and implemented. They have remained at the top of the social pile. And having been tuned to the philosophical and aesthetic eclecticism which they themselves developed, they needed neither renewed religious drives, as in the case of the *santris*, nor a sense of cultural and economic security preferred by the *abangans*. What they needed instead was an opportunity to continue to play the role that they had been playing.

What suited them most, together with a few liberal values, was a situation where law and order was maintained with justice and firmness. Since their own attention was focused only marginally on politics, there was so much else that they could do for their country, as they did throughout its history. While there were some critics among them of the continued army rule, well past the need for it, as Indonesia stabilised under Suharto, they also felt that they and their children needed to play the role of the elites in society and should therefore continue to prepare for it.

The social organisation of Indonesia is far more complex than we can glimpse from various works done by social scientists. This is because while Indonesia is one state, within that there are a large number of sub- or micro-social organisations which are physically enclosed within the boundaries of its many islands. In the words of a perceptive writer, J. S. Furnivall, Indonesia is a classic example of 'a Plural Society'. And a plural society by definition is one 'in which distinct social orders live side by side but *separately*, within the same political unit'.[24]

There are very few social organisations in the world whose absorptive, assimilative and adaptive capabilities have been so severely tested in various cultural encounters as that of Indonesia. There are still fewer examples of societies emerging from such encounters with heightened capabilities for practical adjustments, and with a cumulatively higher and more sophisticated rationale for what had been accomplished.

So great has been the complexity of the social organisation of Indonesia that highly specialised concepts of the social sciences, with their extraneous roots, have come under question as to their adequacy in examining social and cultural life in Indonesia. One such concept is that of 'culture' itself. The Dutch scholar B. Schrieke criticised the works of early European ethnologists for using the concept of culture as equipment to judge overall performance, including physical action, of a people and then to relate it to the various phases of evolution through which they came.[25]

W. F. Wertheim was more explicit in his criticism of both Margaret Mead's and Ruth Benedict's attempts to formulate, independently, the concept of culture and then use it as tool of analysis in an empirical situation which was different. To Wertheim, the examination of the social organisation of the Indonesians presented yet another challenge, and that was true of any examination of Asian society and politics. These required a far more comprehensive approach. In his own words:

Asian societies are ... precisely those where social conditions are intertwined in such a way that it would be impossible, without damaging our total insight, to attack them with specialized scientific disciplines such as economics, social psychology, cultural anthropology or the study of religious systems. Those societies are in need of a more embracing historical approach shunning any one-sidedness.[26]

III. POLITICAL PROCESS

Let us now examine the different components of the Indonesian political process, which is heavily influenced by the personality, philosophy and style of operation of the two towering leaders of Indonesia, namely, Sukarno and Suharto. In the following pages we shall analyse the succession of political events, initiatives and responses of these two leaders, and the people around them, to be able to understand the nature of the political process in Indonesia. Combined with this we shall also examine the nature of pragmatic shift, from the early years of Sukarno's normative emotionalism to Suharto's slogan of 'development before politics'. Finally, we shall determine whether during this change Indonesia's own cultural background, encouraging adaptation and accommodation, and building the commensurate human skill, supplied, as it were, a fruitful backdrop to it or not.

i. The National Movement and the Sukarno Years

Sukarno was a product of a period in Asian history when Western educated leaders were not only becoming aware of the extent of colonial exploitation but were also creating political space for themselves to fight against it. Scholars have estimated that by the late 1920s 12 to 15 per cent of Holland's national income came, directly or indirectly, from the Indies.[27] It was also a period when colonial rule in most of the Asian countries was unable to suppress such criticism. Coupled with that there was racial humiliation which educated Indonesians were less willing to put up with. Their political sensitivities were also being continually heightened by their exposure to the writings of American liberals, and French, German and Russian revolutionaries.

In the 1920s, in Indonesia in particular, it was difficult to organise a political movement based solely on *political* or economic lines. Such a movement also needed a spiritual or moral fervour to strengthen it. This was supplied by Muslim religious leaders who saw Dutch rule, and its brand of Westernism, as a corrupting influence on Indonesian humanity.

While Sukarno welcomed the help of the religious leaders, his vision of a free Indonesia was much broader and more cultural than religious. His own writings were a mixture of Marx, Engels, the Koran, Mohammed Abu, Sun Yat-sen, Gandhi and H. G. Wells. This was evident in his essay on 'Nationalism, Islam and Marxism' (1926).[28]

In the early days after independence, the Sukarno administration lurched from crisis to crisis. He felt that the politicians were constantly interferring with the administration of his policies. For him, at that time, one of the most important things was to earn the respect of the non-Western world which had come through a similar experience. During that period there was a widespread feeling among the emerging countries that they would be able to rebuild their economies without either Western investment or Western technology or its market. The result was the well-known Bandung Conference of 1955, where, in the presence of Chou En-lai, Nehru, Nasser and others, Sukarno thundered, 'Let a New Asia and Africa be born.'[29]

Earlier such a movement had boosted Sukarno's morale, but it did not solve his economic problems. Instead of paying attention to difficulties facing Indonesia, Sukarno went in search of dramatic effects achieved by quick fixes. One of these was Guided Democracy. His excuse for introducing it was that unless people were properly educated there was no point in giving them democratic freedom. In 1963, he even appointed himself president for life. Sukarno was now very much interested in China and what communist doctrine could do for Indonesia. This alienated the army, the intellectuals, and the bulk of the people in society. It also aroused the suspicion of the Americans whose geopolitical interests could not brook another large country in Asia falling into the hands of the communists.

In a confused situation of national and international intrigues, political instability and incoherent policy pronouncements, the Communist Party of Indonesia (PKI) was alleged to have tried to capture power. This was the last straw for the generals, who mobilised the students and the masses against Sukarno with the tacit approval of the Americans. In a subtle game of indirect pressure, Suharto made Sukarno sign a document which effectively put him out of power and under house arrest. For more than a year and a half, Suharto kept a low profile, called himself the 'the acting president', and bided his time. Sukarno died in 1970, and to this date it has not been decided whether to call him 'the Father of the Nation' or not. A simple epitaph reads: 'Here lies Bungkarno, the mouthpiece of Indonesian People.'

Soon after assuming power, Suharto exhorted his countrymen to abandon politics and get on with the task of reconstructing the economy. At that time his famous slogan was 'development before politics'. The army then dismantled all the existing political parties and put an end to free expression.

ii. The Period of Transition

Initially, Suharto's slogan, 'development before politics', was regarded as sinister in intent. In the words of Brian May, a foreign journalist, who watched the period of transition first hand: 'All serious criticism and all protests, even those against manifest corruption in the President's circle, were eventually forbidden on the ground that they were a camouflage for some sinister political group, either Communist, Moslem or Socialist.'[30] In taking this bold step, Suharto realised that his slogan of putting politics on the backburner would be acceptable as long as he produced economic results.

There were two possible ways to realise this: by means of short-term measures to silence the initial criticism; and long-term measures to make economic results a continuing phenomenon. By way of the second, Suharto resurrected local Chinese involvement in the building of the Indonesian economy. From time to time and in recent history, the Chinese had incurred the suspicion of others because of their genius for economic enterprise, inordinate speed of progress, and social cohesion by not letting in others in the field. He then also tapped the growing group of US trained technocrats that was waiting to be asked. This measure had a further payoff. Those technocrats were also widely connected with their counterparts in the US, who had found their way into major international development bodies such as the World Bank and the International Monetary Fund.

While the economic upturn in Indonesia was slowly strengthening Suharto's position, he also needed a political power base for himself. Moreover, he was not always sure how long he could rely on the army. Earlier he had discouraged various political parties, and top flight politicians, from political participation. Then, in order to fill the political vacuum, he built what came to be known as GOLKAR (an acronym for a political group), which cultivated contacts with grassroots communities with the help of bureaucracy and the resources of the state. Then he filled up the new legislature, called the MPR (Madjellis Permus Jawasatan Rakjat or People's Consultative Assembly), with his own appointees. Over the years, Suharto tried to depoliticise Indonesian society. If there were problems or complaints, he and his men wanted to know about them, at least formally. What he did not like, however, was an independent criticism of either his policy or performance. Above all, what was most frowned upon was criticism of his family, and its wide-ranging business dealings which were not always above board. Nevertheless, he could not always silence the students who periodically came out with bold public criticisms. As far as the disbanded political parties, religious groups, independent minded media and academics were concerned, they periodically tested the waters of free expression and then retreated into their safer havens.

One of the major achievements of Suharto's regime was the attention it paid to developing the different regions of the country. Within Indonesia, Java, throughout its history, has received too much attention and importance. Compared with other islands, it is economically the most developed and has also been the centre of administration and culture. Everything in Indonesia is described in terms of Java and the Outer Islands. Over the years this has bred a sense of alienation among the people of the Outer Islands who believe that public policies are all essentially Java-centric. For a number of years this did not matter, but when the Indonesian political process, directly or indirectly, began to allow the expression of public demands, grievances and feelings, Java-centrism could have become one of the issues which politicians could have exploited. Consequently, under the military administration the technocrats were told to devise policies which would address the problem of the regionally uneven development.

iii. The Army's Involvement in Administration and Politics

The army's involvement in day-to-day administration and, later on, in politics was not without its own problems. Until recently, it consisted mostly of veterans of the struggle for independence who were trained by the Japanese. After independence the army officials, that is, former revolutionaries, felt neglected and even belittled by the civilian authority. This was particularly true of Sukarno's years of Guided Democracy.

After the coup the army officials, who thought they had the same kind of credentials as the top flight people in civilian authority, staked their claims to similar positions. And Suharto found it difficult to keep them out.

The emergence of a sustained military power had a far-reaching effect on the social and political life of Indonesia. Not only one's political rights but interpersonal relationships, career progress, business opportunities, and so on, were all tied up with it. As long as the army could provide a reasonably efficient administration, by Indonesian standard, and maintain a modest rate of economic growth, it had no need to be accountable to anyone.

As the economy began to pick up, Suharto realised that there was a political game to be played which could build yet another support structure for himself over and above the one that was provided by the army. His shrewd and highly pragmatic disposition suggested that too much dependence on the army might one day make him very vulnerable to its own internal cleavages, ambitions, and search for power and glory. Moreover, if he did not create channels for the flow of public energy in his own organisation, the army might, especially during moments of dissatisfaction with specific aspects of his own policy, begin eliciting the support of religious groups which were dormant and never completely eliminated. Long ago Suharto had realised that, unlike other religions, the adherents of Islam felt duty bound to keep exploring the possibility of building an *ummat* and changing the laws of the state to conform with Islamic principles. He therefore had to be one step ahead of them. To ensure such vigilance, he put some of his ablest and trusted friends in charge of the portfolio governing religion.

After containing the forces of religion, Suharto's politics entered a new phase. Apart from law and order and improved economic performance, he now wanted to appear as a reasonable person and an accommodationist, albeit without giving the impression of being weak. But regardless of such appearances, he did not want public criticism of his policies and performances to get out of hand. And it is here that the students, academics, media, technocrats, restrained religious leaders and recycled politicians had a role to play. They would then play that part within the political space which he provided. Under no circumstances, though, would they be allowed to reactivate the basic political mechanism of demand and response. It was always turned off at the critical moment when those at the top had heard enough, and it was always for

Suharto to give and not for them to take. Some of the academics who visited him and had his ear, told us that whenever the members of his family were criticised for engaging in corrupt practices, he always grew very annoyed but listened to the criticism fully.

In Indonesia, while the elites seem to treat Suharto's sequence of development and politics as an intrusion in the vision provided by Sukarno, which, in the period of economic growth, does not have much validity, Suharto and those around him saw it as a long-term solution for Indonesia's many problems. Some, however, saw it differently. Earlier, one of the most respected Indonesian scholars, namely, Soedjatmoko had emphasised the need to source social stimulus from within the indigenous cultural system itself. In his words: '"... we must evoke from within our cultural pattern appropriate stimuli which will serve as a catalytic factor in our social structure, providing an impetus towards a modernization specifically Indonesian in character"'.[31]

What then may be considered to be too much pragmatism? Is it pragmatism that is unhinged from the goals and purposes for which it was adopted in the first place? Against the background of a normative–pragmatic continuum, whereby lost balances have periodically to be re-established, Suharto may have become an uprooted pragmatic – or else his normative emphasis is based in economic growth and not much else. The social goals that he often talked about were also far too limited and did not visualise the broader goals of society beyond them. What was absent was an emphasis that economic growth was the means to something else and not an end in itself.

iv. Changing Political Process

After several years in power, the military regime had got used to a top–down approach. Its decisions were arrived at with limited consultations within its own ranks and came down as commands rather than public policy to be implemented. If there were accommodations to be made, they were largely in the nature of power sharing and financial payoff within the army. Accommodations with party leaders, elites, students, and the people were rare.

In the absence of channels for the expression of public grievances, what the established regime faced were indirect grumbles, gripes, rumours, scare-mongering, and so on. Those at the top were then required to listen in, decipher the political significance of what was said, and then either go all out to suppress it at source or listen and warn or accommodate without appearing to be giving in. In that sense the two-way communication or contact was indirect and at best unacknowledged. In such a situation, the elites and the media played the role of buffers and brokers. They would tell the people what was open or available to them. These could be of the nature of appointments, business permits or contracts for government undertakings. Beyond the protective armour of such intermediaries, it was necessary to cultivate either a reticence or an ingratiating style of approach to those in power. The latter often required the greasing of palms or giving a share in your business to the relatives of decision-makers. At the other extreme, resentment could be expressed in the coded language of parallels by referring to examples from the Hindu epics such as the *Ramayana*. There again, it was wise to take examples which were not too obvious. If a reference to such epics landed one in hot water, then it was usually possible to get out of it by means of equivocations, which are often built into those examples. Individuals could not come out with direct criticism of those in power unless they were students. The students' criticisms and confrontations were often put down to their callow youth and immaturity. In Indonesia, as elsewhere in developing countries, they were therefore the politically most privileged group.

In post-election evaluations and appraisals, the question asked was whether the government had enhanced its own credibility by means of the elections. Most were of the view that elections had to be called to impress foreign investors who had difficulty in justifying to their shareholders and directors the suitability of investing in a country which was run by people in military uniform.

In the presidential election of 1993, Suharto was the only candidate, despite indirect comments by the media and explicit remarks by students demanding change. What was most interesting was his appointment of ministers after that election. In recent years, the Indonesian economy had grown at roughly 6 per cent. Those associated with the policy of either stringent fiscal discipline or an interventionist approach to economic growth have been forced to occupy a back seat. And those who have moved into the forefront are those who are aware of the need to attract more capital in the highly competitive atmosphere for foreign investments. All in all, Indonesia now has a group of technocrats who have developed not only policies which served it well at critical periods in its economic growth, but also when it needs to reformulate in an internationally competitive environment. In other words, there are specialists to suit different phases of economic growth, and within them different individuals to innovate policies to secure the desired results. Most of this new generation of technocrats are highly trained with a mixture of Indonesian and American degrees. Consequently, what Indonesia may be building, among its top policy-makers and advisers, is a kind of minor meritocracy, albeit very limited. This might be a pragmatic lesson that has been learnt from Singapore. The new generation of technocrats is also assured of less interference from 'political' people, or from those closer to the wielders of power, which was the bane of Indonesia's development process till recently. One such technocrat has been put in charge of reviving Indonesia's 'ailing' banks.[32] Latterly, because of considerable patronage, they escaped accountability and a demand for efficiency and integrity. This means that the Indonesian development process is now creating its own standards of evaluating performance in public office. Increasingly it is what is delivered in terms of economic results by means of the policies that are introduced, rather than how close you are to the President and his family.

IV. CHANGING ATTITUDES

Let us now briefly examine the various policy measures undertaken in the post-Sukarno period under increased pressure to produce results. In such a shift of attitude the architects of the new policy had to take into account some of the basic problems created by the peculiar nature of Indonesian society, culture, geography and economy. This meant a clearer perception of the diverse ethnic groups and their culturally conditioned group orientations; the geographical divide imposed on a population of 180 million settled on 13 600 islands and living at different levels of social and economic development; and a political system which responded more to its own perception of what was needed rather than to the demands and discontents of the people in a typical demand–response relationship which is found in effectively managed political societies.

The architects of the new policies in Indonesia began to see their own historical and cultural evolution as a valuable heritage to be revived, after the colonial intrusion, but within the framework of an enhanced pace of economic growth. With the coming of independence hopes were also revived towards reaching the cultural and economic heights of the past. For this Indonesia also needed a few role models to look up to. As we saw earlier, the nature of Dutch rule had turned it away from the West in general, but that was partly rectified with the involvement of American trained technocrats. After that Indonesia became receptive to the Americans. What was still needed was to overcome its ambivalent attitude towards the Japanese. And towards the resolution of this problem, the vastly increased Japanese investments were a big help.

While the syncretic background of the two major segments of Indonesian society, the *prijajis* and the *abangans*, were indeed a great help in getting down to economic problems *qua* economic problems, rather than as problems to be solved with the help of an Islamic economic system, what Indonesia needed was a secular ideology which was broadly formulated. The ideology of *pancshilla*, with all its vagueness, was most useful in shifting the attention from religious to social and economic problems. It was also useful in specifying problems and seeking solutions regardless of one's cultural background. For a long time, Suharto and his associates were nervous about reviving the ideology in a big way lest it also revived memories of Sukarno and recycled all the marginalised Sukarnoists back into politics. Consequently, the resurrection of *pancshilla* was gradual, subtle, and purged of Sukarnoist trappings. It was made to appear as the most suitable ideology which the people of Indonesia had given themselves. In its second reincarnation *pancshilla* thus helped create a civil and economic society across the ethnic and geographic divide in Indonesia.[33]

The uses of *pancshilla* at the hands of Sukarno and Suharto were different. The former used it in order to encourage the syncretic efforts of the Indonesians. Simultaneously, Sukarno also used it to counter the growing influence of the purists who saw independence as a great opportunity for Indonesia to become an Islamic state. His successor, Suharto, disowned a great many things which Sukarno had set in motion, but he left *pancshilla* untouched until it was propitious to do so. For this he waited until the Sukarnoists were either depoliticised or rendered powerless.

Pancshilla also helped the decision-makers to rivet the attention of the people to social and economic issues. It assisted the rulers to leave matters relating to one's faith to oneself rather than bring it into the discussion of social and economic issues. It appointed a Ministry of

Religion, with five departments, to pay attention to the needs of the followers of its five major religions: Islam, Protestantism, Catholicism, Hinduism and Buddhism, all these as a routine administrative responsibility.

Once freed from the unproductive discussion on religion as the basis of society, Indonesia successfully, and very quickly, developed its own national language, namely, Bahasa Indonesia and persuaded the elites as well as the common man to use it. The bulk of the Indonesians now speak that language. Furthermore, by 1990, Indonesia attained the high literacy rate of 85.5 per cent among its population.

One of the greatest threats to the integrity of the sprawling archipelagic nation of Indonesia was the uneven development in its different regions. Over the years, the island of Java had dominated its cultural, economic and political life. Suharto is credited with having addressed this problem to some extent. Futhermore, the spurt in economic growth also gave a leeway to such policies and a number of new ventures in the underdeveloped regions.

Between the years of 1969 and 1974, the Indonesian GDP rose by a spectacular 8.4 per cent. This was then followed by an inflow of foreign investments. To top it all, there were substantial earnings from the sale of oil and natural gas. The following five years, 1974–9, saw a relative decline in growth rate, down to 6.8 per cent. But this was also the time when the nature of economic growth was changing qualitatively. More of the earnings were spent on infrastructural developments. While the green revolution was already making a considerable difference to the country's agricultural economy, the export of manufactured goods also picked up from 2 per cent to 17 per cent in 1984. The net result of all this was a highly impressive rise in the per capita income of the Indonesians. It rose from $100 in 1965 to $650 in 1985 and was more evenly spread to different regions than before.[34]

For a number of years the community of Indonesia watchers, both in the media and academia, had difficulty in believing that it had turned the corner and was well on its way to maintaining a growth rate which was pretty close to that of the other ASEAN countries. The disbelief was similar to what we saw in the late 1980s and early 1990s in the case of China, and, earlier, in the case of Japan in the post Second World War period of the 1950s and 1960s. Some of the earlier years of development in Indonesia were written off as fluke years. But when a high rate of growth started registering itself year after year, the onlookers had to revise their opinion. In 1990, especially, Indonesia watchers in Australia saw it registering a very healthy growth rate of 7 per cent, accompanied by a steady rise in exports as well as reduction in poverty. Such positive picture looked more impressive to outsiders when they saw the 'emergence of large business houses in Indonesia'.[35] Among others, the performance of the conglomerate presided over by Liem Sioe Liong, with 'political connections' extending to the very top, came through as the effectiveness of the 'new money',[36] as opposed to the lack of pragmatism of the old money. The next to be converted were the Europeans. In one of their reports it was stated that under the New Order of Suharto, Indonesia, from its per capita income of 1967, which was nearly half that of India in the same year, jumped to nearly 30 per cent higher than India's in the same year. The other side of the picture, as a World Bank Report indicated, also showed 18 per cent of Indonesians below the poverty line.[37]

Indonesian scholars, for obvious reasons, enjoyed much less freedom of expression in print media than did outsiders. One of the rare exceptions to this was Professor Yahya Muhaimin, an MIT trained political scientist, at the prestigious Gadjah Mada University in Jogjakarta, Indonesia. He tried to put the growth of the Indonesian trader class in a historical perspective. According to him, a good proportion of the *santris* in Indonesia were also 'devout Muslim traders' with their highly developed entrepreneurial skills going back for centuries. Their faith enjoined them not to just 'sit back with their hands folded, but to work as hard as possible'. For 'material wealth will only come to those who work'. In developing such a Weberian explanation of the growth of business skills of the *santris*, Yahya took issue with Geertz on the ground that colonial rule, and some 'structural factors' created by it, prevented them from becoming more successful than they were.[38]

During colonial rule, the *santris*, especially when they were in competition with Dutch businessmen and their auxiliaries, namely, the Chinese, were always put at disadvantage. They were often pushed back to their own little neighbourhood commercial enclaves. The coming of independence did not solve their problem either, for they were up against individuals whom the bureaucrats wanted to favour. Despite such a continued disadvantage, as traders in Indonesia the *santris* made some gains. But they were able to make much greater gains when they entered into some sort of Ali-Baba arrangement. What it meant in effect was that ambitious *santris*, under the generic term of 'Ali', entered into business deals with 'Baba', another generic term for the Indonesianised Chinese. A number of such Ali-Baba concerns came into existence, but they neither provided the entrepreneurial dynamism to the economy nor served the broader interests of the country. In the words of Yahya: 'The indigenous Indonesians were only the front men . . . In the New Order Period, dummy enterprises in the names of indigenous Indonesians had not only Chinese behind them but also foreign capital from Multi-National Corporations.'[39]

Under such circumstances a class of bureaucracy-blessed traders came into existence which swelled the ranks of the middle class in Indonesia without enjoying its entrepreneurial skill and independence. Such a class of traders was not only at the mercy of the state but was ever willing to do what the bureaucrat-cum-army wanted it to do. Society thus lost an opportunity for building an independent, entrepreneurial competitive force, which could then have become a channel for the next generation of entrepreneurs to demand an increasing share in political decision-making. That was true even of the Chinese entreprenuers. The Ali-Baba set-up further reinforced their marginality and dependence on the bureaucrat-cum-army. Instead of moving closer to the mainstream society, they, the Chinese, incurred more suspicion and jealousy of those who had characterised them as self-servers in the first place. Earlier on, as Leo Suryadinata had pointed out, a group of Indonesian Chinese had made an attempt to identify themselves with Indonesian nationalists and economic interests. Such a group was called *peranakan*. Since they came through the communist route, they had much less acceptance.[40]

Independently of the Ali-Baba set-up, which was limited, the *santris* had an opportunity to expand their commercial undertakings when the Chinese vacated them in small towns and moved on to bigger ventures in larger cities.

The *santris* of Indonesia, however, were not the only source of its burgeoning middle class in the 1980s and 1990s. Despite the lack of entrepreneurial background, the *abangans* and the *prijajis* received encouragement from the bureaucrats and thereby increased their economic mobility. Nevertheless, the entrepreneurial component among them, like the *santris*, depended heavily on favours from the bureaucrats and the right kinds of signals from the army. In his bold conclusion, Yaya argued that such a situation had created a class of what he called 'client businessmen' who needed favours from the bureaucracy, the army, and the people close to the President. In the winter of 1992, Yahya was interviewed by the media and other groups to justify this blunt statement. They tried to destroy his credibility by saying that he was not a good enough scholar. But throughout the crisis his colleagues and students at the Gadja Madha University stood firmly by him. Both sides wanted public attention to shift from the controversy to something else, and it did. While the economy and decision-making in Indonesia was becoming increasingly technocratised, its rigid political system was still not ready for his kind of well-motivated public criticism. Increasingly, Suharto allowed the expression of criticism as long as it was confined to a dialogue situation between himself and his advisers or audience. University faculty, writers and reporters had become much bolder in their criticism but always as a part of the audience that he agreed to face. Any criticism in the press or learned journals did not meet with his approval. All along he remained haunted by the memories of what had happened to Sukarno when he allowed public criticism of himself. He therefore always wanted suggestions as to how things could be improved rather than a public criticism of what went wrong.

Like all other societies in the region, Indonesia too had gradually become a government directed and supported market economy. It moved in that direction with the help of its Western trained economists who, on their part, also saw similar approaches bearing economic fruit in the region and in the West. Officially they all believed in a free market economy but ended up proposing a role for the state which ranged from supervision to intervention. Such a philosophy, with a combination of these two, also came to be reflected in Indonesia's various five-year plans.[41]

Despite many views to the contrary, Indonesia had thus begun registering respectable economic growth since the middle of the 1970s. The Dutch economist Boeke thought that the people of Java just did not have that kind of background, and that 'it is a mistake . . . to assume that economic urge is universally human'. Like all other 'Eastern peoples', the Javanese too were more concerned with religion and social prestige.[42] Benedict Arnold thought that those Indonesians who went after wealth were looked down upon.[43] Others had argued that the Indonesians were given to *kira kira* (vagueness) which then prevented a rational and precise way to material prosperity. The Indonesians, by their economic development, made a mockery of such characterisations.

V. INDIGENOUS PERCEPTIONS

We will conclude by looking at the perceptions of indigenous scholars themselves on their development process. As could be expected, these are at variance with the perceptions of various outside observers. The technocrats, who were closely associated with policy-making, maintained that Suharto exerted an enormous political will in the process of decision-making. He retired some bureaucrats and privatised some areas of the economy where state undertakings were draining away the resources of society. Despite their training abroad, these technocrats had a deep sense of Indonesian history and culture. They were the people who brought to bear a *sense* of what will work and what will not, given the cultural background and ways of the people in general. To them not all the rational and well thought out measures were effective in all kinds of situations. A new generation of decision-makers, who came from academia, business, banking, the civil service, politics, and even the army, understood this and went in search of the *effectiveness* of the measures proposed and then made those measures implementable, given the contexts of problem and people, so as to produce the desired results. After a spell of success in producing desired results, the technocrats themselves became critical of the linear, 'rational', simplistic analysis of Indonesia's problems undertaken with the help of global economic models. Some of them even felt that Indonesia was particularly fortunate in having its economists taking a hard look at the universal validity claiming economic models. One of the senior economists of Indonesia taught a generation of students that in policy matters it was not enough to be right, one had to be effective. One should therefore not hesitate in making pragmatic compromises.

The top policy-makers in charge of religious matters kept a low profile but were aware of the fact that their policies not only helped confine religion to religious matters, leaving other areas unconstrained by religious considerations, but also helped preserve the rich cultural and aesthetic heritage of the country. Indonesia's accommodationist social pragmatism had successfully insulated strains and stresses on society which periodically resulted from the excessive zeal of some segments. While the policy-makers did not parade their success in this respect and ask their neighbours to treat them as models, there was, nevertheless, quite a lot to learn from the way Indonesia, the world's largest Muslim country, managed its problems.

In the political field there was reluctant acceptance of Suharto's prescription of 'development before politics'. But there was also the acknowledgement of what was achieved in the economic field and in the sphere of international relations. Sukarno's emotional appeals were all right as long as the alien rule was there. After that somebody had to get down to the task of nation building and economic growth. Suharto provided that with a price. His highly personalised style of administration and constraint on criticism was not to the liking of the intellectuals and the media. But they knew that after Suharto there were no other charismatic leaders to follow, at least not in the foreseeable future, which will mean democratic concessions. So prudence required that they should endure the remaining years of the present administration. In the meantime, Suharto's good neighbourly policy and welcoming attitude towards overseas investments may have its own payoffs. The picture of Indonesia which thus emerged from various indigenous perspectives was one of qualified satisfaction verging on pride, despite some reservations in the political field.

4 Thailand: Normative Heritage and Pragmatic Adjustments

Let us now examine the development process of Thailand, one of the larger countries within the ASEAN. The bulk of the Thais are Buddhists, consequently, Buddhist cultural influences are noticeable not only on its society but also on its development in general. Moreover, as is the case in all the ASEAN countries, the Chinese component of its population has registered a quicker pace of economic development. It in turn has been deeply influenced by its cultural heritage of Confucianism, traditional Chinese values as preserved and modified by them as an immigrant group, and, above all, its recently manifested pragmatic ability to make a breakthrough as agents of commercial, technological and managerial revolution in the region. Not only that, the relatively greater acceptance of the Chinese in Thailand, and to some extent their assimilation into Thai society itself, has had a far-reaching impact on the Thai economy.

We shall examine these and other factors in the development process of Thailand under the following headings: i. its historical and social background which have had a lasting influence on its development process; ii. social organisation; iii. some public policies; iv. political process; v. some general observations. We shall now examine each of these in some detail.

I. HISTORICAL AND SOCIAL BACKGROUND

Thailand, like Japan in Asia, was never colonised. However, unlike Japan, Thai monarchs cultivated European colonial powers to teach them the new approaches to civil administration, economic modernisation and the arts of modern warfare. For such lessons, though, it did not want to pay the price in terms of territories despite a great many efforts by wiley European powers with territorial ambition. In the absence of its colonisation by an outside power, it was able to select what it wanted from them. Such a process also facilitated a speedier acceptance of what was deliberately selected. This also meant that Thailand was able to bring to bear in its development process much greater forethought, planning, and a kind of practical approach so that its own population could take to the changes in the shortest possible time.

In a sense, the constant but select borrowings, and their assimilation into its social fabric, have been one of the major and continuing characteristics of the Thai development process. Such borrowings occurred along with a deep commitment to preserve its rich social and cultural heritage. In the words of a perceptive scholar of Thai society and politics, 'Far more than in most societies, the past in Thailand is reenacted in the present. To understand the nature of modern Thai society and politics, therefore, a knowledge of Thai history is indispensable.'[1]

Sandwiched between the two great classical and living civilisations of China and India, Thailand continually borrowed from them and built a unique culture of its own. One of its major borrowings also came from Sri Lanka, especially the Theravada version of Buddhism. This too was assimilated uniquely within the fabric of its social organisation. Such a borrowing and adapting disposition was extended to the industrialised countries of the West and also Japan.

Historically speaking, the Thais had displayed an enormous syncretic ability, which was necessitated by constant borrowing from diverse sources, and then evolving what was syncretised into what was uniquely their own.

> The Thais absorbed this [what was borrowed] cultural heritage, creating in turn their own distinctive civilization: a product of Indian-ized concept of king and state, Theravada Buddhism, and indigenous beliefs, customs, and social organization. This remarkable synthesis of externally derived and indigenous spiritual, political, and social ideas and activities was characteristic of Ayuthaya dynasties that followed (mid fourteenth to mid eighteenth centuries) – and it still is, with the assimilation of two new elements: the impact of the West and the influx of Chinese.[2]

In other words, the Thais developed a capability of syncretic cultural synthesis, and then opened themselves up to absorb, continually, outside cultural and technological influences. They also effectively met the challenge of having in their midst a continuous flow of outsiders, in particular, the Chinese. Such an evolving capability then acted as a matrix within which the outside influence was no longer considered a threat but an enriching component, with a possible social and economic advantage. The external challenges often stretched the Thai genius for assimilation to a limit, it, nevertheless, also saved them from a possible inward looking disposition, given their inordinate commitment to religion. A number of values rooted in the classical civilisation of India – especially the role of monarch, nobility, and the people below them – had a lasting effect on Thai society. The notion of hierarchy, which is deeply rooted in the Indian social structure, was effectively checked from infiltrating Thai society by the influence of Buddhism. Buddhism, which originated in India, was, among other things, a protest movement, protesting against the excesses of Hindu rituals and caste system. Despite a prolonged period of slavery, the *corvée* system of labour, and the bonding of labourers to the land principals, the lines of social and economic stratification remained much less rigid than they did in Indian society. The rise of the army over the monarchy in terms of substantive power, of bureaucracy over the nobility, of the Chinese and the commercial classes over those with rural privileges, the heads of Sangha (central Buddhist organisation) and the NGOs, and, in recent years, the rise of the multinational corporations (MNCs), the professions, academics, urban middle classes, the students, and so on, continually altered the nature of the social stratification and power equation in Thai society.

Both the monarchy and the Buddhist Sangha often revived their importance in Thai society by playing their part at critical moments in its history. Even in recent times, the monarchy became the principal agent of modernisation of the army, government institutions, bureaucracy, education and medicine. That was not all, it continued to act as arbiter, mediator and peacemaker between the two major contending sides for political power, namely, the army and the political parties. As far as the Sangha was concerned, not only did it continue to maintain a powerful influence on Thai society by means of its organisation of cultural and religious life, but also by providing education and employment for those who could not manage it on their own. Thus together with the elements of reverence and sacredness associated with these two institutions, respectively, they also added their practical usefulness in changing times. Moreover, in a society which was continually exposed to outside influences these two institutions also added the elements of stability and the preservation of its cultural heritage.

Theravada Buddhism, in particular, also played a unique role in the life of individuals and their relationship with society. This was due to its emphasis on individual *merit* and the place that it needed to be accorded within society. The concept of merit, as a corrective to one's *karma*, stretched from the past to present life, and held out hope for always improving one's position in order to win justice from one's fellow beings and society. It provided a constructive and self-improvement route to individuals for their own advancement.

The broad interpretation of the ideal of merit has stimulated the rise of different kinds of elites in society, ranging from the religious to the professional. Not only that, it has also placed an enormous emphasis on education and the learning of skills.

The Thai emphasis on individual merit, as opposed to the Hindu–Buddhist emphasis on individual enlightenment – resulting from knowledge, depth of understanding of life and things, rigorous analysis of individual experiences, and, above all, an all out effort to develop mental and spiritual capabilities – did not result in excessive individualism. The Buddhism of Theravada variety, which has its source in the doctrine of the elders, moreover, also inculcated respect for power and authority. Later on when the Chinese came to have a prominent position in the social and political life of Thailand, they found Theravada variety of Bhuddhism much more acceptable to them because in Confucianism, to which they subscribed, there was also an emphasis on respect for authority. Given the prominence of the Chinese in Thai society, and a relatively greater acceptance of them within it than in other ASEAN countries, there was also the reverse influence, namely, the Sinonization of some of the Thai values, particularly in the economic field and in attaining a specific variety of normative–pragmtic balance. We shall deal with that in the final section of this chapter.

In the past, the Thai social structure had made a hierachical distinction between kings, princes and nobles, on the one hand, and the bulk of the common people, on the other. Until around the nineteenth century one out of every three common person was bonded to his land principal. Such bondees were referred to as *phrais*. The nature of their work was then prescribed depending on the kind of bondees they were. Those who had a punitive characteristic attached to their status were called *phrai luang*. The others were called *phrai som*. The latter, with their relative advantage, worked on the farms of princes and nobles. Some scholars have argued that such a social history has led to a kind of patron–client relationship in Thai society despite the termination of the bonding system. Such a view, however, has limited support in the rapidly changing Thai society.

The duality of the Thai economic classes thus produced different degrees of emphasis on the traditional values and also on the practical values that guided one's occupation in agriculture, trades and crafts. Under such a division the princes, the nobility, bureaucracy, professions, and the middle class in general remained committed more to the traditional values of Theravada Buddhism. So far as the former *phrais* or the common man in agriculture, crafts and trades were concerned, they practised the ritualised values of the trickled down variety of Theravada Buddhism, as was imparted to them, and then mixed them up with a strong proportion of pragmatism which the pursuit of their trade required.

Over the years, curiously enough, the ex-bondee commoner, when faced with the economic imperatives of the industrialising Thai society, had much less practical ground to cover. It was the high and mighty elites of the days gone by who had to cultivate new approaches to produce results, together with their strong and continued commitment to traditonal values. When the Thai economy produced a major economic revolution in the 1980s, with investment stimulus from the MNCs, the rural migrants to factories and businesses were far more at home with the new economic assignments than were the traditional economic elites. It was this latter class that underwent a lot of soul searching and agony of adjustment to a world which increasingly demanded results.

Ever since the publication of Fred Riggs's *Thailand: The Modernization of Bureaucratic Polity* (1966),[3] a number of scholars have assumed that the politics of Thailand have revolved within the power game which the bureaucrats played, either among themselves or in conjunction with the army and nobility. That could have been a phase in Thai politics. The politics of Thailand no longer revolves round the bureaucrats: they along with the monarchy, army, political parties, spokesmen for commercial interests and MNCs, professional elites, academics, students, NGOs, the Sangha etc., are one of the many players within it.

Historically speaking, in the absence of a colonial style modernisation, the old kingdom of Siam had employed European experts to help it modernise various branches of administration, including the economy, defence, education, and so on. The models chosen illustrated what the

British had achieved in Burma and Malaya. The kingdom of Siam had undertaken such modernisation not as a result of pressure from below but by way of foresight on the part of the people at the top. There was a continuous anxiety over what the European powers, which were colonising one country after another in the neighbourhood, might do next. Modernisation, therefore, was seen as a means to strengthen Siam and ward off any future designs on its territory. Modernisation was also seen as a measure to bring about development in general which would then minimise dissatisfaction with the regime. It was these top–down pragmatic measures of the earlier period which have left behind deep imprints on society. Until recently, practically all its development initiatives were either undertaken or inspired by people at the top.

The initial impact of such a top–down development process was the reinforcing of power at the top, in particular the monarchy, in a period when elsewhere it was in decline. Simultaneously, such a strategy also strengthened the hands of the bureaucracy which was needed to implement new measures. Subsequently, the bureaucracy came to have a life of its own, injecting itself into the power equation where until recently there were only two players – the monarch and the army. And as Thailand began to put more emphasis on education and the professions there also appeared yet another contender for power – the educated elite. Gradually, more players joined the power equation. These were the economically powerful Chinese minority; the spokesmen for the indigenous commercial interests and the MNCs; the political parties, often representing the different factions in the army; the NGOs; the academics and the students, and the Sangha. These contenders for powers spoke with many voices but always on behalf of the people. What they tried to do was reduce the exclusivity of any single group to speak on behalf of the people.

The bureaucracy and the army, despite their earlier and prolonged prominence, were unable to cope with the new social and economic issues which hit the political scene as a result of the extraordinary pace of development in Thailand. These issues began chipping away at both their status and power. In the 1970s and 1980s especially Thailand had experienced enormously accelerated pace of economic growth, and there was little or no effort to balance that growth in the social and political compartments of Thai society. The bulk of the economic expansion was taking place in urban centres, which meant a vast migration of the population from rural communities. Such migration put enormous pressure on the services in urban areas and took away the economic and human resources from rural communities. The accelerated pace of industrialisation and commerce also resulted in the major depletion of natural resources, causing grave environmental damage. The accelerated economic growth also put great stress on bureaucratic structures, which, together with the politicians and the army, became the major players in the rapidly increasing corruption in Thai society. The bureaucrats and the soldier-cum-politicians became deeply involved in what came to be known as the sex industry of Thailand, presumably one of the largest in Asia.

The bureaucrats, the top ranks in the army, with or without interest in politics, and the politicians were for a prolonged period accountable to no one but themselves. They had tried to stifle the growth of the accountability movement as long as they could. However, in the late 1980s and the early 1990s, they could not stem the tide of a movement which wanted accountability and participation in the making and implementing of public policy. In giving expression to such a demand, a section of the print media and the educated middle class had played a crucial role.

Added to this were the changing external factors which had affected the nature of politics in Thailand. The influence of the US on Thailand has been manifold and complex. In a sense the US represented in Thailand, and still does, a model of what an indiscriminately technologised society would look like. The type of social modernisation which the US represents is deeply despised by the professional elites, the academics, the Sangha and the media. So far they have been powerless to stem the imitative tide of American mass culture and consumerism which have brought in an indiscriminate number of shopping malls with vast crowds of youths in their sneakers (in that heat) and jeans. As a perceptive European scholar put it, the only place where one can walk now in Bangkok is in its shopping malls.

The Thai elites have had an enormous respect for American educational and political institutions, whereas the military brass admired the training given to its personnel and the high-tech military hardware. The significance of open political debates, continually forcing the American ruling group to be accountable to the people who elected them, was not lost on the academics, the professions, the media and the students. They in fact wanted Thai society to emulate precisley those ideals and practices which made such a democratic process possible. But the military personnel who were in charge of the administration and politics of Thailand would have nothing to do with it. Moreover, the threat of communism in the region, and the Vietnam war, had also helped the army chiefs to ignore the political side of the American model. All that changed once the GIs left the Asian scene and Thailand herself experienced enormous economic growth.

Thailand's attude to Japan is no less simple. The Thai elites are conscious of the historical fact that, like the Japanese, they too were never colonised. Therefore there is undoubtedly a lot in common between these two free people. Moreover, like Japan, Thai modernisation has been selective, both allowing into their respective social and political systems only what they wanted. Since Japan, during the post Second Great War period, had relied heavily on investing in its human resources and in building its own society along with its economy, the Thai elites felt that they too should introduce similar measures.

In the winter of 1991, Japan apologised only to the United States for Pearl Harbor and not to the countries of ASEAN which had suffered much more at their hands. Even Singapore, not normally given to critcism of major economic powers, was upset. Among the major ASEAN countries, Thailand had not pressed for an apology and during the Second World War, had even given facilities to Japan. In the post-war period, up to the 1970s, the strong men of Thailand often exhorted the people to emulate Japan, but after that Thailand spoke with many voices, some of them critical. An era of cautious relationship between the two countries ensued. Japan on its part increased its investment in Thailand from $800 million in 1988 to $1.5 billion in 1990, but studiously maintained a low profile and encouraged closer cultural ties and peace corp type activity among its youth in Thailand. When Thai academics discussed the possibility of using South Korea as a model in place of Japan, Japanese commentators ignored this shift in Thai thinking.[4]

The nature of politics in Thailand had thus experienced a sea change since the days when it was described merely as a bureaucratic polity. The very presence of more political players had changed the political scene almost beyond recognition.

In their development process, the Thais have been imitators of portions of the achievements of various Western nations ever since they came in contact with them 200 years ago. Historically, too, they had chosen what they wanted from the Chinese, Indians, Cambodians, British, American, Japanese, Koreans etc. They have consistently refused to become *one nation admirers*. Historically speaking, they had repeatedly made composite models out of what they had chosen and chopped from others and then successfully grafted them on to their own.

II. SOCIAL ORGANISATION

Let us now examine some of the features of the Thai social organisation which have an impact on its development process, and also on the peculiar normative–pragmatic balance within it which makes such a process different from other societies that we have examined in this volume. Since religion is a major aspect of Thai social organisation we shall begin with it and then evaluate its significance in the other compartmens of life.

i. Theravada Buddhism

Nearly 95 per cent of the population of Thailand is Buddhist, 4 per cent Muslims, and a little less than 1 per cent Christian. Buddhism as a religion is well organised in Thailand. Throughout the country it has a network of monasteries and monks, and a variety of institutions, including educational institutions, which are run by it. Scholars have estimated that there are 30 179 monasteries with 357 048 monks looking after the spiritual and social needs of the population. In addition to these there are also Chinese and Vietnamese Buddhist institutions. The Buddhist monks of Thailand run 10 400 Buddhist ecclesiastical schools. Then there are highly respected centres of Buddhist learning such as Mahamukut Buddhist University and the Mahachulalongkorn Buddhist University opened in 1946 and 1947, respectively. The Buddhist Association of Thailand, which was founded in 1933, with its many affiliated branches, enjoyed royal patronage.[5]

The influence of the Thai variety of Buddhism, namely, Theravada Buddhism – which came from Sri Lanka, and also via the cultural influences of the Mon and Khemar civilisations – has permeated deeply into the social fabric of Thailand right across classes, regions, professions, and the rural–urban divide. Apart from its influence on the day-to-day conduct of its people, Buddhism's usefulness to the rapidly developing Thai society and economy is continually being discovered.

There is a widespread belief that whatever the problem, the well understood principles of Buddhism can find a solution to them.

Historically speaking, Theravada Buddhism, in particular, always 'validated and complemented' the institution of kingship. In the words of Professor S. J. Tambiah of Harvard, 'Buddhism and kingship had a close complementary relationship in Ceylon, Burma and Thailand, all of them countries of Theravada Buddhism.'[6]

Furthermore, the way in which the bhikkus could operate in society, then in Sangha, and then back into society, if they so wished, had indicated a highly practical set of rules of association for them. Originated as a Buddhist counterpart of the Brahmin *sanyasis* (those who renounce worldly ties), the bhikkus in Thai Buddhism could go in and out of society, and even take on bhikku status for a short period, to spiritually recharge themselves, and then return back to society. Such an in-and-out circuit, brought the bhikkus close to society. And the restless and the seeker within the society got an opportunity of short withdrawal and self-renewal. One was thus not totally out of society, as was the Indian *sanyasi*, nor was one an inseparable part of it.

Merit-making was initially defined as a pursuit in and around the *wat* (temple), but over the years it came to acquire a much wider social and practical reference. It came to be governed by the considerations of obtaining 'security and safety and prosperity in this world and the next'.[7]

Despite its concession to practical considerations, Theravada Buddhism played a conserving and an anchoring role in Thai social and political history. The two words which constituted it, namely, 'Thera' meaning the Elders of the Buddhist Order, and 'Vada' meaning speak or tell, indicate its bias in favour of the experienced and the established. And its elders were deeply committed to preserving the 'doctrines and precepts preached by Buddha'.[8] Such a bias in favour of the doctrines and precepts, and of the Elders of the Buddhist Order to express them, historically, proved to be of immense value to Thai society. During the middle of the nineteenth century when there were numerous intrigues on the part of the European colonial powers to penetrate Thailand, among other things by means of Christianity, the Royal household, the Sangha, and other leading men in society rededicated themselves to Theravada Buddhism. Consequently, culturally and politically, Thailand was able to insulate itself from the outside influences it did not want.

One of the major institutions of Thai Buddhism is the Buddhist Sangha (organisation). Its goals are twofold. Firstly, to encourage a basic commitment to personal enlightenment, to guide the course of not only ones's own actions but also those who might need help of that nature. In that connection, Lord Buddha's exhortation to the bhikkus, who were enlightened by him, 'go forth ye bhikkus, for the welfare and happiness of mankind', is repeatedly cited. What it encourages is a *social* concern, and also a social involvement on the part of the bhikkus and the Sangha. In days gone by such an involvement was relatively easier than in the Thai society of today.

Secondly, involve the lay individuals in the activities of the Sangha, help them educationally, and also improve their chances of being able to play a useful role in society. One of the unexpected results of this is that younger men of rural background, after their education in the Sangha, have made a career for themselves within it rather than outside.[9] The Sangha now has a huge employment roster.

Such a two-way interaction of the Sangha, with bhikkus in society and layman in the Sangha, indicates the ambitious nature of 'social interaction' between society and the Sangha. While Theravada Buddhism emphasises personal emancipation of the individual from his worldly concerns, it also binds the emancipated individual to the concerns of society of which he is a part. In this latter capacity he is sent back to society not through his own personal interests but because his own enlightenment so directs him.

ii. Thai Society

Let us now examine the nature of the changing Thai society and the controversy that it generated in its interpretations. We shall subdivide our presentation under the following themes: (a) the changing Thai society; (b) 'the Loosely Structured Society' Controversy; (c) the Chinese as a vital component of the changing Thai society; (d) and the significance of all these to our major concern of understanding the attempted normative–pragmatic balance and its peculiarities.

(a) The changing Thai society

No society lends itself to a simple and straightforward analytical characterisation, least of all Thai society. And yet scholars obsessed with achieving glory for having formulated a 'paradigm' which explains everything about Thai society have not only attempted it but have even gained currency, and some kind of paradigmatic influence, for having done so. The paradigm in question was formulated by John Embree in his much discussed paper entitled, 'Thailand: A Loosely Structured Social System'.

As stated earlier, Thai society, like the Japanese, was able to keep itself insulated from Western influences because it was not colonised by European powers. Thus unlike all other ASEAN countries, such as Singapore, Malaysia, Brunei, Indonesia and the Philippines, Thailand was able to select what it wanted from the West. This meant that there was a specific role for the selectors to play in letting into Thailand only what they wanted. The two major selectors, until recently, were the Buddhist Sangha and the Thai monarchy. The Buddhist Sangha, as the repository of traditional values, has struggled very hard to keep guard against extraneous influences, and in so doing has had considerable success. The Buddhist Sangha – barring the recent onslaught of American mass culture affecting the youth, and Western style consumerism affecting most of the town dwellers – was able to retain its hold to a great extent on Thai society. Moreover, there was near total acceptance of the values that it propounded.

The monarchy, on the other hand, actively went out of its way to determine the specific areas in which Thai society should imitate Western dress, education, medicine, technology, civil and military administration, political institutions and practices. But at no stage did the monarchy want to weaken the hold of traditional values on Thai society. In fact apart from being a protector of the Buddhist Sangha, the rulers of Thailand publicly associated themselves with it and its values so as to provide an additional support for its continued acceptance by society.

Apart from the conserving and modernising roles of the Sangha and the monarchy, respectively, *personal relationship* played a vital role in the organisation of Thai society. Earlier, the Thai agricultural economy was based on the *corvée* system (forced labour) and slavery for its steady supply of labour in rural areas. This inevitably led to a personal relationship between the landowner and the labourers. The enlightened king of Thailand, Chulalongkorn, abolished slavery in 1874 and *corvée* labour in 1900. Nevertheless, for a long time social change was routed through those personal links, until such time as further change in the land tenure system, the modernisation of the Thai economy, urbanisation, migration from rural to urban centres and the spread of education, entered a critical stage to replace the conduits of social change. In the 1970s and 1980s, the boom decades, the Thais were more influenced by the forces released by the changing economy, urbanisation, migration, and so on than by personalised relationships which no doubt continued side by side and competed for influence with the new forces.

Critically viewing the oft-used 'patron–client theory' for describing the complex and dynamic nature of social and economic relationships, the editors of *Strategies and Structure in Thai Society,* maintained that: 'It is a serious mistake to either reduce the social order to a congeries of interpersonal transactions or resort to a broader (though not necessarily class) framework which ignores the individual and his or her relations with others.'[10] Furthermore, they argued that the extraordinary emphasis on 'patron–client' theory 'weakened the descriptive and analytical value of patron–clientage and associated concepts and led to an ignoring of other, sometimes very important, elements of personalism in Thai society such as friendship and family connections'.[11]

Nevertheless, 'personalism' does not have the same level of moral obligation as kinship. What we see in 'personalism', on the other hand, is a strategy of temporary identification, making use of its symbols so as to pass as one of the 'insiders' or obtain protection of someone who advances one's advantages. Since there are no deep commitments in such relationships, 'personalism' unlike kinship is used more as a strategy.

In the pervasive atmosphere of fleeting relationships, any movement outside one's locale meant a re-evaluation of strategy and a search for a new set of personal relationships. Personalism as a strategy received a setback in the impersonal situations of migration to big urban centres or being on an impersonal factory payroll. Under those circumstances, 'personalism' may have acquired, to some degree, a character of a mutuality based friendship.

The world of the migrating Thais had experienced a far greater pace of change than did those who were caught in a similar rural–urban push in other Asian societies. This is because the personal ties which bound the average Thai rural worker were not merely those of family and kinship but also of the work-place. Few societies have changed as rapidly in the course of less than a century as did Thai society, wherein nearly one-third of the ex-slaves and ex-*corvée* labourers were pushed into a rapidly urbanising and industrialising society. In such a transformation, initially at least, the personal ties of family and kinship were diluted until they were somethimes re-established across the rural–urban divide. But so far as the ties of the work-place were concerned, they were not lost for ever; there were now fellow villagers, friends in the work-place and common union membership in its place. During this period that saw the weakening of the primary groups to which Thais were born, namely, the family and ethnicity, the other two major institutions of society, namely, the local *wat* and/or Sangha and the monarchy, acquired an added and sometimes manifest identification. They gave to the migrants larger than life institutions to belong to as followers and subjects, respectively. The esteem in which both these institutions are held in urban Thailand have hardly any parallels in other Asian societies. The migrants there have revitalised or forged bonds of personalism as devotees and subjects and feel protected and secure as a result.

(b) 'The loosely structured society' controversy
Let us now examine the controversy created by the much discussed paper by John Embree which characterised the entire Thai society as one which did not have a closely knit social structure similar to Japan. In his 'Thailand-A loosely Structured Social System' John. F. Embree maintained that what struck him as an observer was 'the individualistic behavior of the people' and the absence of 'regularity, discipline, and regimentation in Thai life.'[12] For the author what was responsible for the individualistic behaviour of the Thais was the loose family structure and also a weak framework of mutual obligation in rural communities. He thus saw too much of 'looseness' in Thai society as opposed to what existed in Japan.

Embree had not gone deeper into the nature of Thai society. While the Hindu–Buddhist influence on Thai society led to individualism at one level, the structure of Thai society, vitally influenced by the presence of the well-organised Sangha, inculcated social compliance and togetherness. The all-pervasive influence of the Sangha thus does not leave much room for Thai society to become a 'loosely structured society', as some scholars had observed. In fact Theravada Buddhism does promote social cooperation through its emphasis on individual responsibility.

Despite its lack of careful observation of Thai society, 'Embree's article is probably the most cited work on Thailand'.[13] For this reason some scholars were even inclined to give it the status of a 'paradigm' on Thai studies.[14] Normally not given to taking up theoretical issues with Western scholars, this time even Thai scholars felt that Embree's conclusion could have been deduced from his own pre-existing 'model'.[15]

Embarrassed by the success of Embree's 'paradigm', whereby too many scholars took his characterisation of the Thai social system as 'loosely structured' at its face value, J. A. Niels Mulder came out with a blunt criticism: 'he [Embree] never did systematic social science research in that [Thailand] country'. Furthermore, 'Embree's formulation was of necessity impressionistic in character'.[16]

Thai scholars felt that even American cultural anthropologists found it difficult to escape the influence of Embree's 'paradigm'. Boonsanong Punyodyan wrote that after Embree the Americans cultural anthropologists 'have become so preoccupied with his thesis that in their observation and analysis of Thai soeity, or aspects thereof, they have unceasingly centred their attention on this (loosely-structured social system) notion and seemed least interested in viewing Thai society from any other angle. (For notable examples, see Hanks, 1962; de Young, 1958; Hanks and Phillips, 1961; Phillips 1965; and Piker 1968a.)'[17]

(c) The Thai world view

Thai cultural history records a gradual evolution of its 'Siamese Great Tradition' stretching from the early kingdoms of Ayutthaya down to kingdoms in Thon Buri and then Bangkok.[18] With exposure to the civilisations of India, China, Mon and Khemer, Thailand gradually developed its own cultural traditions in the seats of learning of its various kingdoms. Over the years, the world view of the Thai has changed under the variety of different influences – Buddhist, Chinese and subsequently Sino-Thais values, and in recent years values which gained currency with the advent of urbanisation and economic growth.

The greatest single cultural influence on Thai society had been that of Theravada Buddhism. It had established a cultural matrix and a world view, within which subsequent cultural influences were absorbed. In the words of Chai Podhisita, 'religious values and belief are often incorporated into concrete everyday behaviour and situations and inspire the motivations of individual actors involved'.[19] Further, he argues that since human suffering is the central theme in Buddhism, the question is how to attain freedom from it. One of the major reasons of suffering is attachment: human attachment to human beings and material possessions. And the escape from it therefore lies in the conquest of the feelings which lead to attachments.

There is another source of suffering, however, and that is one's *karma*. Theravada Buddhism is sometimes characterised by scholars as '*Karmic Buddhism*'. And human escape from the suffering arising out of one's *karma* is gained through the attainment of *merit*, which can help us escape suffering not only in the life to come but even in our present life. In the Thai world view, therefore, merit (*bun*) and demerit (*bap*) become very important. The ultimate goal is to escape from the cycle of births and deaths by attaining *nirvana*. To reach this state, guidance given by the enlightened to cultivate and attain *bun* and avoid *bap* becomes crucial. Since *bun* and *bap* relate to this life as well as to the next, the guidance of the Sangha and *bhikkus* therefore becomes very important.

On the other hand, not everybody's world view is shaped by the teachings of Theravada Buddhism and the organisation which is devoted to it. For some it could proceed at the level of personal enlightenment attained by the individual after initial guidance from the organisation. For others ('rice farmers' or rural dwellers), and this relates to the bulk of society, there is a variety of animistic beliefs which attribute control over humans to supernatural forces and the spirits of place. Therefore, practical wisdom demands that they are brought to one's side by means of rituals and offerings. These forces govern not only one's own life but also the lives of those who govern.

Despite the emphasis on merit for the life in this world and in the hereafter, in a survey 'ambition' and 'hardwork' for specific goals was ranked after such attributes as 'self-reliant and independent'; 'honest and sincere'; 'responsible'; 'grateful and obligated', etc.[20]

The world view of the Thais, as in any other society, did not register a monolithic picture. But what was most significant was the possibility of putting merit to work and using it in this material life, while also accumulating points for the ultimate relief from the cycle of births and deaths to which one's *karma* had condemned oneself to. As in Max Weber's Calvinist ethic, which 'canonised' some of the material pursuits, merit in the Thai world view was of as much significance in this life as it was in the next. This was in marked contrast with the Hindu world view which condemned the present life to a kind of *maya*, or illusion, which then becomes a test of ability in not swerving from the steadfast path to righteousness. Only the life to come, or *moksha*, the

Hindu counterpart of the Buddhist *nirvana*, was the real one. The norm of merit thus added an enormously important dimension of *practicality* in the Thai world view.

(d) The Sino-Thais
Throughout Southeast Asia one cannot examine the development process of any of its regions without taking into account the contribution made by the Chinese. As traders, early immigrants and later on as settlers in the region, their role has been of vital importance to any study of ASEAN countries. In the words of William Skinner:

> With the demise of Western colonialism in Southeast Asia, the overseas Chinese have assumed greater importance for the future of that region. China's recent emergence as a major communist power [and now as a major economic power], too, has added a new dimension to their political influence. Centuries before these developments, however, overseas Chinese were already playing an important role in the economic development and social evolution of the major Southeast Asian countries. It is no exaggeration to say that the central current of Thai history in recent centuries cannot be properly understood or anlayzed apart from the changing position of the overseas Chinese.[21]

For the Thais and the Chinese, the ethnic divide also coincided with economic differences. The Thais, until around the middle of this century, preferred to stay in agriculture, government service and small self-employed trades. The Chinese and their descendants, on the other hand, went into commerce, industry, finance, mining, etc., over and above wage-labour. The Chinese distinguished themselves for their

> extreme industriousness, willingness to labour long and hard, steadiness of purpose, ambition, desire for wealth and economic advancement, innovations, venturesomeness, and independence. The Thai, by comparision, were generally said to be indolent, unwilling to labour for more than immediate needs, contented with their lot, uninterested in money or economic advancement, conservative, and satisfied with a dependent status.[22]

The fertile land of Thailand and, above all, an extremely favourable man–land ratio had made the Thais a softer people, unlike the hardy and ambitious Chinese. In their drive towards economic advancement, the Chinese were also aided by the Confucian ethic of achievement in either scholarship or government position, or indeed in economic enterprise. A successful Chinese would bring up his extended family under one roof. And such a family would also be his cushion in case his enterprise and risk did not bear fruit in foreign lands. After each successful enterprise he must take further risks. The best of the Thais could not keep pace with the economic dynamics of a moderately successful Chinese. Even their emphasis on 'merit', which we examined earlier, did not go as far and as fast, as did the lure of economic advancement to the Chinese.

In the game of economic advancement, the Thais had a late start. Until the turn of this century, the mass of the people were rigidly fixed in the economic hierarchy of Thailand. The *corvée* system and slavery took away the desire for mobility and initiative from the average Thai. Having worked all his life for either royalty or a patron, the average rural Thai did not know which way to turn long after the *corvée* system and slavery were abandoned.

Initially, the Chinese worked on the periphery of Western economic interests, sometimes assisting them by accommodating their demands and learning new skills from them. But when they began registering success after success in competition with their assumed superiors, namely, the Westerners, they aroused the suspicion not only of the bureaucrats but also of some people in the palace. King Wachirawut, began sharing the suspicion of the Westerners towards the Chinese and eventually became an anti-sinicist. He encouraged a public outcry against the presence of too many Chinese in Thailand and is reported to have described them as 'the Jews of the East'. He also sought to deprive the Chinese of some of their rights and privileges. This policy did not continue for long, and by 1920s the Chinese had regained most of their rights as residents of Thailand.

Over the years the Chinese, who were more accepted in Thailand than in other parts of ASEAN countries, developed what came to be called an 'intermediate culture',[23] which was an amalgam of their own culture and that of the society where they had settled. The Chinese throughout Southeast Asia had periodically reincarnated themselves to suit the requirements of different phases of economic growth of the various societies where they had made a home for themselves.

The social and economic changes in post Second World War Thailand, and the economic boom of the 1970s and 1980s, gave rise to a

Western educated and affluent Thai elite. Such an elite which was largely located in the professions, commerce, and international joint commercial and industrial ventures, did not view the Chinese as seeking only their self-interest but as stimulating a lot of economic opportunities and advancement in Thailand. Moreover, over the years the Chinese had become nativized. The Thai-ised Chinese had therefore less difficulty in terms of social acceptance and even intermarriage. Such a process helped the Chinese socially and the Thais economically.

During the last two decades of Thai economic expansion, the MNCs, instead of taking the Chinese as partners, preferred Thais who might have retired from the army or government service so as to sail through the problems with permits, and so on. Now the Chinese have their own MNCs, bank connections and shipping interests in the region, and they too are picked up as partners by the Europeans and Americans for developing the Thai economy.

The booming economy of Thailand has so far not given rise to a movement corresponding to *bumiputeraism* in Malaysia. And yet the acceptance of the Chinese in Thai society has not been a straightforward process. Commonality of religion, a rich cultural heritage, an assimilating disposition, and economic boom from which most have benefited in Thailand, have no doubt minimised the fear of the Chinese. Nevertheless, their cultural unmalleability and economic power do register themselves as targets of periodic criticism. At the other extreme, we have the culturally self-assured Thais, who are in no need of cultural self-definition at the expense of others, and who prefer to concentrate on their own concerns rather than pick on the Chinese.[24] Furthermore, since the Chinese form less than one-fifth of the population, half of whom are in Bangkok, they are not perceived as a threat.

The question, then, is how did the presence of the Chinese change the nature of Thai society? The Chinese have been with the Thais for a very long time and over the centuries have continually adapted themselves: economically, as traders, agriculturalists, businessmen, industrialists, bankers, shipping magnates, professional people, politicians, partners with MNCs, networkers with overseas Chinese the world over, in short, the initiators and the takers of wherever and whenever economic opportunities presented themselves. The significance of such economic dynamism was not lost on the Thais. Furthermore, the Thais even gained a rare historical opportunity of giving a good account of themselves *vis-à-vis* the Sino-Thais. This was due to the increasing presence of Japan,

Japanese technology and investment, and Japanese economic leadership in the region, which seemed to favour the Thais. As the only two nations of Asia which were not colonised, the Thais feel naturally attracted to the Japanese. Even at the academic level the nature of contact between these two countries is different. This often results in Japan wanting to do more for Thailand, and the Japanese preference in all this has invariably been for the Thais. So while the Sino-Thais have gradually built themselves up economically over the centuries, the Thais are more likely to receive an external boost to their economic drive which has recently been set in motion.

It is this group of Thai elites, with a number of opportunities opening up as a result of a special relationship between Thailand and Japan, that views Western countries and Japan in a different light. It sees the US as a declining economic superpower but pays lip service to it to keep its interest and investments in Thailand. In moving closer to Japan it is beginning to learn two vital lessons from it, namely, the need to invest in the improvement of human skills and to be more pragmatic. Fortunately, for Thailand, even without formal education in the past, there had been a continuing emphasis on human skill and quality. It has been a country which has produced incomparable excellence in its craftsmen no matter what they did. Such an emphasis on excellence has even been brought into the field of manufacturing electronics and high-tech products. And as far as adaptability and a result-oriented approach are concerned, the Thais have this in their traditional merit system, except that this time around it will require greater emphasis on results in this world rather than the next.

III. SOME PUBLIC POLICIES

Thailand may be said to be one of those countries which manifested an international sequential chase: of labour chasing capital to where it was located; and, subsequently, the flow of capital to where labour was located. To put it simply, Thai labour migrated initially to the more rapidly developing economies of the Asian countries, that is, Singapore, Hong Kong and Japan. Then there was a flow of capital from those very countries into Thailand to make use of its cheap labour. To put this in perspective, let us examine the sequential chase of labour to capital, and vice-versa, in some other countries.

The post-war European countries had experienced a new phenomenon, namely, an international division of labour. Such a division of labour also became a crucial *international dimension* in the development of the countries of Asia Pacific, and is vastly different from some of the concerns raised by the dependency theorists, especially in the 1970s, about the nature of development in this area. Such dimensions also differ from region to region and therefore need to be identified. For instance, first of all the MNCs moved into the ASEAN region to exploit cheap labour. At a later stage, the ASEAN countries themselves formed their own MNCs to move into each others territories and even beyond.

Now in the NICs of ASEAN there is a considerable effort on the part of their leaders and academics on how to continue to influence international investment in their favour. In fact a section of the elites in those countries, who are well trained and have acted as advisers to MNCs in the past, play the game of either forecasting and/or providing what the MNCs require next, and then boldly approaching them with persuasive proposals. Gone are the days when the MNC host countries would merely wait for the investors to take all the initiatives.

Lee Kuan Yew, Mahathir, Suharto and Leekpai in the ASEAN countries were surrounded by extremely competent MNC movement guessers, who continually devised highly attractive deals to peg down the interests of the investors in their own economies. Such guessers were also on international circuits, of consultancies and conferences, and then advisers to the MNCs. Together they developed a good rapport and often distributed benefits on either side. The leader who perfected this to a fine art was Singapore's Lee Kuan Yew. Meanwhile, no matter who had a headstart on this, other ASEAN neighbours were not far behind. The investment gravy had to go round.

The record of Thailand in eradicating poverty was much less impressive. The problem of poverty, indicating uneven development of its various sections of society, still troubles Thailand. According to international observers, the East Asian countries reduced the segments of their population afflicted with poverty from one-third to one-tenth in the course of barely two decades – 1970 to 1990. Even countries like Malaysia and South Korea had almost totally eradicated poverty. Taiwan, Hong Kong and Singapore had done it ten years ago. In the last two decades, the performance of China and Indonesia in that respect was very encouraging. But the performance of Thailand and the Philippines remained poor, particularly Thailand because during the last two decades it had enjoyed a cumulative growth rate of nearly 7 per cent.[25] The gulf in education between rural and urban dwellers in Thailand is likely to widen. This is because whereas 80 per cent of students complete their primary school education and move into secondary school in Bangkok, only 20 per cent do so in rural areas. And those with mere primary education are then excluded from better paid jobs. This is in a way ironic because Thailand is also a country which has the region's highest literacy rate: about 90 per cent.[26] In the long run the less educated rural poor, perpetually migrating to the industrialising centres of Thailand, will increasingly present economic as well as social problems.

Despite political upheavals, resulting in the fall of three governments, and recession in the major economies of the world, in 1992 Thailand registered a hefty growth rate of 7.5 per cent from the previous year. Such a performance would then continue to provide an economic cushion to its decision-makers to sort out its economic and social problems.

IV. POLITICAL PROCESS

Thailand's political development may be said to have passed through various phases. These ranged from conscious attempts made by the monarchy to set up new political institutions; to the redistribution of power between the monarch, the army and the bureaucracy; to the first round of a democratic upsurge in 1973 which merely provided, in the words of Prudhisan Jumbala, 'half democracy',[27] leaving the army effectively in charge of the new political institutions; to the mass political upsurge of 1992 demanding the withdrawal of the army from politics, and the unresolved power struggle which ensued thereafter.

While there were repeated demands for an increasing measure of participation and accountability, what had not clearly emerged was something corresponding to a 'civil society' which could then generate sustained political pressure to ensure participation and accountability. In developing societies, which often embark upon an accelerated process of democratisation, we also need to talk in terms of 'political society'.[28] It is within this that the lessons of dos and don'ts, for both those in and out of power, have to be learnt. In this section we shall go into the ramifications of Thai political development towards greater citizen participation and the seeking of accountability from those who governed them.

There have been several approaches to the study of Thai politics. The bulk of these studies has been undertaken either by Western scholars or Thai scholars who had just about freed themselves from the influences of Western approaches. In the words of a perceptive scholar of Thai political studies:

> Western scholars have dominated the study of Thai politics in the past two decades. The minor role played by Thai political scientists in developing new frameworks is indicated by the fact that they were virtually ignored in the major literature reviews of Thai politics. During the last five years, however, Thai university academicians have increasingly produced sophisticated works on Thai politics. Despite this growth neither western nor Thai political scientists have provided theoretical breakthroughs. Instead, the literature on Thai politics remains used to the past and to Western frameworks.[29]

But sound theoretical 'breakthroughs', as opposed to mere reductionist theoretical positions, can only come through historical scholarship and political anthropological-style field research, especially when social and cultural factors deeply enmesh with the political as they do in Thailand. Girling, in his 'Thailand: Society and Politics' emphasised this. In his words, 'politics cannot be understood outside the historical and cultural contexts'.[30]

One of the longest and still surviving influences on the study of Thai politics is Fred Rigg's *Thailand: The Modernization of a Bureaucratic Polity* (1966). Such a polity broke down as a result of social and economic changes in Thai society. After that Girling developed his concensus–conflict model; Neher came out with his clientilist model; and Morell identified the dimension of search for legitimacy in Thai politics.

Among Thai scholars we have Chai-anan's variation on legitimacy model; Likhit Dhirevegin's emphasis on efforts at modernisation for strengthening bureaucracy; Thinapan Nakata's concept of a 'ruling elite'; Chattip Narsupha's economic history approach; Suchit Bunbongkarn's approach of proliferating roles of the army; and Prudhisan Jumbala's theory of the emerging civil society of Thailand as having established only 'half democracy'.

These approaches have provided a wealth of insights into Thai politics. The approach that we have adopted, however, is that of going back into the historical and cultural background of society and the way changes there affected the orientation to political action from time to time. It is a way of understanding significant phases of the political process in Thai society and then analysing them. Since the thrust of this work has been an exploration into attempted normative–pragmatic balance, in economic growth and political development, we shall try to identify the part played by various social and historical factors, the vision of elites, the commitments of different segments of society, and the gains made by the new forces in society towards responsible government.

i. Historical Background

Prudhisan has argued that in order to understand the present political culture of Thailand, with masses of people generating political pressure for democratisation, we need to understand the historical antecedents and the reshaping of various political institutions over the centuries, including that of the monarchy. Among others, historically speaking, the most important are the 'Sukhothai paternalistic rulership and the Ayudhyan Hindu-Khemer concept of divine kinship'.[31] The Sukhothai form of patriarchy viewed the king as the father figure presiding over the large family and acting according to the moral code of Buddhism. Later on the Ayudhya dynasty, from the fourteenth century onwards, introduced the 'Indianised' notion of *Deva-Raja* or divine king. The king was viewed, under the influence of this concept, 'as future Budhha or Boddhisattva'. He then became absolute, shrouded in 'Brahminical rituals, ceremonies and royal language'. But its greatest effect was on the relationship between the monarch and his subjects: the subjects, under the influence of this concept, were transformed from 'children to servants and slaves of the throne'. Such a vast acquisition of the human resource had then to be graded in a hierarchical order. This was known as the Sakdina system and it continued till the end of Ayudhya dynasty in 1767.

Then came the Chakri dynasty with Bangkok as the centre. By the nineteenth century, European nations were lurking in the background trying to turn Siam into a colony. The kingdom of Siam then hurriedly introduced reforms to strengthen itself and thereby thwart the designs of the colonial predators. Such changes also changed the nature of the monarchy: from direct rule, the kingdom came to governed by means of a bureaucracy; slavery and the *corvée* system were abolished; peasants became owner cultivators; and the military build-up received special attention. Later on King Chulalongkorn introduced further reforms by placing an enormous emphasis on education, social reforms, economic reforms and began borrowing Western ideas and practices to accelerate the pace of the modernisation of Thailand.[32]

Great strides in education had begun to build an educated middle class. Such a class was beginning to express its demand for an increasing measure of democratic participation. But this process was abruptly forestalled by the coup of 1932 by which the army forced a constitutional form of government on the king. The army was thus the direct beneficiary of the constitutional division of power. It then consolidated its hold during the war years in the region which extended from 1938 to 1944. Between 1944 and 1947 Thailand experimented with a short-lived civilian rule.

While the army and the bureaucracy were continually making a case against further democratisation, as leading to corruption, after a point the changed character of society would not stand for it. Together with education and a continually improving standard of living, Thailand now had a vocal middle class and a relatively bold press, which sounded a joint call for open discussion on civilian participation. In 1971, the students, with encouragement from academics, successfully brought down a dictatorial government. There then followed some grudging concessions and democratic reforms. In 1976, retired generals began moving into the political arena. They now wanted to play the democratic game and began forming their own political parties.

While the generals appointed themselves not only to political positions but also to lucrative state-run institutions and seats on the boards of certain joint ventures with the MNCs, the character of Thailand's political society was rapidly changing. There were now educated middle class, vocal and bolder academics, professionals, journalists, NGOs, social workers and students who kept up the pressure on the army to share power. Since its top brass was periodically and openly accused of corruption, the army's characterisation of corruption as something unique to civilians did not go very far.

ii. The Monarchy

The monarchy in Thailand continues to play a major role in the political process. After the constitutional coup against it in 1932, when it agreed to share power with the 'democratic soldiers' and govern constitutionally, royalty has been seen as a voice for modernisation as against obscurantism, accommodation as against army bullheadedness, and a protector of Thai culture as against vulgar materialism and mass culture. Surprisingly enough, on some issues it has been more forward looking than some of the other forces in society. In very few societies has a royal household played such a role or has continued to be held in such a high esteem as the monarchy in Thailand.

Despite the changes in the power equation over the years, the monarchy, because of its role in spearheading and then consolidating changes, has occupied a special place in all ranks of Thai society. The army, the bureaucrats, the professions, the intellectuals and the social activists look up to the king in times of crisis, either to guide them through it or actively intervene so as to find a solution. The king thus has been a still centre of Thai society and politics. The more Thailand modernises itself economically, and the more different groups want their voices to be heard, the more occasions of conflicts will develop, and the greater becomes the need for mediation from an institution which is held in respect by all sides, and that is the Thai royal household.

iii. The Role of the Army in Thai Politics

The role of the army in Thailand has been of special significance to Thai society. This is because the army was the earliest in forcing the kings of Thailand to share power with it. From the 1930s onwards the army has been claiming increasingly greater jurisdiction: from defence to internal security, to modernisation of the Thai economy and society, to a non-corrupt administration.[33] Regarding the last claim, especially, it was taken for granted that only civilians were corrupt and not the men in military uniform. Only recently this has been called into question.

Although the army had been meddling in political affairs since the 1930s, only recently did it try to legitimise its role in politics. To further this ambition, it consistently exploited internal as well as external factors. Scholars have estimated that since the 1932 Revolution, when young 'democratic soldiers' forced the king to share power with them, 'there have been nine [after the coup of 1991, ten] successful military coups'.[34] This brings the average to at least one coup every five years.

In the political field, the army as a protector of society assumed some additional responsibilities. One of these, ironically enough, was that of developing/defending 'democracy'. But the army wanted to run Thai democracy with the help of 'reliable' people. And the army's self perception was that nobody was as reliable as itself.

Against such an entrenched position of the army, initially only a few voices could be heard, due mainly to the 'Thai non-participant political culture'. Instead of getting involved in the political process and building an access to influence the decision-making, the Thais looked for strong leadership which would 'safeguard the country from crisis and disintegration'.[35] Given such a background, in the earlier period the army did not have to worry about popular opposition to its entrenched position. What began creating problems for it was factionalism in its own ranks which in turn created tensions and then led to coups.

However, it was the changing character of society that began creating problems for the army. Economic growth, modernisation, urbanisation, the accelerated pace of education, the growth of the professional class, and increasing boldness on the part of the press, began creating a questioning culture in Thailand. The old style rationale for suppressing the demand for accountability in the face of charges of abuse of power or corruption in high places did not carry conviction.

One of the perceptive scholars of army and politics in Thailand, Suchit Bunbongkarn, has argued that while scholars have discussed the 'role expansion' of the army in a number of developing countries, we also need to study the 'role contraction' of the type that took place in Thailand in the 1990s. In fact right from 1970s, the army's role in society and the economy was in the 'contraction' mould or, in any case, an accommodative role. Suchit argues that under the leadership of General Prem, between 1981 and 1988, the accommodative arrangement had worked quite effectively and had set Thailand on the course of army 'contraction' rather than 'expansion'. Moreover, there was the emergence of a number of 'social action groups' speaking on behalf of various interests and concerns. Thai society, in other words, was moving more towards an increasing degree of 'pluralism' of social and economic interests, making the task of reversal to an exclusive military rule impossible. And the generals who tried to reverse such a flow of events, such as Suchinda, came to grief.[36]

iv. A Democratic Upsurge in Thailand

During the past several coups in Thailand the streets had remained calm. There was rarely a show of mass support for one side or the

other. But in 1992 it was different. Unlike the coups of the past –
whereby one general was ousted by another, who then made necessary
changes to the institutions and routinely appointed commissions to
investigate public grievances – the one in 1992 resulted in a public
outcry. General Suchinda Kraprayoon, who had grabbed power, had to
face something unusual, namely, a huge rally of democratic slogan
shouting masses. The rally was organized by the representatives of four
political parties, also led by ex-generals. In Bangkok alone, the popular
ex-mayor, Major-General Chamlong, could mobilise 200 000 people.
His appeal to the masses had increased phenomenally not only because
he was an effective mayor of Bangkok, but also because of his ascetic
and renunciatory lifestyle which appealed to Thais of all classes. He
was a member of the Shanti Asoke Sect of Buddhism who, like Mahtama
Gandhi, invited suffering on himself in order to pursue the cause to
which he was committed. Later on the army was asked to shoot the
demonstrators. That did not help. For the first time the Thais refused to
vacate the streets and there was every possibility of a widespread civil
war.

King Bhumibol Adulyadej appeared on television with the two contending generals in front of him. Before resigning Suchinda wanted to
ensure an amnesty for all those who were involved in killing unarmed
civilians. But the leaders of the masses refused. This time they wanted
punishment meted out to all those who were involved in the killing.
More than that they wanted changes in the constitution which would
then put a stop to the periodic takeover by the army.

This episode indicated that a sea-change had taken place in Thai
politics. After the coup Thai political society was not the same as
before. The new forces, as well as the cumulative change in the old
ones, had materially altered the political relationship between the rulers
and the elites who spoke on behalf of the ruled. The latter doggedly
tried to inject into the ongoing political relationship an element of a
demand–response mechanism.

The earlier fundamental change which had occurred in Thai politics
was when there came into play three players in the political equation:
the royalty, the bureaucracy and the army. That change had taken place
as a result of the coup of 1932. Although the army was then seen as the
net gainer *vis-à-vis* the monarch, the bureaucracy too had substantially
increased its power and importance. Sixty years later, in 1992, previously unempowered groups such as the political parties, business and

professional elites, articulate leaders of the middle classes, academics, students and social activists came into the political process.[37] In the past, whenever there were conflicts and crises there was always a military 'solution', rather than an institutional, procedural or political solution, but the events of 1992 and beyond reflected the fact that Thai political society had progressed far enough to demand more than a military 'solution' to that particular crisis.

To be politically effective, individuals need to come together and then generate enough political pressure on those who control power in order to obtain a response. But towards such an effective coordination, some of the religious and social factors, and the traditional loyalties and attitudes to authority play a deciding role. Over the years Thai political society gradually moved towards the building of political effectiveness by means of non-traditional elites coming from political parties, business and the professions, academia and NGOs, and supplementing it by means of relentless media criticism and mass agitation.

Likhit Dhiravegin came up with a convincing explanation of why social groups in Thailand remained weak. According to him, the *corvée* labour system facilitated the penetration of the state into the family. Consequently, the family system in Thailand, so far as *corvée* labourers were concerned, did not stretch beyond lineages and clans. The Chinese immigrants, however, introduced social entities whereby the extended family existed apart from the state. The sinic culture in Thailand brought countervailing social groups who were able to put their grievances effectively before state officials.[38] The Thais did not have a counterpart of this. Nor did they have the hoary institutions of village republics as in rural India, namely, the panchayats, which administratively and judicially bound the individual to units of administration, which could then generate its own varying degree of influence on the central authority. And in that respect the autonomous villages of Japan went still further. They provided a much greater countervailing force to the central authority.

While the *corvée* system weakened family ties, individuals were linked by the religious order. So when the *corvée* system was abolished and the migrations to urban centres began, family influences, together with the renewed drive of the Sangha, provided newly forged social ties. Thus what we have witnessed is a resurgence of social ties which had received a partial setback under the preceding system of land tenure and bondage.

Kanok Wontrangan has argued that politics in Thailand was elite-centred. The elites came from the ranks of the army, the bureaucracy, academia, the professions, and socially concerned groups, who engaged in a game of 'exchange of power and wealth'[39] for themselves with much less for those whom they represented. As opposed to the elites, the masses cannot get into such a business because they have no leverage and nothing to give in exchange. The implication here was that the elites could extract votes from the masses without actually having to give something in return.

The mass upsurge of 1992, indicated that despite these factors weighing on Thai politics, society had undergone profound changes, and these changes had then begun to reflect themselves in the political arena. Under the very gaze of the army and the indifference of the ruling elites, Thai society had changed politically enough to make both parties take the new, and mass empowering, political forces in society more seriously than they had done before.

Until recently the political party structure in Thailand had not crystallised fully. Even during the mass democratic upsurge of 1992, the five political parties were all presided over by military retirees. Since the bureaucracy and the army were the two major sources for the supply of elites, the average Thai had no other recourse. Moreover, unlike in other countries, the military retirees, because of the continual expansion of the Thai economy in the last three decades, were good at recycling themselves. Wherever they went, they cleverly used their army image for probity, disciplined work and reliability. Over the years, with the threat of communism in the region and constant encouragement from the Americans, the army was made to look far more important as the custodian of the interests of society than was the case. And while the Americans spoke of defending democracy, they ended up giving a setback to other forces in society on which democracy in the region could be built. Finally, the changing forces in society and the growing number of their own shady deals caught up with the army.

Furthermore, during the economic growth of Thailand many civilians and professional persons were seen as being able to handle responsible positions effectively. This too provided a setback for the army. Now they were no longer seen as possessing exclusive managerial talents. In fact the civilian technocrats were seen as possessing far more skill and training in handling the jobs they were assigned to. The rise of the civilian elite to major economic positions also led to a relative evaluation of performance and criticism.

Every researcher in Thailand is amazed to see how much freedom the press enjoys in a country run by people in military uniform. Day after day, in their newspaper articles and editorial columns one notices a freedom of expression known in very few countries of the ASEAN with the exception of the Philippines.

Thus right from newspapers down to academics, professionals, social activists, students and politicians, it became apparent that freedom of expression and criticism, though not altogether unrestricted, had made great strides in the Thai political process. This change was constantly threatened by irate generals, who claimed that such criticism might cause chaos in society, but they connived at it only to see that it had become unstoppable.

In the span of a few days in the streets of Bangkok, the masses, the middle classes, the social activists and the students grew phenomenally in their political capacity *vis-à-vis* the unelected generals. When Suchinda started buckling under the pressure of the mass upsurge, he wanted to make a deal so that no action would be taken against him or his men. The representatives of the masses said no. They now wanted to realise the next critical stage in the growth of their own political capacity, namely, the demand for accountability. They now wanted Suchinda and his men to stand trial publicly.

Since the Thais did not have colonial rulers to fight against, and the army had fought against the absolute rule of the monarch, the middle classes and the masses had no previous experience of political involvement that would help them develop their own political capacity.[40] The mass upsurge of 1992 was therefore a kind of baptism of the Thai citizens into the political process from which they were hitherto excluded.

In terms of the growth of a liberal political culture, the Bangkok democratic upsurge may be considered as a critical beginning. Much will depend on the success of the people who led the upsurge to build a political society where the citizens, through their involvement in the participatory process, continually enhance their political capacity. Not only that but they must also learn to sustain the fragile institutions of liberal democracy by learning the normative–pragmatic dos and don'ts for those both in and out of power.

ASEAN newspapers, however, feared for their own national political stability in what was happening in Thailand. Singapore's *The Strait Times* saw it as a sinister game by opposition politicians to use the crowds; Malaysia's *Business Times* described the masses as 'gangsters';

and the Indonesians compared notes to say that there was no immediate threat to their own army. The influential Thai newspaper, *Nation*, denounced Suchinda's action as 'the arrogance of power'. The Western press saw it as a trend towards 'democracy' in the region.

In the ultimate analysis, the question was: did the events of 1992 give rise to the emergence of a political society which could act as a watch-dog regarding the uses and abuses of mandated authority, seek responsibility and accountability from those who exercised public authority, and inculcate a respect for norms of democracy on both sides of the power divide? The answer to this question can be ascertained as events unfold. Unlike Western societies, which had nearly three centuries to build their *civil society*, what a developing country like Thailand needed was a century-skipping *political society*, benefiting and assimilating the significance of major events such as those of 1992, and learning at a quicker pace about how democracies function effectively.[41]

V. SOME GENERAL OBSERVATIONS

As we have seen in the foregoing pages, Thai society was exposed to two major cultural influences: the ethical principles implicit in Theravada Bhuddhism, anchoring it into a firm normative base; and the pragmatising influence of the Confucian culture of the hardy, enterprising and result-seeking Chinese. Between the two extremes a number of bridges were built as a result of mutual interpenetration. On its own, Theravada Bhuddhism evolved a highly pragmatising notion of merit-making which was useful for the here and now, and the Chinese, and later on the Sino-Thais, provided a role model in a rapidly modernising economic life by closely watching the economic initiatives and organisations of the Europeans and the Japanese, and emulating them. The Thai normative–pragmatic balance was thus as much a product of their own efforts as it was of the influences from outside.

Like India, Thailand is a deeply religious country. But unlike India Thai religion has made it possible for the man of the world to retire temporarily from his earthly concerns, recharge his ethical batteries, and return to the world from whence he came. It is possible to become a *bhikku* for a month in Thailand, but not possible to become a genuine *sanyasi* in India for less than a lifetime. In Thailand religion and society are thus integrated, but in India they are kept apart. Moreover, in Thailand, religion, because of the Sangha, is far too organised. The *wats* and monasteries, as branches of a central organisation, are spread right down to grassroot level. Thus whether involved in either social, moral or even educational concerns, one is never far away from centres of organised religion. Such a proximity has created a feeling for social concern for the average Thai, and this is strikingly noticeable in the expanding, educated middle class.

Even the royal household is perceived as embodying the traditional values of Thailand. The king is the protector of Buddhist religion and also of the Thai traditions and values. Ever since the Hindu concept of kingship made headway in Thailand during the Ayuthiya regime, emphasising the moral obligations of the ruler to his people, the kings of Siam and later on of Thailand had, relatively speaking, a much better record of administration than did those in surrounding countries. Not only that, they kept up with the changing times and accepted their roles as constitutional heads, modernisers of social, political and educational institutions, arbiters between the army and the civilians, organisers of new social and economic ventures, and so on. Even in the 1990s, the king of Thailand has represented for the people – right across the social and economic hierarchy – the best that there is in Thai culture and civilisation. His exhortation to them became one of the major sources of their normative direction.

Thailand has a large number of NGO organisations, perhaps the largest in this region. According to one study, a decade ago, there were more than 113 registered NGO organisations, including foreign NGOs. The bulk of them were involved in rural community development; 18 in primary health care; 6 in consumer activities; 17 in education; 8 in the protection of human rights; 3 in technical assistance.[42]

In a sense the bulk of the NGOs, with their university degrees and middle-class professional or service backgrounds, are a modern day progeny of the Buddhists of the past. They concentrated on issues which the Buddhist Sangha and/or the state either ignored or could not effectively deal with. But they carried the Buddhist conscience and heightened awareness of human suffering and offered their own little contribution, often at the expense of a career and wealth. They were the reincarnated Buddhist *bhikkus* for a rapidly changing Thai society. They did not solve many problems but kept alive that social awareness which made the young and the old realise that some voluntary effort on their part was needed to tackle a range of problems which plagued Thai society.

At the level of its political society, its normative emphases have had their source not in a national movement but in its own political dynamics and the evaluation of the performance of those in office. Unlike the Philippines, Indonesia and Malaysia, within the ASEAN region, Thailand did not have a national movement to prepare its political society with a discussion concerning normatively desirable political institutions and ideals. Until around 1932, its administrative and political goals were set forth and incorporated by the king, the bureaucracy, and the army. Then came the Second World War, American anti-communist involvement in the region, and the enormous strengthening of the army. After that in the 1970s and 1980s, it was the economic growth of the country which occupied everyone's attention. But as the economy expanded, and with it came the expansion of the educated middle class, the clamour for responsible government and accountability increased. As we saw in the foregoing pages, the social activists, the Buddhists, the professionals, the educated, and the masses all joined in to define and undertake the fulfilment of the new political goals of the emerging Thai political society. And in the accommodationist culture of Thai political society, no political movement made straightforward one-way gains. It was an incremental realisation of some of the liberal political ideals with face-saving space for the politically retreating generals. Yet the political incrementalism of Thailand had secured an increasing measure of political freedom and what Likhit Dhiravegin called 'demi democracy'.[43]

Equally significant is the growth of Thai pragmatism. Like most societies in the region which are deeply committed to religion, Thailand too was wrongly characterised as mainly concerned with otherwordly problems. That, as we saw in the section on religion, was incorrect. Theravada Buddhism, as it evolved in Thailand, made even the doctrine of *karma* much less immutable than was the case in the country of its origin, namely, India. The exercise of merit-making brought its own atonement, not only for the life in the hereafter but also for the one that was currently being lived. Merit points are collected and then distributed throughout the threatened cycle of births and rebirths, starting from the birth that one already has. Theravada Buddhism thus gave control over this life which could then make a difference to the rest of the lives to come. It offered a practical way out of effectively altering the dreaded cycle of births and rebirths, and thereby put the responsibility squarely on the shoulders of the individual and his willingness to work for merit.

At the social and economic level, the kings of Siam and later on of Thailand introduced a kind of top–down modernism. One could now imitate certain aspects of Western modernity which those at the top asked for. The selection of certain aspects of modernisation was done by the king and his advisers. Since Thailand did not go through the colonial experience of externally imposed modernisation, whatever was selected by those at the top had good reason for it and should therefore be adopted without delay.

Earlier, Thailand, given its geographical location of being sandwiched between the two great classical civilisations of India and China, had to learn the lessons of selective emulation. This it did with such a finesse, in the absence of an external force, that selecting, borrowing and assimilating became an integral part of its social and economic life. Such a predisposition helped it to bring in ideas, techniques and crafts from different sources and then turn them into typical Thai artefacts. Even to this day, a large number of designs from outside are so deeply assimilated into its artistic fabric that it is difficult to tell what was borrowed from outside. The quick borrowing and assimilating Thais often minimised, to the extent to which it was possible, the social repercussions of what came in from outside.

The borrowing which presented problems were in the political and social field. In the absence of an indigenous participatory culture, corresponding to the panchayats of India, Thailand had a problem making the grassroots community share its vision of an evolving liberal society. Its urban political movement towards making the rulers of Thailand more responsible and accountable had little or no support at the grassroots level. At the non-urban level, communities have not evolved enough, politically speaking, to link up their conception of participation with the one that is implicit in a modern style liberal democracy.

As well as the democratic norms there are those interests which are served by liberal democracy. While there could be imitation of what urban leaders have emphasised about democracy – as a desirable goal in itself – individuals at community level have yet to realise fully that such a political arrangement, when effectively implemented and carefully watched, can also protect one's interests. It is the protection aspect of liberal regimes that has yet to make headway in the consciousness of the non-urban Thais, who for centuries have been the wards of the higher up.

5 The Philippines: Uncrystallised Normative Base; Unhinged Political Cynicism

In the early 1950s, scholars and observers believed that the Philippines and India, among the newly independent countries of Asia, would have the fastest all round development. Since then both these countries, with a different set of problems, have undoubtedly stayed the democratic course, they, nevertheless, have so far failed to quicken the pace of their economic growth and bring about an increasing measure of social equality. Such shortcomings continue to create additional problems for their deeply cherished liberal political institutions.

Despite poor economic performance, and inroads made into her political institutions by cynical politicians, the Philippines, on a comparative scale, may be said to be ASEAN's most democratic political society. She has also paid a heavy price for wanting to continue, or revive, her democratic institutions. While her elites have shown a deep commitment to them, they have yet to devise ways and means to make those institutions produce results. There are a number of historical, cultural, economic and participatory reasons for this and in the following pages we shall analyse them. Our presentation will be divided into the following subheadings: i. background factors and the way they continue to influence the development process; ii. social organisation and implications for political effectiveness; iii. public policy; iv. political process; and v. some general observations. We shall now examine each of these in some details.

I. BACKGROUND FACTORS

Like Indonesia, the Philippines as a nation is composed of islands – 7107 in number. Her island character has significance for her identity,

159

balanced development, sense of togetherness and statehood. For the purposes of regional reference and administration, her islands are clustered together in three groups: Luzon; Visayas; and Mindanao. Some of these islands are 530 km from the coast of China and much less from the coast of Taiwan. From time to time, the Philippines has looked up to other countries as models to emulate. After a prolonged enchantment with America, the current role models are either Taiwan or South Korea. Japan is considered to be too far ahead to become a model.

Racially, the Filipinos are considered to be of Malayo-Polynesian stock, but references to it are rarely made. On account of its 'colonial and migration history', the inhabitants have a mixed ancestry, 'with Spanish, American, and Chinese blood in their veins'.[1]

Like Indonesia in the ASEAN region, the Philippines too experienced the most damaging economic impact of colonialism. But unlike Indonesia, the Philippines went through two colonialisms, the Spanish and the American, and emerged with more than economic damage to herself. These two episodes also devastated the self-esteem of her people. And in the case of the Philippines particularly, the feeling of hurt continued longer as a result of the lack of economic success in the post-independence period. Such success would have lifted the spirits of the people as it did in most countries of Southeast Asia. Take the example of another equally ravaged country in the region, namely, Indonesia. Because of its achievements in many compartments of life in the post-colonial period, the feeling of colonial damage did not last much beyond the 1970s, and what its people remembered about it were their own heroics against the Dutch wanting to sneak back in during the last few days of the Second World War. That was not the case with the Philippines. Even in the 1990s it is difficult to come across a serious book written by a Filipino scholar where the undercurrent of what happened to her as a people during the colonial encounters is not apparent. It is not surprising, therefore, that the highly original works on social psychology in post-colonial societies have come from such scholars. More about that later.

When the Spaniards were present, the Filipinos could not even address themselves as 'Filipinos'. That term was reserved by the former for those Spaniards who were born in the Philippines. The local population was called the 'Indios'. Furthermore, the Spanish colonial administration was very keen on breaking the hold of the natives on the land.

Consequently, more and more land was transferred to the friars and to churches, collectively. Administratively, too, the existing *barangays* (communities) were dissolved to make room for the new ones through which the colonial rulers could exercise strict control. In the words of O. D. Corpus, 'Colonial society was founded on the disappearance and ruins of many of the old barangays. The people who survived were uprooted from their homes and joined to other survivors to make up new barangays.'[2] So great was the destruction of their way of life that it took them several centuries to start reacting in an effective way. In such a colonial thrust, as could be expected, the bulk of the functionaries of the church were not with the people. And they even discouraged the educated Filipinos from going abroad for higher education because of the fear that they might come back with liberal ideas and ask for more freedom. The only way out for the Filipinos, therefore, was to cultivate a culture of duplicity and deceit and wait for the right moment to rise against the hated colonials. Such a culture, according to scholars, had rubbed off on the social and political life of the average Filipino. In the words of O. D. Corpus again:

> because the native world was a part of the regime but concealed and estranged from it, it promoted artifice, shrewdness, agility, and opportunism. Part of this way of life survives in the political behavior of the modern Filipino, who will accommodate abusive and corrupt central regimes, while feeling an essential indifference and estrangement from them.[3]

Of the different regions which formed the Philippines, Mindanao remained culturally unassimilated during the Spanish colonial regime. Being geographically closer to Malaya, it retained its indigenous and pre-Spanish culture which was mainly Muslim. But during the succeeding American colonial administration, it fell prey to American corporations like Dole, Del Monte and rich Filipino interests who wanted to establish plantations on its fertile soil. To this day, Mindanao has remained a source of political and administrative problems for the Philippines.

During the Spanish colonial period, administration in the Philippines became rigidly centralised. Within the Spanish empire, communication links extended from Madrid to Mexico, and from there to Manila. But given the state of communication in those days, the rulers in Manila were left to their own devices and resources. The state in Manila became not only authoritarian, even by Spanish standards, but came to be looked upon as a 'provider', maintaining a strict distance between the ruler and the ruled. Those two conditions have stubbornly persisted even to this day. Despite a flourishing entrepreneurial culture, which has transformed the neighbouring states in a span of two decades, where the state plays a critical interventionist role but also allows and exhorts individuals to rely increasingly on their own economic initiatives, the average Filipino economic initiative is heavily dependent upon state direction, protection, subsidy, and periodic bailing out.

The population of the Philippines, which is close to 60 million, is divided into 85 per cent Roman Catholic; 7 per cent Protestant; 5 per cent Muslim; and 3 per cent Animistic groups. Since the Roman Catholics are in an overwhelming majority, it is very rare for high public offices to be occupied by people of other faiths. In the 1992 presidential election, when Fidel Ramos contested and won, orthodox Catholic elements had tried to exploit the religious sentiment, but it did not go very far.

Philippine society is based on a network of strongly entrenched family relationships which are formed not only by blood but also by 'ritual kinship'. A number of political cleavages, as we shall see, are resolved by appealing to extended family connections.

Women in Philippine society enjoy an extraordinary place of importance and access to economic and political opportunities. Apart from the Malayo-Polynesian background, wherein women did play a prominent role in social as well as economic matters, the Spanish colonial custom, which allowed women to 'inherit property, engage in trade, and succeed to a chieftainship in the absence of a male heir', vastly strengthened the position of women in what continues to be, in other respects, a man's world.[4]

Apart from the archipelagic charcter of the Philippines, in the pre-Spanish period it was a region inhabited by many tribes and agricultural and trading kingdoms. These latter used to trade with India, China and Japan, but did not develop an overarching religion, like Hinduism, Buddhism or Islam, which could then bring diverse people within a common belief system. It was left to Spain to bring together the far flung population under one rule and one dominant religion.

The Spanish colonial rule was essentially a combination of the state and the church in which the friars were as greedy for material possessions as the laity itself.[5] Opposition to such a rule had to wait until Filipino clergy came to occupy crucial positions and encourage not only higher education but nationalistic political ambition as well. A number of Filipino clergy were executed together with educated nationalists, the most prominent among them being Jose Rizal.

The nationalist movement in the Philippines, however, could neither have a clean break from the past nor become a politically regenerating experience, as in the case of either the American War of Independence or the Indian national movement. Both these latter two countries came out of their respective national movements as politically questioning and self-assured people. When the war of independence against Spain ended in 1898, the American occupation began – and was most deceptive. While it did not have the brutality and callousness of the earlier regime, it was not short on misleading characterisations, including the one of calling the Filipinos 'brown Americans'. The point to be made here is that the Filipinos were not left to themselves to grow into their political responsibility as a self-governing people. Uncle Sam wanted to do that for them instead and asked them to wait for the economic miracles to follow. What came in the bargain was the entrenchment of American corporate interests, with greedy Filipino counterparts to serve them.

The two national movements, first against Spain and then against the US, instead of building the political character of the Filipinos resulted in taking away the self-confidence of a newly born political society. Here we are not talking about mistakes in policy or in ideological direction, or even the lack of integrity in people who occupy major public office. What we are witnessing here is a gifted people, as good as anywhere else in Asia, unable to trust their own sense of direction, leadership and ability to solve their own problems. They belittle themselves and constantly look to others as being great. In the words of a Filipino scholar:

> critics point to the persistent colonial mentality of the Filipinos: their self-denigration, their uncritical regard for the West and its culture and life-style, and their desire to emigrate *en masse* to the United States, other English speaking countries, and elsewhere. This outlook is nurtured by continuing underdevelopment and mass poverty, which is aggravated by the dominant influence of imposed models of development, and by economic and political dependency.[6]

II. SOCIAL ORGANISATION AND IMPLICATIONS FOR POLI-
TICAL EFFECTIVENESS

In the examination of Philippine society, scholars are often faced with dimensions which are baffling. This is because, apart from the basic historical and anthropological material, one has also to take into account those international dimensions which have an unsettling and even dispersing or diasporic impact on the skilled and the elites of society. That means over and above the impact of Spanish and American colonialism on her society, we need to take into account the impact of the Filipinos wanting to work in other countries of Asia and North America. Moreover, unlike other post-colonial societies, the Philippines seems to live through a continued reaction to her two colonial experiences while she is engaged in rebuilding her society, economy and polity.

Equally baffling are the dimensions of her kinship organisation, which consists of 'affinal' and 'ritual' components. Some anthropologists therefore characterise her as an 'uncrystallised' society.[7]

Philippine society also had to deal with the problem of having to absorb, almost continually, new influences and interests which came from outside. Even before the Spanish conquest, at different ends of her territory there were influences coming in from outside. The northern part of her territory being close to Taiwan, there were influences and migration from there into the Philippines, and the southern part of her territory being close to Sabah, Malaysia, there was the interpenetration of Filipinos with the *Orang Asli* (the original settlers of Sabah).

Before the Spanish conquest, the Philippines was an amalgam of tribes and kingdoms. Three and a half centuries of highly centralised and brutal Spanish rule had welded these unconnected people into a Filipino society with a hierarchy of its own: Spaniards, Spaniard-Chinese Mestizos, the Principals, Chinese, the Indigenous Malayo-Polynesians-Tribals, in that order. Such a social and economic hierarchy continued until American colonialism changed it into: the Americans, followed by American-Filipinos, Chinese, Malay-Polynesians, and then the Tribals. It was only in 1945 that the social hierarchy in the Philippines began to crystallise without many outside components. Until then the society and hierarchy within it was changing most of the time under external pressure and impact.

American colonialism, armed with the principles of equality and Jeffersonian liberalism, gave the impression that it would bring about an 'assimilation' between its people and the 'Brown Americans' of the Pacific. Regardless of the seriousness of such intents, there was a sea-change in the nature of administration after the Americans arrived. This electrified all the educated Filipinos and people below them. What society in general lost, nevertheless, was the opportunity to rediscover its own Asian roots once the fascination for things American receded. Such a realisation remained confined only to the reflective elites and the educated youths who had earlier come under its influence. But it did not percolate much below, and was even resisted by the American pop-culture's saturated commercial interests. The most influential institution in society, namely the church, either remained indifferent to the problem or saw any talk about Asianism as a threat to itself. The elites, on the other hand, realised that due to historical reasons, Philippine society had weakened its Asian cultural roots. At the same time, they also believed that the Philippines represented a Westernised variety of Asianism for which eventually respect would build, provided it added on to its cultural system those aspects which were peculiarly Philippine.

While Christianity had continued to make gains in Asian countries even after the colonial era in the continent had ended, it was always grafted on to the cultural roots of the people who accepted it. Singapore, Taiwan and South Korea are examples of this. In the case of Sri Lanka, perhaps the sole exception, there was a return from Christianity to Buddhism once the colonial period had ended. The case of the Philippines was different. There society remained deeply anchored in the Christian faith.

Unlike Christianity in Europe and North America, where it also became a critical factor in liberalising and humanising political societies, Asian Christianity encouraged the cloning of the West and the despising of all the Eastern religions. While human dignity remained the core principle of Christianity in the West, its Asian version did not much encourage the need for self-respect and self-direction. Having accompanied the two colonialisms in the Philippines, it could not take a critical position on thoughtlessly imitating the West, and thus lost the opportunity of developing an independent Asian version of itself. That was accomplished by the Syrian Christians of Kerala, in south India, where Christianity was introduced directly in the first century after Christ by the Apostle St Thomas, and not via Europe or America. The Syrian Christians of India have played a major role in all aspects of their country's development including the cultural. They remain deeply rooted in India's cultural and even philosophical traditions. Other versions of Christianity in India, especially those which accompanied colonial and other interests, have weaker Asian cultural roots.

The reflective elites in Philippine society are therefore burdened with too many responsibilities. One of them is to develop a culture which has deep roots in the indigenous sources, pride in its Asianness, and at the same time being able to combine these with the humanistic aspects of Christianity brought in by the Jesuits and clerics in their educational, medical, and social work institutions. The Philippine version of Christianity has strong Filipino cultural roots. Then there are the implications for egalitarianism and social justice in Christian principles, and these have great relevance for practically all Asian societies. But these societies tend to confine those principles to a religious level and do not explore their significance in the social and political spheres.

Let us now briefly examine some of the indigenous values and emphases which have survived not only the two colonialisms but also an urban drift towards Western style consumerism. Before the Spanish colonial administration established itself, there was a considerable social and cultural diversity among the inhabitants. The relative isolation of various islands had given rise to variations in cultural systems which the Malayo-Polynesians of the area had established. After Spanish rule consolidated itself, attempts were made to eliminate those differences with the help of both the colonial administration and church. This resulted in the adaptation of certain Christian practices and values, on the part of various tribes and kingdoms, and resistance on the part of the Muslims (Moros) in Mindanao. Despite efforts at culturally levelling off people, some of the indigenous values survived. Socially speaking, instead of Christianity engendering a culturally homogeneous society, its values and emphases became grafted on to its antecedents, giving rise to 'folk Catholicism' or 'Christianized animists'.[8] In the absence of a sufficient number of priests and friars, and in place of pure Spanish style Catholicism, the Filipinos developed a mixture of pre-Spanish religious beliefs and adapted versions of Catholicism. Consequently, beneath the Christian form there survived not only the worship of the spirits of dead ancestors but some of the Hindu beliefs which had come to the various islands from Indonesia. In some cases the name of the supreme deity, namely, *bathala* (in Sanskrit means supreme 'lord') survived.[9]

From such a past values and emphases survived which dominate the system of social interaction. They are 'obligation', 'honour' and 'shame'. To the Filipino community, social life revolves round, and is influenced by, these values.[10]

In the centre of the social system is the Filipino 'family' which is more than a nuclear family. Family ties are forged outside the immediate family and these are helped by the occasions of birth, marriage, and ceremony. Once those ties are made they are maintained by means of models of relationship existing within the immediate family, which are then guided by obligation (*utang na loob*), self-esteem (*amor propio*), getting along together (*pakikisama*), and embarrassment (*hiya*).[11]

The family is deeply rooted in Philippine society. Neither the repressive Spanish colonialism nor the promotion of material values under American colonialism could weaken its hold on its members. In fact it played an important role in preserving the traditional character of its social life when extraneous values were being promoted by both those occupying powers.[12]

Equally distinctive has been the role of women in Philippine society. Outside observers are often surprised to see how much women dominate the social, economic and the professional life of urban Philippines. As we pointed out earlier, apart from the Malayo-Polynesian tradition of the central position of women in society, Spanish rule allowed women to inherit property and bid for leadership positions. Filipino women also bring to their various undertakings the unmistakable imprints of attention to immediate problems, as opposed to the alleged long-term planning and the involved reflective disposition of men.

The strength of family, traditional social values, and the adaptation of Christianity to antecedent beliefs helped Philippine society to minimise the extent of change that was imposed on it by the two colonialisms. 'For centuries Spanish priests sought to change the Filipinos, and for half a century American soldiers, governors, and teachers sought to impose their values. In spite of these pressures, Filipinos retained their own character.'[13]

Apart from the effective resistance offered by traditional Philippine society, neither the Spaniards nor the Americans left behind a socially attractive and economically and politically powerful class which the average Filipino could look up to. Except for the limited old wealth and a handful of important mestizo families, the influence of Spanish colonialism, barring educational and religious institutions, was sharply reduced by the succeeding American influx. The Americans in turn, for historical and economic reasons, ended up creating an ambivalent attitude towards themselves on the part of the Filipinos. On the campus of an average Philippine university, an undergraduate dreams of settling in America but at the same time he or she cannot stand the sight of an American either on the campus or in town.

One of the major problems for the Philippines, apart from the poor performance of the economy, major natural disasters, insurgencies, and an administration lacking in political will to implement its own policy, is the problem of Mindanao. Historically speaking, Mindanao had resisted absorption into the Spanish cultural set-up. Its Muslim population had fought and preserved its customary laws based on *adat*. While it was more successful in retaining its cultural identity, its fertile agricultural lands were objects of encroachment and exploitation by special interests within the two colonial establishments. In the words of a perceptive scholar:

> Mindanao's indigenous inhabitants have received few promises. They have seen their birthrights usurped and tradition assaulted in the name of development. The island has a reputation for violence. History has involved an array of interests including foreign powers, the state, secessionists, revolutionaries, cults, politicians, land-grabbers, bandits, renegades, all attempting to enforce their political and economic objectives through the barrel of a gun. Mindanao has been a frontier, a society in formation with all the attendant chaos that such a process entails.[14]

The people of Mindanao essentially view all the development plans and efforts of Manila as Luzon-centric. Consequently, the problem of Mindanao has become compounded not only in regional differences but also in the religious and economic spheres. And the more the Filipino economy slows down in its rate of economic development, the greater is the concentration on what else to extract from the economy of Mindanao, and the consequences of all these on an already existing sense of alienation and exploitation by a distant people. The most serious aspect of all this is the claim to distinctiveness of the Moro (Muslim) people – 'the failure of the national government to respond to the basic social needs of the Moro people has led the Moro people to contest the legitimacy of the Philippine government's occupancy of what they consider their homeland'.[15]

The complexity of Filipino society, which we have barely touched upon, has far-reaching implications for political society and the development process in general. To single out one feature, we will consider the influence of the nature of obligation on which institutions rest. Distinguished British anthropologist F. G. Bailey had once pointed out that when you do not extend your sense of moral obligation beyond your extended family to neighbourhood, political constituency, administrative unit, and, ultimately to state, then to that extent you will have weakened the kind of modern secular state which, over and above its legal system, rests on a sense of moral obligation to ones fellow citizen. Could the Filipino family, which protected the average person from the untold pressures unleashed by the two colonialisms, have become a factor in preventing the emergence of a political society where, over and above the ascriptive family, one also builds cross-cutting moral ties and becomes politically effective?

There is also the other side of the coin and that is an enormously increasing volume of NGO activity, often claimed to be the largest in Asia. Over the years this has acquired great legitimacy. The only time it had a setback was during the Marcos years in power. Marcos did not approve of the defiant attitude of the NGO activists who from time to time exposed how his policy was afflicting the poorest of the poor in agricultural and urban communities. While Marcos wanted to favour his cronies and the multinationals in return for suitable payoffs, the NGOs kept up their criticism of how harmful those policies were despite dangers of physical threats to their members. Marcos tried to debunk them as insurgents who were trying to destabilise the country.

With the change in regime, the NGOs did not moderate their criticisms. They continued to point out that in effect the post-Marcos change had not addressed itself to some of the major issues of society such as corruption and abuse of human rights by the law enforcement agencies, in particular the police. Together with this their criticism of the imbalance in the agricultural sector, created by those involved in agribusiness, on the one hand, and the average small landowner or the landless farmer, on the other, continued. The NGOs kept the attention of society focused on those vital issues, when the general tendency was to think that since Marcos had gone everything would be fine.

To the NGOs, the activists within the church were most helpful. In the Philippines, the church is almost a parallel state, stretching to all parts of the country and to all walks of life. Such an organisation can be, and is, most helpful to the NGOs whenever it (the church) decides to go beyond religious activities to social issues.

Not all NGO activity has borne fruit. This is particularly true in areas where it fails to evoke a broader response or where it is spread too thinly. It is heavily concentrated on economic and in particular agricultural issues. Consequently, a large number of social problems receive relatively less attention. And that concentration is likely to continue because of special favours given to big farmers and external interests by politicians. Together they controlled not only the price structure of agricultural produce and agricultural inputs, but also where and how such produce could be marketed.

III. PUBLIC POLICY

Certain aspects of public policy are responsible for the kind of development process which came to be established in the Philippines. Within the ASEAN family, the Philippines may be considered to be one of the poorest in her economic performance and social development in general. A number of reasons have been given for this: the two colonialisms, far too many natural disasters, corruption, economic setback caused by the dictatorial regime of Marcos, Western trained and influenced elites with a poor understanding of the actualities of the problems, neglect of a sound rural policy for an overwhelmingly agricultural country, and liberal democracy. While a case for or against can be made for all these explanations, what we shall do here is to refer to the rural policy. After all nearly three quarters of the population depend on agriculture and agriculture-related sources of income.

Like most economies of developing societies, the Philippines too had a problem with land tenure policies of the pre-independence political regimes. Different countries in Asia had different degrees of success in setting right the land tenure policy of the preceding period. And if we had to identify the two extremes of total success and total failure, these would be Taiwan as the example of the former and the Philippines as the instance of the latter. In between we have several other examples where land tenure policy did not change substantially in the post-independence period, but some of those countries emerged with differing degrees of adaptation to the needs of changing times.

During the Spanish period, the colonial regime had distributed large tracks of land to religious establishments, army officers, and the men it trusted the most. By such a measure it introduced into Asia European style feudalism which by the sixteenth century was on its way out in Europe. The colonial regime had called it the *encomienda* system.[16]

This system had radically altered the nature of land tenure which had existed in pre-Hispanic Filipino society. Earlier there was a lot of share-cropping among those who worked on the farms. Sometimes share-cropping became a means by which serfs obtained their freedom. Under the system introduced by the colonial regime, however, a new class of people were introduced into the agricultural sector whose sole business was to collect land revenue regardless of the condition of the people cultivating the land. Not only was land revenue collected according to what the new owners dictated, those to whom the land was gifted by the colonial regime, but they also claimed a portion of the crops and animals. Even the church, through its 'friar estates', was involved in the business of peasant exploitation. The new recipients of land stabilised the Spanish colonial administration in far off lands. By the end of eighteenth century, the colonial administration dictated what kind of crops it wanted. Since Europe needed sugar, tobacco, hemp, etc., the farmers were forced to grow them.

Between the colonial state and the church establishment at one end and farmers at the other, there came into existence a class of native chiefs. These were known as the *cacique*, but were considered good enough only to control the farmers. Above them were the Spanish *inquilino* who had wealth, education and culture.[17] Together they built and sustained one of the longest and most exploitative colonial administrations Asia had ever seen.

American colonialism, which extended from 1899 to 1946, wanted to bring about changes in the Philippine land tenure system but ended up implementing only a few of them. One of its great achievements was to take the land away from the friars, which it did through negotiating with the Vatican.

The relatively liberal colonial regime set up by the Americans gave the farmers freedom to express their grievances. And when there was no response, they rose against the regime. The American colonial administration had three peasant uprisings on its hands: in the 1920s, 1931 and 1935.[18]

Until around the 1950s, there was a widespread practice of shared tenancy in the region of Luzon, a vital agricultural component of the

Philippine economy. Large landowners replaced this by means of tenants, on the one hand, and agricultural labour, on the other. The demand for agricultural labour was then gradually reduced as some of the big landowners introduced farm machinery. By the 1990s, nearly half the households in Luzon were those of landless agricultural labourers. In the words of a scholar of the transformed agricultural scene of the Philiippines:

> Studies agree that the benefits of heavily commercialized agriculture have not been equally distributed, although they do not agree on the extent of inequality. Most concur that larger landowners have generally faired well. Producers and sellers of fertilizers, tractors, and other inputs and equipment have also profited. Among peasants, those with regular nonfarm income generally do better than those without . . . Most studies show that landless agricultural workers are usually on the bottom of the socioeconomic ladder on account of low, even declining real wages; intermittent work; and scarce alternatives.[19]

One of the major peasant rebellions was known as the Huk rebellion which took place in 1946 and lasted for seven years. And in some of the villages of Luzon there are still Huk veterans who keep the memory of their brush with the Japanese, and later on with Filipino authority, alive. What happened during that year was a part of the continuing peasant revolutionary tradition spread over the centuries.[20]

The American administration had encouraged plantation economy, agricultural exports, and the treating of agriculture as a *business* rather than a means of livelihood, which it was for three quarters of the Philippine population. A number of American fruit and farm interests benefited by such a policy, but as far as the average farmer in the Philippines was concerned his condition hardly improved.

The Marcos years, from 1972 to 1986, were no better. During his years in power, the number of farmer families below the poverty line very nearly doubled. Before coming into office, Aquino had promised to bring about fundamental changes in land tenure policy in the Philippines, even promising that she would introduce measures which would give back the 'land to the tiller'. But in actual practice nothing was achieved. By 1991, more than 70 per cent of agriculturists sank below the poverty line, and in one of her last policy speeches, the outgoing President Aquino acknowledged the grim statistics that two out of every three rural families lived in poverty.[21]

The policies followed in the Philippines by the two colonial administrations and Marcos had created a large number of landless farmers and some others with merely small pieces of land, barely existing at subsistence level, on the one hand, and those with large tracts of land, entering into commercial agriculture, on the other. This meant that the antecedent social inequality was further compounded by the kind of rural policies that were followed over the years. The number of Filipinos who are homeless is quite heart rending. Scholars have estimated that nearly 26.2 million people in the Philippines are homeless, which is just under half the total population.

The marketing and distribution system of the Philippines is full of ruthless middlemen and monopolies, which means that the producer never gets a fair price for his goods. A big chunk of what should have been a part of his return goes to the people in the middle who have been planted and strengthened by one administration after another. To date there have not been any politicians in office who have had the political will to do anything about it.

In the Philippines itself, there is no lack of resolve for improving the economic condition of the people. But like all other developing countries, too much faith was placed in the government's ability to help the people. On the other side, the people in the government took advantage of their position to help themselves and those outside were unable to check them. Since this has happened continually in Philippine history, during the two colonial regimes and after, the question uppermost in everyone's mind is what would prevent this in the future.

One of the important components of Filipino society and the economy are the Chinese. No one knows how many Chinese are there in the Philippines, mainly because of the problem of definition. There are those who are of mixed Chinese blood and others who identify themselves culturally with the Chinese. One estimate suggests an overall total of 600 000 Chinese.[22] Compared to their presence in other Southeast Asian countries, this is considered to be about the smallest.

The Chinese in the Philippines are largely concentrated in urban centres and are mostly in trade. They have their own economic and political associations including a branch of the Kuomintang party, called the Chinese Nationalist Party. Chinese traders were in the Philippines well before the Spanish arrived there. The Spanish rulers suspected them and forced them to live specifically in an area called Parian. Parian was burnt down at least seven times, but the Chinese persisted and prospered. The American colonial period was good for them since they tried to be useful to the new administration both economically and politically. With the coming of independence they moved into industry and finance. All this resulted in envy on top of a continuing anti-Chinese feeling in the Philippines. The Chinese also had a number of problems with regard to their citizenship but that did not slow down their economic activity. Outside Manila their relationship with the local population was friendlier. Those among them who had embraced Catholicism found a relatively greater acceptance of themselves. But by and large a feeling of unease and even tension continued between the Filipinos and the Chinese, despite the fact that the Filipino 'bilateral kinship system is completely open ended from the point of view of recruitment'.[23] Since the closing of the American bases in the Philippines, more and more of the Filipinos have looked to Taiwan for investment and economic stimulus. That in turn has resulted in a softening of their antipathy towards those Chinese who have settled in the Philippines.

Being a part of the ASEAN family where more prestige is accorded to a country which reaches the status of an NIC, President Ramos is seen as one who wants the Philippines to attain that status in the shortest possible time. Like other ASEAN countries, he too wants to liberalise the economy. Before that, however, he had to tackle the problem of monopolies and the effect of liberalisation on agriculturists.

In the summer of 1993, he finally ventured to take on some of the most powerful corporate interests in the Philippines. At the risk of annoying his close friends who are powerful industrialists, and whose assistance he needs to speed up economic activity, Ramos went after two of the most powerful monopolies: Philippines Long Distance Telephone Co.(PLDT), which was controlled by the Cojungco family; and the beer-based conglomerate, the San Miguel Corporation. These two companies had symbolised rule by economic oligarchy in the Philippines. Ramos wanted to put across to his countrymen that he meant business, even if it meant alienating some of his industrialist friends. But that was not the end of it – fears persisted that he might be 'replacing the Cojuangco plutocrats with his own'.[24]

When Ramos succeeded Aquino there was an air of optimism in the Philippines, that being a man of army, and also elected, he might come up with quick decisions followed by their firm implementation, as opposed to Mrs Aquino who was perceived as a weak person. The nation was grateful to her for having thrown out Marcos and restored democratic institutions. But there were doubts as to whether she would be able to face head on some of the friends and beneficiaries of the Marcos regime who had firmly established their advantageous positions in the economy. From Ramos, however, much more was expected, and when he did not act quickly enough there was open criticism. Consequently, when he did move against the two powerful economic groups, he was reacting against the public criticism of his lacklustre performance.

When he took over from Mrs Aquino, Ramos was full of praise for what Singapore was able to achieve with its limited resources. Apart from Singapore's economic success what appealed to Ramos, the ex-army man, was the highly disciplined nature of its society. He therefore invited Lee Kuan Yew to come to Manila and advise him on what kind of policy he should adopt. Lee's advice was twofold: scrap democracy and dissolve all the monopolies. On the first count, Ramos publicly disagreed with Lee, maintaining that he wanted an all round development and not just economic growth. On the second point, he had to bide his time.

Political cleavages and economic conflicts in the Philippines, especially when major families are concerned, have to be examined against the background of their interlocking interests. While their public posture may be one of conflict, they also tend to resolve their differences behind the scences without doing much harm to one another's interests. Then there is the Marcos factor. He entered into so many deals with so many of his cronies that each one of them can make claims and counter-claims in the law courts. It was therefore difficult for Mrs Aquino to make a clean break with the past. Even the bulk of the illegitimately acquired wealth of Marcos's widow could not easily be touched.

IV. POLITICAL PROCESS

i. The Marcos Kleptocracy

The collapse of democracy in the Philippines, and the prolonged authoritarian regime of Marcos, came as a shock to many observers. The Filipinos, according to them, had liberal political institutions, and training in operating them, provided by the Americans during their half a century of presence in that society. How could then the Philippines of all the countries in Asia succumb to the illiberal forces. Moreover, as stated in earlier, in the 1950s, the perception among the elites of Asian countries was that the Philippines, along with India, given their liberal political institutions, close contact with Western societies, will go about the farthest. That did not materialise for both the countries, so far as their economic performance was concerned. And in the Philippines unlike in India, even democracy could not defend itself.

Before democracy came to grief in the Philippines, Marcos, who came to power through the ballot box, began interfering with institutions such as the courts, the legislature, the press and political parties, in an effort to see if he could render them ineffective in the name of 'social reforms'. So when he imposed martial law in 1972 most of these institutions did not, or could not, resist his onslaught. His excuse was that they were full of 'reactionary oligarchs' who impeded the development of the Philippines. The fact of the matter was that Philippine political society had lost its moral fibre and the political will to resist him. As a perceptive observer put it: 'Clearly the collapse of Philippine democracy was the product of a deep malaise and not just the work of one man.'[25]

Marcos went on marginalising or dismantling one institution after another and the opposition to him either did not close ranks or just did not care. It was only when Benigno Aquino was murdered that the opposition was outraged and wanted to do something about the situation. An increasing number of opposition leaders and some of Marcos's former supporters came under the umbrella of the 'People Power Movement'. Since Marcos always sided with the Americans, he seemed to enjoy their direct and indirect support and it was, therefore, not easy to dislodge him.

Moreover, the end of American colonialism was not a straightforward event. During the American administration, a number of Filipino politicians had prospered with the blessing and support of the Americans. But in order to continue as leaders of the Filipino people they effectively had to denounce the Americans, thus playing a more deceitful game than politicians normally do.

> Forced into an unavoidable collaboration with an all-powerful colonial state, Filipino politicians who wished to secure American patronage – an absolute requisite for their political survival – had to achieve a precarious balance. They could not offend their American patrons with serious demands for power or independence. But neither

could they be seen as collaborators for fear of offending the nationalism of the electorate. The solution was a duplicitous posture – rhetorical militance before their mass clientele and a cozy cooperation in private with their American patrons.[26]

During the Spanish administration some leaders came into prominence by similarly playing a double game, which almost became a political art during the American colonialism. Even the Japanese occupation allowed wheeling and dealing on the part of the political elites, as a means to survival and prosperity. In short, these elites did not advance via defiance and suffering but through a game of deception and self-advancement. They therefore could not be expected to show a level of political integrity when independence came, or political backbone when Marcos began his onslaughts on democratic institutions. A number of them also tried to use Marcos's illiberal regime to their own advantage.

Since the role of Marcos in Philippine politics is central to the understanding of the development process, we shall analyse several views of him, one of which emanates from an American State Department consultant.

Charles C. McDougald, in his *The Marcos File: Was he Philippine Hero or Corrupt Tyrant?* (1987), has argued that right from his boyhood Marcos was given to extraordinary claims of personal achievement. He was the most decorated soldier but most of the awards given to him were on affidavits rather than the testimony of fellow soldiers. He was supposed to have engaged in 'buy–sell activities' and collaboration with the Japanese.[27] Even before he rose to power, he had a legal practice and was a notorious 'ten-percenter' in the commission he charged over and above his legal fees. On a similar basis he gave extensive help to the army, American interests, his cronies, and almost anyone.

All the time he exploited the fear of communism in the region and presented himself to the Americans as a brave cold warrior for 'democracy'. When Marcos, while in power, got himself re-elected, George Bush, the then Vice-President, sent him a message: 'We love your adherence to democratic principles and practices.' A day later most editorials in American newspapers were asking the question, 'How could you do that?'[28] Congressman Stephen Solarz called the Marcos regime a 'kleptocracy', meaning government by thieves.

William H. Oversholt, the American State Department consultant for the Philippines, argued that between 1950 and 1965 Philippine economic development in Asia was next only to that of Japan, and that the others (Taiwan, South Korea, etc.) were not even in the picture. Even democracy seemed to be more firmly rooted in the Philippines than in countries such as India, Malaysia, Columbia and Venezuela. In his words: 'The press was freer than elsewhere. Two parties regularly alternated in office. There were no political prisoners or other human rights abuses. The democratic parties had deep roots in nearly every village, and their patronage system integrated an extraordinary diversity of competing regional and ethnic groups.'[29] Very few Filipino scholars shared that view of Marcos's performance. Moreover, in terms of ultimate results, the above-mentioned opinion turned out to be misleading whereas in fact a struggling, developing country suffered a moral and material setback lasting for decades.

The author's claim that Marcos's greatest achievement was the destruction of the old oligarchy, was then differently viewed by himself. In his words: 'The old landed oligarchy that Marcos had destroyed was quickly replaced by a new oligarchy composed of gigantic business conglomerates run by President's cronies.'[30] Elsewhere in Asia at that time the authoritarian regimes of Lee Kuan Yew and Park Chung Hee were successfully building their economies – while Marcos was destroying his. Marcos had thus used autocracy in the guise of checking corruption and overcoming economic hurdles – for the consumption of his American supporters. They, however, looked the other way and compromised themselves. Neither the American taxpayers nor the people of an economically struggling country like the Philippines were well served by this kind of 'expertise'.

ii. The Restoration of Democratic Institutions

Apart from the collapsing economy, military brutality was on the increase and both the left and the right in Philippine politics were looking for alternatives. Marcos gave an impression until the very end that in any event President Reagan would come to his aid. The students once again started looking for a radical alternative, including the one provided by the communists. While the middle class and businessmen looked to the Church to give them a lead. 'Both the left and right found it useful to blame the US for many of their problems.'[31]

Initially the Catholic Church filled in the vacuum. It began to show greater and greater concern for social and political issues. In and around those issues, more and more elites began to rally. In its own publications, namely, the 'pastoral letters'[32] critical of the regime, the Church now began to test the extent of tolerance of Marcos's government. Suddenly, it dawned on the groups around the Church that Marcos was unable to control the situation or reassert his authority. It was such a situation which persuaded the Aquinos to return home. But Benigno was assassinated by Marcos's men while getting off the plane which brought him home. Crowds now openly asked for Marcos's resignation. Because of his failing health, Imelda, Marcos's wife, was in charge of a number of portfolios. Despite Marcos's claim for Reagan's support, the American legislators, media, and thinking men and women were feeling deeply embarrassed over what they had created in a poor country they were supposed to help.

Cory Aquino mobilised 2 million people in the streets of Metro Manila and Marcos's tanks could not go from one place to another on roads choked with people. Some of the top army officers deserted him. By means of mass agitation and also an election, Cory Aquino and her supporters threw out Marcos from power.

The rise of Aquino was variously interpreted. American perception of her rise to power was a reflection of its ambivalent attitude to democracy in the Philippines. On the one hand, they viewed Marcos as guarding American interests in the Far East, no matter what he did to his own people; on the other hand, when Aquino succeeded Marcos, through the ballot box, they read into it *their* success in advancing the cause of democracy. 'In a setback for the US foreign policy, the peaceful transition of power in the Philippines was a major success story.'[33] For the Filipinos the implication of this was that when Marcos was trampling down democracy, with the connivance of the Americans, they had nothing to do with it, but when the Filipinos successfully threw out a tyrant, peacefully they wanted to take the credit for having taught them democracy. When Marcos fell the Americans switched their stance and revived their interest in democracy.

Filipino men and women in public life, the Church, and academics saw the dismantling of Marcos's tyrannical regime in a different light.

For one thing, it electrified them regardless of their economic status, and was something like their own French Revolution. It was also a pointer to what could be achieved when people got together and asserted themselves against their tyrannical rulers.

The Church was gratified with its role in the movement to oust Marcos. It felt reassured for having taken the social and political issues seriously, along with its religious function. Through such an involvement it had almost redefined itself. With all her simplicity, and to some extent political naiveté, Corazon Aquino called for a 'new politics founded on the morality of justice and truth'[34] which would bring into the political process the vast human and spiritual resources of the Catholic congregation. Even priests and nuns were recycled into the democratic process. Aquino had tapped the religious-cum-social resources of society and proved to her fellow countrymen that it could be done. It also stimulated a quantum of voluntary activity to oversee the political process which was unheard of previously. The citizens of the Philippines now came out with what they called, 'The National Citizens Movement for Free Elections' (NAMFREL), a non-partisan organisation to see that Marcos did not cheat the voters. It was able to organise half a million volunteers. Thus apart from getting rid of a deeply entrenched and powerful tyrant in a peaceful manner, Aquino's greatest service to her people was to restore their faith in their own political capacity, and to awaken them to the possibility of improving the quality of public life in the Philippines. But those resolves were more easily stated and put into practice during a political crisis than made into an integral part of a country's ongoing political life.

While the formal restoration of democratic political institutions proved to be relatively simpler than making the army and all the powerful interests, which had got used to having their way, respect them. But more than any one of these was to make democracy produce results. In the words of Philippines's distinguished political scientist, Professor Carolina Hernandez, Aquino's toughest problem proved to be 'economic recovery . . . within a broad democratic framework rather than under dictatorship'.[35]

Within the ASEAN countries there was very little patience with the bungling, inefficient and corrupt ways of democracy. With the exception of the Philippines almost all of them had either not introduced a full measure of democracy or expressed reservations over it. And all of them were economically more successful than the Philippines. Moreover, in the name of democracy, what the Philippines had under Marcos was a ruthless dictatorship which plundered the resources of society and for which there were no parallels in Asia. The ASEAN countries therefore viewed the Philippines as an example of what a democracy can do to its people when it runs amok.

Aquino did not have much success in making the restored democracy produce the much-needed social and economic results. Her reign in office was marred by military insurgencies, natural disasters, vacillating public policies, family favouritism, and the near absence of political will when it came to implementing tough economic policies. But the nation owed her a debt of gratitude for having restored democratic institutions, for having followed the due process of law – even when it was sometimes very frustrating, as in the case of making Imelda return her ill-gotten family wealth – and, above all, for having introduced a level of decency in the shifty and ruthless world of Filipino politics. She brought about the much needed changes in the country's institutions and normatively committed herself to protecting them. Before coming to power she helped a large number of Filipino citizens realise that they too mattered in rising against a government which did not work for them. What is more she revived the faith of the elites and the professions in the possibility of making the democratic process work, provided they got involved in it, and brought to bear effective political pressure by organising people round different interests and concerns.

Despite untold problems, the growth rate in 1988, was 6.5 per cent. Foreign investments too increased. Mercifully during that year there were no attempts at coup. But what continued to plague Philippine government was graft in which sometimes Aquino's relatives were involved. But still careful scholars of Filipino situation, nevertheless, were 'cautiously optimistic'.[36]

Then, in 1991, there were some major disasters, notably the eruption of Mount Pinatubo and floods in Leyte. They brought about untold suffering to the surrounding agricultural communities. Finally, came the withdrawal of the US bases and with them the loss of revenue and a large number of jobs. During the election Aquino had campaigned against those bases, but once in power she realised the extent of the economic hardship it would cause and therefore advised against it. In question for a tottering economy was the problems of millions of dollars in revenue and 70 000 jobs. However, the Philippine Senate stood tall before rest of the world and symbolically – and realistically – reversed the last symbol of neocolonialism. The removal of the bases from the Philippine soil will in the words of Senator Earnesto Maceda, 'determine the conduct of our domestic and foreign policies and the character of our democracy for centuries to come'.[37]

On the positive side, one of the most important pieces of legislation to be passed by the 6-year-old Aquino government was the 1991 Local Government Code, which sought to decentralise the administration. Since the days of Spanish colonialism, administration in the Philippines was highly centralised. The new law gave local governments jurisdiction over health, social services, agriculture, and public works. It also opened up the scope for NGO activities in those areas.[38]

iii. An Emerging Political Society

Let us now briefly examine the nature of the democratic process in the Philippines, its limited resilience and equally limited ability to hold people in public office accountable. In developing countries with limited scope for trial and error, given the urgency of their problems, democracies also face an additional test – that of producing the promised results. They continually have to compete with 'soft autocracies', particularly in the Asia Pacific region, where country after country has produced impressive economic results and so far allowed only a limited discussion on 'democracy'. We therefore need to look at the problems of Philippine democracy against the background of her emerging political society which has to put her democracy to work.

To elaborate some of the points made in the preceding paragraph, all post-colonial societies, as a result of the normative political commitments of their elites in various national movements, are deeply drawn towards liberal ideals. They therefore impose new liberal political institutions on their stagnant societies from the top down. And when those institutions begin to flounder or register little or no resistance to onslaughts made on them by part of the same elite, the question is then: how far was it appropriate to introduce them in the first place?

One of the surviving democracies in the developing world is democracy in India. And India took more than four decades to build her own capability to revive from the onslaughts of Mrs. Indira Gandhi. But

Indian democracy is still not out of the woods. The problem of accountability and of making democracy produce results still remained with her. And so far as the Philippines is concerned she has just about succeeded in restoring her democratic political institutions, and now has to ensure that it was an enduring restoration. But more than that like India she too has the problem of seeking accountability from her elected and appointed public officials. Also Philippine has to give a comparable account of her economic performance, through her democratic institutions, given the impressive economic growth in the executive-driven soft autocracies of Thailand, Indonesia and Singapore.

This is an appropriate stage to look at some of the specific features of the struggling Philippine political society.

(a) Democratic strife-accommodation
Electoral conflicts in the Philippines have yet to earn the legitimacy of a contrived or special kind of conflict. In elections anywhere else in the world emotions are roused followed by feelings of elation or disappointment on either side of the electoral result. But the question for democracy is whether the electoral conflict has consequences for the interpersonal relationships of the two sides, members of their family, clans, and all those who support them. In other words, there is the democratic imperative of dissolving the animosity and defanging the elections.

Marcos, it is alleged, had gone to the extreme limit of hacking to death the person who had defeated his father in an electoral contest. The family or even an extended family is a highly venerated institution in the Philippines. What happens to it is always closely connected with one's honour. So, naturally, more people are likely to be hurt than elated when results are declared. But Philippine society also has developed a special way of combating those feelings by means of special meetings of clans and extended families after the victory and defeat are announced. It works in the following manner.

The elite families and clans, who are normally involved in election frays, often have to protect their corporate interests. So victory or defeat in elections has repercussions on the fortunes of corporations. Solutions for the problems created by electoral results are therefore sought in the world of economic accommodation, whereby a part of the gravy of one's electoral victory is shared with a vanquished rival. The problems of two or more clans are thus taken care of by means of corporate solutions. Soon after the election of 1992, *The Far Eastern Economic Review* described the conflict-resolving ways of the Filipino elites as follows:

> This clan phenomena extends to the corporate world. While the Ramos campaign has been playing up the evils of Danding (Cojuangco) as a monopolist, on account of his role in coconut cartel, among other things, another Cojuangco – the faction headed by Antonio Cojuangco which controls the telecommunications monopoly Philippine Long Distance Telephone Company – has moved to capture the control of privatised flag-carrier Philippines Airline Inc.[39]

It is against the background of this kind of economic activity, that the newly acquired power of one group to make decisions is to be viewed. The patching up of differences takes place by means of give and take activity, all at the expense of the Filipino taxpayers. The ruling families and clans with their corporate interests will swap favours of permissions and licences for the closing of hostilities incurred during the electoral frays. There was electoral strife but now it is time to accommodate with the help of certain favours that one's corporate business badly needs. The same is true when electoral fortunes are reversed. The exchange game works behind the scenes as long as there are no unexpected favour-seekers with economic muscle or threat of releasing the scandal to the public.

The elites who come at the top during Philippine elections are drawn from the world of business, the land and the army. They then become significant factors in the composition of the patchwork support structure for the candidates. In such a situation some always ride across the electoral divide and then forge new bridges across it.

Fidel Ramos, who won the election of 1992, had a deft politician at his side named Jose de Venecia, a rising political star who represents the old wealth, an Iberic name with a Ladino-Filipino appearance, and was re-elected from Ramos's home province. Soon after the election, he arranged 'reconciliation' dinners for Ramos at his own residence to which were invited Ramos's electoral competitors such as Imelda Marcos, Eduardo Conjungco, and others.[40] What there ensured was the reducing of the stresses and strains of the aftermath of the election in which each side battled it out with the other. The dinners were more than just occasions for eating together. And in effect they did not register a clean break with the past. This also means that Philippine political society has yet to make its elected deputies work for them rather than let them protect and enhance the interests of a handful of powerful political and economic elites.

(b) International influences
The liberal political institutions of the Philippines were established both as a result of the demand of the political elites and the response of American administrators. There then followed the Second World War, the Japanese occupation, American interest in the bases, and an American claim to save 'democracy' during the cold war years by propping up any regime which simply came out with anti-communist rhetoric. In that sense, until 1993, the Philippines was never left to sort out the problems of its democratic society in its own way. There was always a strong international dimension present ever since the gaining of statehood.

Apart from becoming a factor in American geopolitical interests, American offshore economic interests became deeply entrenched in the Philippine economy, stimulating the growth of indigenous corporate structures and monopolies in the name of a free market economy and capitalism. Consequently, combined with American interests and influences there were also powerful indigenous interests which placed a great strain on the democratic process. The result was that after nearly four decades of experience with democracy, the political society of the Philippines had not surrounded her fragile political institutions with a deeply internalised notion of dos and don'ts. Even her routine elections registered far too much stress on interpersonal relationships.

External influences on the Philippines also continued in another form. Unlike other societies in the region, the average Filipino is given to too much self-deminution and the extolling of the newly successful countries together with the United States. Consequently, apart from economic reasons, far too many Filipinos think of emigrating than do those among their neighbours. While poverty and lack of economic prospects become convincing arguments, such an inclination and mind-set also takes away the best of their vision and energy for improving their own society. Societies are continually reformed by individuals who feel that they have had a raw deal or that they cannot bring up their families within them. Their living conditions therefore have to improve, and while some leave their country, others remain and make the necessary changes. In that respect the Philippines continues to lose every year precisely those who could have contributed a little more towards their country's betterment.

(c) Economic and social influences
At the economic level, the concentration of old and new wealth in a few hands made it extremely difficult for those with limited resources to use the machinery of democratic institutions to protect and enhance their interests. As stated earlier, the land tenure policy in the Philippines did not prevent the concentration of land in fewer hands. Then came the slogan of agribusiness as being a good thing for the Philippines. Administration after administration increased the number of landless and resourceless people in rural areas. Such a deeply entrenched economic inequality did not give half a chance to democracy in rural areas. Various peasant uprisings brought a few formal changes without making a difference to the concentration of agricultural resources in a few hands.

On top of that there was the rigid centralisation of rural administration which continued right up to the final days of the Aquino administration. This meant that local institutions, and the voice of local leadership that needed to make itself heard at the levels above it, either did not fully develop or was turned into an intermediary to serve the interests of its superiors. Local leadership is rarely able to give a good account of itself unless it links up with either political parties or social activists with specific goals which are of significance to rural communities. Only in a few cases has this happened in the Philippines.

The involvement of the Church in social and political issues in the Philippines has been both intermittent and limited. At the national level it performed magnificently during the overthrow of Marcos. But once such visible and easily identifiable villains of society were dealt with, there was a return to normal religious activity. The Church in the Philippines, which is both well organised and powerful, has yet to involve itself in the day-to-day participatory social and economic issues of society, which then will result incrementally in the enhancing of the political capacity of rural dwellers.

The Philippines has a large number of newspapers with an exceptionally high level of specialised and editorial writing. These newspapers participate in various discussions on burning issues in the most informed and responsible manner. Whatever else may be said about the state of democracy there, it has to be admitted that the Philippines has some of the liveliest newspapers in Asia. Unfortunately, TV and radio do not present such a useful picture from the point of view of preparing citizens to participate fully in the democratic process. A number of radio and TV stations devote far too much time to religious issues. The Philippines also has a lively and socially concerned student body. The themes and issues discussed in campus debates bear witness to the lively interest in current national and international affairs. The faculty too are deeply involved in scholarly work on issues which face society. In the social and human sciences their scholarly contribution to national and international issues would rank very highly in Asia.

However, the excellence on the campus and in the press has so far had limited influence on the conduct of democratic politics in society. Their influence was greater when the Marcos regime was being dismantled. Once that was done the faculty and the students returned to their scholarly pursuits, leaving the press to continue its lonely and isolated fight.

On the other side of the coin, leading politicians with their organisation and resources would first of all turn a serious political meeting into a political fest, with singing and dancing and merrymaking, as if a political campaign were yet another occasion for entertainment. In those meetings, there is a loss of seriousness, a loss of purpose. One could certainly make a case for the joviality of the Filipinos, but that misses the point. A serious occasion is deliberately made to look light so that it is possible to avoid serious questioning and cross-examination. Pleasure is so subtly mixed with work that one does not know where one begins and the other ends. Judging by the net result, it is precisely such practices of making a carnival out of a political meeting that help the people in power to dodge accountability. As long as they can keep their audience momentarily happy, they can then get on with the business of extracting a payoff from their political involvement without having to answer too many questions.

In the Philippines public criticism often becomes an end in itself. Simply by engaging in it an illusion of the safeguarding of democratic institutions is created. Repeatedly this has proved itself to be more ineffective in developing societies than in the developed, because of the tradition of democratic accountability in the latter. But even there, the fear of political setback, exposure, and legal action reinforce political accountability.

Given the much greater political distance between public officials and the average citizen in developing societies, the effectiveness of public criticism is minimised. What proves more effective is the continuous involvement of various segments of society to keep issues alive, debate them inside and outside the legislature, and then make sure that voters remember who did what when they have the next opportunity to elect their representatives. Therefore, between voters and elected officials in developing societies it is necessary for far more people to be politically involved and act as intermediaries than are needed in developed societies.

Then there are the handicaps with which developing societies work. They have to deal with an ever present belief that an official position provides you and your family with an opportunity to make use of the resources of society. And they do this without exception. At the same time, unlike in the developed societies you do not have access to information on how public funds were spent. There is hardly any developing society with something parallel to the Freedom of Information Act in the United States. So you never get an official version of how public funds are being spent. Not only are the resources of society likely to be sqandered greatly, but the incidence of abuses of authority is also likely to be greater. Given such potential, and the daily infractions of democratic responsibility by public officials, elected or appointed, more than mere public criticism of the issues involved in developing societies is needed. It is necessary to be involved politically in order to influence those nearby and farther away so that abuse of authority is continually checked.

Then there is the question which is being raised all over Asia Pacific, and that is: do we really need an unqualified liberal democracy which in the economic and political field does not give a good account of itself? There most countries are beginning to settle for 'soft autocracies', led by technocrats, and high economic growth. Situation would have been embarrassing for them if a considerably liberal democratic country like the Philippines had given a good account of herself both politically and economically. It would then have given an additional amunition to the critics of 'soft autocracies'. But that did not happen. On the contrary, the illiberals got an example to point out what happens when liberal democracy is demanded at the expense of everything else.

In the region then, the Philippines has been an exception. Her national movement especially against Spanish colonialism, and later on the influence of Jeffersonian democratic ideals on her elite during the period of American colonial administration, put her in a different category. And with all her problems from time to time she also registered a growth rate which was reasonably impressive. What she failed to do however is to involve her burgeoning middle class in her democratic process to make her rulers more responsive and accountable.

The bulk of the elites either remained far too committed to the utopian side of democratic ideals, thereby refusing to make some of those ideals realisable, or joined forces with cynical politicians who treated public office as a means to personal gain. Marcos was the worst expression of this. In earlier years he had had a lot of support from a credulous segment of the elites which thought that he would introduce 'soft autocracy' within the floundering liberal democracy of the Philippines and accelerate the pace of development. But Marcos did neither.

V. SOME GENERAL OBSERVATIONS

Like other emerging political societies, the Philippines too was born amid great idealism and with social and political aspirations. There were three centuries of encounter with Spanish rule when individual nationalists like Rizal and others rose against its oppression and paid heavily for their nationalist commitments and assertion of human dignity. To indicate its disapproval of colonial rule, the Filipino elites went back both to their pre-colonial roots, whatever remained of them, and the Europeanised values which they had assimilated through education and travel. Different segments of society possessed different mixtures and emphases of Western and indigenous values. It was on such a mixture that the American colonial administration and its educational system tried to impose a convenient variety of the American social and political liberalism. Emphasis on participation and equality were suitability modified so as not to create problems for the American administration. Nevertheless, the American educational system, contact with American citizens, and travel to the North American continent could not prevent further interest in the best that there is in Jeffersonian participatory liberalism.

The ultimate test of the assimilation of normative liberal values is when citizens see fit to challenge political authority in the name of those values. In other words, political resistance is offered in the name of commitment to certain basic liberal values such as freedom of expression and criticism, the right to replace government by means of election, freedom of association, courts to safeguard the rule of law and enforce a bill or charter of human rights, and so on. When these were denied during the period of Marcos's rule, after a time there was a rededication to them and resistance in their name was offered.

The point to be made here is that for historical reasons the Filipinos did not get round to finding support against political oppression within their own indigenous tradition. And the Christianisation of a part of their normative values emphasised religious issues rather than political matters of deep social and human concern. The people to emphasise that were the Jesuit educators, the religious and non-religious NGOs, and the deeply agonising and soul searching intellectuals. The Philippine democracy, in times of crisis, thus could not fall back upon a clear-cut indigenous tradition to involve the bulk of the people. To reach out to them the above-mentioned intermediaries were necessary to translate the need of the hour, and appropriate public action was needed, from the world of the highly educated and often withdrawn to the world of exhorters and organisers of the masses. Until such a link was formed, Philippine democracy was deprived of the effective tool to keep the abusers of public authority in check.

Underneath such limitations of Philippine democracy, there were the wider questions of what the two colonialisms and the Marcos years had done to them as people and as citizens of a democracy. The two colonialisms had deprived them of the opportunity to rebuild their own normative cultural system which could go beyond social and religious issues to the political. And if there is a preference for liberal democracy, it is necessary to derive moral support in times of crisis and resistance from a cultural system within which people live and grow. Some of the highly perceptive works on social psychology, addressing these issues, have been done by scholars such as Virgilio G. Enriquez,[41] Patricia Licuana,[42] and A. Timothy Church;[43] by rural sociologists such as Manuel Bonifacio;[44] and by normative linguistic scholars such as Michael R. Walrod.[45] They go into some of the agonising aspects of rebuilding not only the normative references by means of clarification of local terms and references, but also go into the field of the social sciences to identify the inadequacies of various concepts and proposals which then influence public policy.

To conclude this point, the normative basis needed either to assimilate some of the liberal values and/or come up with resistance when they are breached is still in the process of striking root in the Philippines. And the reason for a prolonged process involved in bringing that about is that the Philippines has had a diversity of historical cultural exposures and experiences, and for these exposures to become a part of a commonly shared and identified experience will take time and effort on the part of its thinking men and women.

At the other extreme, we have a variety of pragmatisms, ranging from the peculiar contribution which the prominent role of women in the Philippines has made to its practical approaches in society, to an unhinged pragmatic cynicism that was practised by Marcos and his cronies. Such a range of pragmatisms has had its own influence on the implementation of public policy and the quality of political life in general. Let us examine this briefly.

Any observer of Philippine society is amazed at the important role that is played by women in various compartments of its social and economic life. The women are as visible in the labour force, at all levels, as are men. But that is not all. Even in the professions and as executives in various commercial and business houses, they are not only present in great numbers but also occupy important positions in their decision-making bodies. Finally, in public life too, apart from the high profile Cory Aquino, Imelda Marcos and Merriam Santiago, women shoulder the burden of organising and operating public activity at various levels of Philippine politics.

Apart from the intriguing question of why is there such a narrow gender distance in the Philippines – and in this respect it is unique even in Southeast Asia where the gender distances, by and large, are less pronounced than in South Asia – the other significant question for us here is what has been the implication of this unique phenomenon for our central theme of attempted normative–pragmatic balance in society. To be more specific, has the predominance of women in all walks of life in the Philippines brought into the picture a peculiar kind of pragmatism or not? Could this kind of pragmatism justifiably be addressed as feminine pragmatism?

The answer to these questions will have to be found in the nature of public policy which might have been influenced by them. The relatively greater anxiety of women over questions concerning family, not just theirs, but also of the public, seems to dominate their consciousness and therefore policy-making where they have influence. In private as well as public organisations, women have influenced policies which concern the facilities for raising families, and, in particular, food, nutrition, education, health care and housing receive special attention. While they emphasise these, it is altogether another matter how policies are actually implemented. And also whether such emphases are at the cost of certain basic problems or long-term issues which require postponement of the satisfaction of short-term or even immediate issues. Women in the Philippines often end up specifying what needs to be done immediately and then leave it to men to find financial provisions for them and take the responsibility for implementing those policies. The net result is that some of those matters which concern women do not effectively go beyond the stage of immediate articulation of how important they are.

The feminine pragmatism that we spoke of earlier is essentially a trusting pragmatism of family and social concerns which require immediate attention. But in net results it remains a halfway pragmatism, of concerns and intents, for the immediate. It is then handed over to the men and their way of going about it: often promising, neglecting, and even counteracting.

Two important women of the Philippines in this decade brought to public attention the need to attend to something very basic in the normative commitments of society. Aquino took the entire society with her in its reaffirmation of faith in liberal political institutions and restored them against great odds. Then an unsuccessful candidate like Santiago pinpointed the need to do something about the number one drain on the resources of society, namely, corruption. The former had an opportunity and the latter did not. But even if both of them had had equal opportunity, to look beyond the immediate issues which proverbially grip women, they might not have had, by themselves, what it takes to see them through. In that respect Margaret Thatcher was the lone exception: she *was* also an implementer of her own policy. The point to be made here is that the feminine pragmatism of the Filipino variety had all the characteristics of feminine concerns for immediate issues and then leaving much of the critical work of implementation to men.

Another dimension of Filipino society and politics is the impact of unhinged political cynicism, unhinged from normative commitments, that the Filipinos practised during the Marcos years in office. The two colonial regimes left behind their own legacy of political cynicism not only on the part of various functionaries of the state, both indigenous and foreign, but also with the average Filipino in his encounter with authority. He had to devise various ways of self-survival, protection and advancement of his interests. Even the friars and some Church organisers were parties to it. Deception and corruption became the means of transacting bussiness, especially among unequals. Such a mode of operation continued right up to the end of the American administration, and resumed with equal force after the Filipinos became independent.

While Marcos was the principal player in the corrupt practices of the Philippines of his time, he succeeded in poisoning the entire system of governance. The question is why did that happen and what could have stopped it? Apart from the lack of development of political capacity on the part of the citizens – the development of such a capacity takes place only through a continuous self-involvement in democratic processes – the bulk of them had taken it for granted that graft and corruption will always be there. Nothing can be done about it, therefore, why even try. Such a sense of resignation, which ran through the different levels of society, emboldened Marcos and his cronies to stop at nothing.

Democratic institutions, in the absence of a broader and more effective involvement of the different segments of society, continue to be highly vulnerable. Educated men and women of integrity do not want to do anything with politics. They merely want to groan and grumble when someone with only formal normative commitments begins to use them for his or her gain. They want democracy but do not want to lend their own personal integrity and commitment to working it and to producing the much needed social and economic results through it. In other words, they do not seek ways and means of realising in actual terms what they themselves hold dear in their personal commitments. The situation in the Philippines thus reillustrates the basic problem of the fragility of democratic institutions, when the educated and informed components of society merely stop at the passing of moral judgments and do not involve themselves in the democratic process itself to set things right.

6 Brunei: Affluent Welfare State, Traditional Norms, Undeveloped Political Process

Let us now briefly examine, the smallest and the richest of the countries within ASEAN, namely, Brunei. With a territory of 2226 square miles and a population of less than a quarter of a million people, Brunei is believed to be one of the richest countries in the world. In its 1984 report, the World Bank placed Brunei as the second wealthiest country with per capita earnings of $22 150.[1] Such an enormous resource has resulted in great opportunities for a high quality of life and a resistance to social and political change. In this chapter we shall examine: i. Brunei's historical legacies; ii. social organisation; iii. political economy; and iv. undeveloped political process. We shall examine each of these in some detail.

I. HISTORICAL LEGACIES

Since the dawn of its history, Brunei has been plagued by the problem of political survival.[2] Surrounded by larger empires such as the Chinese, the Sri Vijaya of India, and the Majapahit of Indonesia, Brunei was always required to pay close attention to international relations. Internal quarrels and the interests of the European powers in the region caused additional problems and eventually led to the disintegration of the kingdom of Brunei. There was an uncontrolled chipping away of Brunei's territory in Sabah and Sarawak, and even the Protectorate Agreement with Britain did not offer full protection. James Brooke, who subsequently came to be known as the White Raja, was instrumental in partitioning whatever was left of Brunei.[3] He annexed Limbang to Sarawak which he already controlled, while others encroached on territory in Sabah. Later on, in 1906, Brunei was forced to accept the British residential system, establishing 'British – type administration'[4] so as to prevent further loss of territory. The loss of Limbang, nevertheless, continued to rankle in the national psyche and continues to do so even today.

The interests of European powers in the region of Brunei were rekindled when it became known that there might be oil resources of considerable value. By 1929, it became clear that Brunei's oil resources were perhaps the largest in the British empire.[5] The royalties received by the state government as early as 1933 were in the order of $230 000, which was the equivalent of four-fifths of the total revenue of the kingdom.[6] From then on Brunei could concentrate on providing social services for its people, and also, as a consequence, dampen their interest in politics which some leaders were trying to arouse. The political issues centred round the basic question as to how long did Brunei want to remain a protectorate of Britain. Such efforts notwithstanding, so overwhelming was the influence of the increasingly high standard of living that various attempts to change the country politically did not get off the ground.

Then there were explorations about the possibility of a federation grouping in the region. In the aftermath of the Second World War, there was heightened nationalist activity in the former Malaya and in Indonesia. This had deeply influenced Azahari, the leader of a newly formed political organisation called Party Rakyat Brunei (PRB). While the PRB was pressing for democratic reform, the then sultan was exploring a merger with Malaysia so as to ward off internal as well as external threats to the kingdom. Simultaneously, there was interest in forming a federation of territories in the Borneo region. Brunei in fact came very close to joining the Malaysian federation and then withdrew from the proposal because of fear of being dominated by Malaysia. In addition, there was the problem of a possible loss of identity in the federation as the Malaysians were inclined to treat the Bruneians as rather undeveloped and therefore in need of being educated in true Malay culture and civilisation. Moreover, Brunei wanted to retain a hold on its oil resources and income therefrom.

The Sultan of Brunei successfully resisted pressure from Britain to establish a council of elected deputies, his excuse being to let the regional groupings crystallise themselves after which he would introduce changes. In 1977, he joined the ASEAN, and in 1984 Brunei gained independence from Britain.

In such a course of action Brunei was guided by its own historical experiences covering several centuries. All through its history there was a net loss so far as Bruneian territories were concerned and consequently there was always suspicion of friendships and mergers with other countries. But that was only one side of Brunei's experience. The other side involved internal dissatisfaction and intrigues by the aristocracy. And the only way to tackle this was to build an income structure for the average individual, together with a network of social services, that would dampen any interest in sharing political power. That too was accomplished, as we shall see later, by the manner in which the political economy was managed.

In accomplishing this an overall emphasis on Islamic values was of great assistance. For the Muslims of Brunei, in particular, there was constant emphasis on Islamic laws based on the holy Koran. Then, in the educational field, stress was placed on the conception of the 'Malay Islamic Monarchy' and the 'Islamisation of knowledge'.

While there has been considerable influence exerted by the English educational system and Western lifestyle on the upper strata of the Brunei Malays, they also balance this with the norms which they imbibe from religious sources. Thus Brunei's emphasis on Islamic values does not engender hostility to modernisation or Westernisation. Islamic values, nevertheless, occupy a position of greater influence on the predisposition and conduct of the individual. Such a duality is thus helpful in promoting a high standard of living and an ultra modern lifestyle, and at the same time remaining firmly anchored in the Islamic normative system. At the lower and less educated level of society, the Sultan and his authority have the support of the continuing animistic beliefs, implying that the chiefs always possess extraordinary or even supernatural powers.

II. SOCIAL ORANISATION

Brunei, like most societies in the region, is a multiethnic society. But unlike them it has rigidly tried to control the nature of society so that the Brunei Malays, unlike the Malaysian Malays, do not suffer from either a numerical or an economic setback. The result of this has been twofold. First, the Chinese component of the population has been controlled by applying some of the most stringent residential requirements, on the one hand, and by introducing some of the most difficult general knowledge tests, on the other. Second, it was decided to man a number of technical and low skill positions with the help of expatriate labour with a strictly defined duration of stay.

The composition of the population is as follows: 55 per cent Brunei Malays; 12 per cent Indigenous people or Tribals; 26 per cent Chinese (the Chinese claim that it is 30 per cent); and 7 per cent Others.[7]

In the social stratification, factors of proximity to royalty, race, income, and immigration status have become significant. As a result of independence in 1984, the Sultan Hassanal Bolkiah is no longer addressed as 'His Highness' but 'His Majesty'. After him come those who claim proximity to him in terms of either blood relationship or marriage. Then come distant relatives and the aristocracy; this is then followed by white expatriates (*orang puteh* or whitemen), usually British and a few Americans, Australians, etc.; then come economically powerful Chinese, Brunei Malays, less prosperous Chinese, expatriate Asian labour, and finally the indigenous people.

D. E. Brown, an anthropologist who had done field research in the area described all this as follows:

> Brunei's empire was ethnically plural at the beginning of the last century, with the Brunei's ruling over all. At the end of the century, plural structure remained fundamental in the three Borneo states (Brunei, Sarawak, the British North Borneo Co.); but by that time (1906 in the case of Brunei) the ethnic groups were topped by the Europeans and included a large addition of Chinese peoples.[8]

He goes on to say: 'Within the Bruneis, the principal stratification boundary was between nobility and others. Each of these two strata was in turn stratified on the basis of nearness of descent from officials.' Finally, 'at the bottom of the Brunei status scale was a class (or classes) of "slaves". Captured, purchased or debt slaves (probably mostly pagans by birth) . . .'[9]

One of the remarkable features of its social organisation is residence. While the Sultan and those close to him live in *Istana* or palace, a large number of Brunei Malays prefer to live in what is known as *Kampong Ayer* or water village. The village is literally on the mouth of a river and houses there are built on stilts. People of the village come and go by water taxis, get into their air conditioned cars, attend to their work in offices, and then go back to *Kampong Ayer*, where most houses have modern amenities including television, referigerators, telephones, videos etc. The villagers have also devised an ingenious way of getting drinking water from the land by means of bamboo pipes. *Kampong Ayer* and its houses on stilts are a major tourist attraction in Brunei.

The *Kampong Ayer* is not just one village but a cluster of thirty-five villages, each with its own village headman. Its current population is estimated to be in the vicinity of 30 000 people. In days gone by, the village headman used to enjoy considerable authority, now he merely implements the laws of the state. In the past, living on water was a way of life for the Bruneians.[10] It is said that the very name 'Brunei' has been derived from a Sanskrit term, *Varunai*, which means 'sea people'.[11] Over the years life in this cluster of villages is supposed to have become less hygenic but attempts and inducements to house the villagers on land have consistently failed. The villagers have even cited such instances as when 'flu hit the whole of Brunei town, nobody even sneezed in *Kampong Ayer*'. Even Brunei administrative machinery which is known for its strictness in implementing laws, has not been able to get any response. Bruneian Malays just do not want to give up their traditional residential settlements.

Nearly 40 per cent of the population of Brunei is non-Muslim, and the largest component within it is that of the Chinese. The Chinese presence in Sarawak, Sabah, and what is now modern Brunei goes back several centuries. They came in search of better economic prospects and very few of them returned home. As in other ASEAN countries, by means of hardwork, commercial enterprise, making their services available to colonial powers, and coming up with effective responses to challenges and problems of the local economy, the Chinese were able to prosper economically. The more they succeeded, the more they became the objects of envy and suspicion, and restrictions were imposed on them periodically to halt their progress. Despite this, in Brunei they control the wholesale and retail business and also work as skilled workers in the oil industry.

Regardless of their length of stay, only 10 per cent of the Chinese have been given Bruneian citizenship. Even when they complete residency requirements they

> fail to pass the Malay language test which they claim is administered in a way meant to keep them in the limbo of non-citizenship . . . The main stumbling block is a section on general knowledge of Brunei in

which they may be required to recite facts about local flora and fauna so obscure that most educated Brunei Malay would fail.[12]

Their prolonged sense of marginality has its own consequences. One of them is an added economic aggressiveness to teach the other side a lesson – to work harder than before and tell others how deserving they really are. Some of them embraced Christianity, but very few adopted Islam so as to make themselves more acceptable. The other expression of their resentment is emigration. In recent years, some of the Chinese have emigrated to Canada and Australia as economic immigrants. And they took a considerable portion of their wealth, economic experience and enterprising spirit with them. Others just live with a sense of statelessness waiting for the citizenship policy of Brunei to change.

Among the indigenous people or the tribals, there are the groups of Penans, Muruts, Bisayas (they had a history of headhunting) and Ibans. The Ibans in recent years have made considerable progress in rice growing.

III. POLITICAL ECONOMY

The political economy of Brunei centres round its income from oil and gas, the ability of such a revenue to provide a network of social services, and the employment which the state itself provides for its citizens. Brunei government bureaucracy is so large that it provides employment for every seventh person in the population.

The discovery of oil in 1929 changed Brunei's economic fortunes from rags to riches. 'Oil and gas account for 99 per cent of the value of exports and about 70 per cent of the gross domestic product. The ouput comes entirely from the Brunei Shell Petroleum Company (BSP).'[13] Its parent company is the Royal Dutch Shell Group.

While, officially, BSP is supposed to receive half the income from oil and gas, in actual practice it ends up with much more, as a result of various taxes and royalties. With declining political control over the former protectorate over the years, the parent company had to agree to various claims. While both sides have benefited enormously as a result of oil revenues, there are, nevertheless, hushed and not so hushed judgments as to which has in fact got the better of the two. The expatriates working in the BSP complex maintain that the revenue from oil is in fact a gift from Shell to build a 'Shellfare state' in Brunei, parodying the term 'welfare state'. Some Bruneians, on the other hand, argue that since the natural resources of Brunei belong to the people, there should have been a short time limit for Shell to take out the money it invested, with a handsome profit on top of it, and then leave.

Such arguments are never heard in public, and among the academics only in an oblique manner. Students are, relatively speaking, a little more forthright in expressing their views. Since Brunei does not have a political culture of publicly expressed criticism on public issues, some of these views come up only in chance conversation inside and outside the country.

No one knows precisely, or cares to talk about, how long the reserves of oil and gas will last. Such questions come up only when the Bruneians start worrying about the future and the need to diversify their economy while there is still some time. Various proposals are suggested including the development of food, canning, furniture, chemicals and dyes, plywood, glass industries and forest products. At such time also emphasis is put on expanded educational training and specialised training abroad. Brunei has already started sending a large number of young men abroad for training. But all such efforts still lack a sense of urgency since, as of now, there is no perceived or experienced urgency. At such times, Bruneian decision-makers also realise how very valuable her Chinese population can be for launching new economic initiatives, both commercial and industrial.

Brunei constantly invests her surplus income from oil and gas through its own investment body which has international advisers from the top financial institutions of the world. Lately, besides the British it has included Americans, Japanese, Singaporeans and Europeans. This reflects the growing view of the kingdom that it will have to broaden the base of its investments rather than depend only on British advisers.

It is said that apart from the personal wealth of the Sultan, which apparently has made him one of the richest men in the world, the income from investments is so large that it can underwrite the cost of running the government and the various services that it offers.[14] This then creates a peculiar problem for Brunei's social and political life. Why would the people want to become involved in political issues and controversies, and to participate in decision-making, when most of their economic and social needs are met? To that we now turn.

IV. UNDEVELOPED POLITICAL PROCESS

The only time the leaders of Brunei took an interest in political issues and openly expressed it was during the period of Japanese occupation leading up to the formation of the Malaysian federation. The defeat of the British army in Southeast Asia at the hands of the Japanese transformed the views on the permanence of the British presence in that region. Leaders of Brunei, and not only the then Sultan, were thinking of their country's future. One of the by-products of their nationalism was a degree of democratisation of the Bruneian government especially after the war. Simultaneously, the re-established British administration was also pressuring the Sultan to introduce an advisory council with a few elected members and the latter was cleverly evading the issue.

Sheikh A. M. Azahari established the Socialist Brunei People's Party in 1956, and enrolled as many as 16 000 members and kept up the pressure for some degree of representation. By 1959, Brunei was meant to achieve internal self-rule and a legislative council was supposed to be established to advise the Sultan. However, he cut the ground from under the feet of Azahari by bringing in nationality enactment regulations whereby Azahari, who was Labuan-born, and therefore an outsider, was ineligible to become a member of the council. He then offered to 'nominate' Azahari to the council which would have then destroyed the latter's credibility.

The focus of political activity soon shifted to the question of joining the Malaysian federation. Azahari championed the cause of joining it, but the Malaysian leaders became unpopular with the Bruneians because they started claiming superiority. Once again Azahari lost his platform. After that he could function only from outside. From Manila, in 1962, he inspired and directed a half-hearted revolt in Brunei which the British army crushed with the help of 2000 Gurkhas who were specially flown in. That was the end of Azahari's influence. Later on some of his colleagues tried to contest elections for the council but their influence did not go very far.

The abortive revolt was mentioned again and again to point out what so-called democratic activity leads to. Politicians were seen only as law breakers and not interested in the development of Brunei. In the words of the present Sultan: 'it is important for all the people of this country to adopt an attitude of concern about what goes on within the society and remain sensitive to our environment . . . efforts should be concentrated on economic matters and the building of a healthy and highly disciplined society free from social scourges.'[15]

Like Suharto, the present Sultan has tried to take people's minds away from political issues by emphasising social and development issues. Unlike Indonesia, the country has provided its average citizen with one of the highest standards of living and social services in the world. Unlike oil rich countries of the Middle East, Brunei has also tried to put enormous emphasis on modern education. The question then is: will not all such developments lead, sooner or later, to a greater interest in social and political issues and public participation?

As of now the Sultan can avoid the problem of sharing political power, but before long he will have to attend to that issue. As in the case of Thailand, Taiwan and South Korea, a higher standard of living and more education unmistakably result in demand for more participation in decision-making on public issues and policies. Even the rulers of Singapore have realised it. But they have forestalled such demands by bringing in decision-makers of such high calibre who regularly deliver results. After that, pressing a demand for participation begins to create doubts in the minds of those who ask for it. Yet the problem of meeting this demand will continue to nag at precisely those societies which think that a higher standard of living and education will serve as a diversion from it. It rarely does. It only postpones it. Even Singapore's response of making avilable the most talented in the service of the state may not always suffice. At some stage, participants might want to enjoy the privilege of commiting mistakes, creating controversies and giving limited political jolts, not to destroy the existing arrangements but to make their presence as individuals known and recognised. Thus a higher standard of living, far from being a diversion, becomes an intermediate stage and a channel for demands where the recognition of one's worth as an equal person, in contributing one's judgement and experience, begins to loom large in individual estimation.

Most ASEAN societies, as we have seen earlier, have so far passed the test of economic growth. They have now to pass the test of what such growth does to their constituents. Different societies within them have their own historical legacies, cultural influences, and social and political institutions through which the impact of economic growth will filter. And these filtering agencies will make a difference to the nature of their participation. Nevertheless, what they will not be able to do is to avoid its challenge and suppress it for long. The same may be said to be true of Brunei.

While the normative base of Bruneian Malays, especially, is supplied by the teachings and practice of Islam, it is also supplemented by the standard of living and education in Brunei. Despite being exposed to the values of Islam, the average Bruneian is not insulated from the values implicit in modern education and lifestyle. And while the Sultan and his immediate advisers worry about investment returns for Brunei, the quality of administration and the need to diversify the economy, the individual in such a well-provided state is restrained from the practical application of what he or she has been trained to do.

The component of the population which is subjected to severe pragmatic application and solution, whatever its material and human resources, are the Chinese of Brunei. For they have not only survived but also prospered in a continuing state of marginality and statelessness. And if Brunei takes the problem of diversification of its economy seriously, then the Chinese economic initiatives and pragmatic approaches might become not only a national asset but may also lead an economy like Brunei from total dependence on oil and gas to what her educated population could possibly do for her with its human resources and training in new skills. Such a development, when it materialises, needs to be watched.

Notes and References

1 Singapore

1. Riaz Hassan (ed.), *Singapore: Society in Transition* (Kuala Lumpur: Oxford University Press, 1976), p. xvi.
2. Chan Heng Chee, in K. S. Sandhu and Paul Wheatley (eds), *Management of Success* (Singapore: Institute of Southeast Asian Studies, 1989), p. 87.
3. Riaz Hassan (ed.) *Singapore Society in Transition*, p. 4.
4. Ibid., p. 12.
5. Maurice Freedman, *Chinese Family and Marriage in Singapore*, Colonial Research Studies, No. 2 (London: Johnson Reprint Corporation, 1970), p. 8.
6. Ibid., p. 87.
7. Paul Chao, *Chinese Kinship* (London: Kegan Paul International, 1983), p. 2. See also Maurice Freedman, *Family and Kinship in Chinese Society* (Stanford: Stanford University Press, 1970); and Mei-chun Tang, *Urban Chinese Families* (Taipei, Taiwan: National Taiwan University Press, 1978).
8. Lee Poh Ping, *Chinese Society in Nineteenth Century Singapore* (Kuala Lumpur: Oxford University Press, 1978), p. ix.
9. Ibid., p. 113.
10. In her words: 'A Third World Proletariat has been created in the growing manufacturing centres of the Asia Pacific Rim. In the factories and workshops of Singapore, Hong Kong, Taiwan, and South Korea, where workers make low cost goods for the export market, families maintain subsistence economies and forge kin and community ties to survive. That the rapid expansion of the world capitalist system has created urban poverty system.' Janet W. Salaff, *State and Family in Singapore: Restructuring a Develping Society* (Ithaca: Cornell University Press, 1988), p. 3.
11. Ibid., pp. 3–4.
12. Ibid., p. 4.
13. In her words again: 'the intervention of the Singapore government in molding a new family on behalf of its development program offers the best known example in a market economy of a state restructuring society' (ibid., p. 261). 'State sponsored public services become means to alter family lives' (ibid., p. 270).
14. Tanya Li, *Malays in Singapore: Culture, Economy and Ideology* (Singapore: Oxford University Press, 1989), p. 97.
15. Ibid.
16. Sharon Siddique and Nirmala Puru Shotam, *Singapore's Little India: Past, Present and Future* (Singapore: Institute of Southeast Asian Studies, 1982), p. x.

205

17. George Netto, *Indians in Malaya: Historical Facts and Figures* (Singapore PO Box, 1961), p. 22.
18. This refers to the work of A. Mani, 'India–Singapore Caste Continuum', quoted by Sharon Siddique and Nirmala Puru Shotam, p. 12.
19. Kernail Singh Sandhu, *Indians in Malaya: Some Aspects of their Immigration and Settlement (1786–1957)* (Cambridge: Cambridge University Press, 1969), p. 36.
20. Ibid., p. 146.
21. Bhanoji Rao, 'Role of Government in Singapore's Economic Development' (Singapore: unpublished paper, 1990).
22. Chan Heng Chee, in K. S. Sandhu and Paul Wheatley (eds), *Management of Success* (Singapore: Institute of Southeast Asian Studies, 1989), p. 78.
23. Ibid., p. 81.
24. Mukul Asher, 'Singapore's Fiscal System: An International Perspective' (Singapore: unpublished paper, 1990).
25. From the editor's note on Gary Rodan, *The Political Economy of Singapore's Industrialization: National State and International Capital* (London: Macmillan, 1989).
26. *The Strait Times*, 9 February 1990.
27. See, for the changing labour scene, Raj Vasil, 'Trade Unions', in Sandhu and Wheatley (eds), *Management of Success*, pp. 140–70.
28. See in this connection, Abdul Majid Mohmed, 'Cointegration, Causality and Dynamic Modelling: The Case of Singapore' (Swansea: University College Swansea, unpublished M.A. thesis, 1988).
29. *The Strait Times*, Singapore, December 1992.
30. T. J. S. George, *Lee Kuan Yew's Singapore* (London: André Deutsch, 1973), p. 7.
31. Ibid., p. 54.
32. Ibid., p. 51.
33. Robert O. Tilman, 'The Political Leadership of Lee Kuan Yew and the PAP Team', in Sandhu and Wheatley (eds), *Management of Success*, p. 55.
34. Chan Heng Chee and Obaid ul Huq (eds), *Leadership: Vision and Style: Selected Speeches and Writings of S. Rajratnam* (New York: St Martin's Press, 1987), p. 16.
35. See in this connection, Noleen Heyzer, 'Economic Dependency, Foreign Technology and Social Change: A Study of the Formation, Organization and Maintenance of Peripheral Capitalism in Singapore' (Cambridge: unpublished Ph.D thesis, 1978).
36. See in this connection, A. H. Somjee, *Political Capacity in Developing Societies* (London: Macmillan, 1986).
37. Chan Heng Chee, in K. S. Sandhu and Paul Wheatley (eds) *Management of Success*, p. 79.
38. "Politics in an administrative state: where has the politics gone?" by Chan Heng Chee. Unpublished paper, 1975, p. 5.
39. Ibid., p. 5.

40. Chan Heng Chee, 'Succession and Generational Change in Singapore' (Singapore: University of Singapore, 1982), p. 8.
41. Ibid., p. 10.
42. See in this connection, Ezra Vogel, 'A Little Dragon Tamed', in Sandhu and Wheatley (eds), *Management of Success*, pp. 1049–66.
43. Ibid., p. 15.
44. Chan Heng Chee, 'Politics in an administrative state: where has the politics gone?', 1975, p. 2. Unpublished paper.
45. Ibid., p. 5.
46. Gehan Wijeyewardene (ed.), *Leadership and Authority* (Kuala Lumpur: University of Malaya Press, 1968. Sponsored by UNESCO), p. 4; my italics.

2 Malaysia

1. See in this connection, Barbara Watson Andaya and Leonard Andaya, *A History of Malaysia* (London: Macmillan, 1982), p. 252.
2. Ibid., p. 252.
3. Ibid., p. 207.
4. Ibid., 226.
5. Judith Nagata in her *Malaysian Mosaic: Perspectives from a Poly-ethnic Society* (Vancouver: University of British Columbia Press, 1979), has effectively used this expression in order to indicate the cultural deposits of Hindhism, as a substratum, and then Islamic and other values in Malaysian ethnic groups and society in general. I have, however, used the term 'mosaic' to indicate the matrix within which its development process is cast.
6. Ibid., p. 8.
7. H. M. Dahlan, 'Local Values in Inter-cultural Management' (Kota Kinabalu: Workshop on Malaysian Managerial Values, 1990), p. 2. See also S. Takdir, *Values as Integrating Forces in Personality, Society and Culture* (Kuala Lumpur: University of Malaya Press, 1974).
8. See in this connection, Sharon Siddique, 'Some Malay Ideas on Modernization, Islam and Adat' (Singapore: University of Singapore, Master of Malay Studies; unpublished M.A. thesis, 1972), p. 179.
9. M. B. Hooker, *ADAT Laws in Modern Malaya: Land Tenure, Traditonal Government, and Religion* (Kuala Lumpur: Oxford University Press, 1972), p. 1.
10. 'What is a Malay? Situational Selection of Ethnic Identity in a Plural Society', in *American Ethnologist*, 1:2. Quoted by Mohd Aris Hj Othman, in *The Dynamics of Malay Identity* (Bangi: University Kebangsaan Malaysia, Faculty of Social Sciences and Humanities, 1983).
11. Ibid., p. 3.
12. Passim. pp. 5–19.
13. Ibid., front page.

14. Ibid., p. 1. See also Heng Pek Koon, *Chinese Politics in Malaysia: A History of the Malaysian Chinese Association* (Singapore: Oxford University Press, 1988).

15. Rajakrishnan Ramasamy, *Sojourners to Citizens: Sri Lankan Tamils in Malaysia* (Kuala Lumpur, 1988), p. ii. See also Rajeshwari Ampalavanar, *The Indian Minority and Political Change in Malaya: 1945–1957* (Kuala Lumpur: Oxford University Press, 1981).

16. See in this connection K. J. Ratnam, *Communalism and Political Process in Malaysia* (Kuala Lumpur: University of Malaya Press, 1965).

17. 'Kota Kinabalu Urban Development Study' by the International Bank for Reconstruction and Development, Government of Malaysia, State of Sabah, Interim Report Vol. I, February 1978.

18. Mohd Yaakub Hj, Johari and Baldev Sidhu (eds), *Urbanization and Development: Prospects and Policy for Sabah and Beyond* (Sabah: Institute for Development Studies and Konrad Adenauer Foundation, 1989).

19. H. M. Dahlan (ed.), *Sabah: Traces of Change* (Bangi: University Kebangsaan Malaysia–Yaysan Sabah, 1983), p. 3.

20. Ibid., p. 7.

21. *Far Eastern Economic Review*, 26 November 1992.

22. R. S. Milne, 'Political Parties in Sarawak and Sabah', *Journal of Southeast Asian History*, vol. 6, 1965, p. 104.

23. M. Clark Roff, *The Politics of Belonging: Political Change in Sabah and Sarawak* (Kuala Lumpur: Oxford University Press, 1974), p. 3.

24. John A. Lent (ed.), *Cultural Pluralism in Malaysia: Polity, Military, Mass Media, Education, Religion and Social Class* (Northern Illinois University, Special Report Number, 14, 1977), p. vii.

25. *Far Eastern Economic Review*, 26 February 1991, p. 72.

26. 'Report on Malaysia', in *The Globe and Mail*, 7 July 1992.

27. Alasdair Bowie, *Crossing the Industrial Divide: State, Society, and the Politics of Economic Transformation in Malaysia* (New York: Columbia University Press, 1991), p. 97.

28. David Sanger, 'Japan and a Malaysian Dream', *International Herald Tribune*, 27 March 1991.

29. R. S. Milne, 'Malaysia – Beyond the New Economic Policy', *Asian Survey*, vol. XXVI, no. 12, December 1986, p. 1373.

30. Ibid., p. 1382.

31. *Fifth Malaysia Plan: 1986–1990* (Kuala Lumpur: National Printing Department, 1986), p. iii.

32. Ibid., p. 29.

33. *Sixth Malayasia Plan: 1991–1995* (Kuala Lumpur: National Printing Department), pp. v, vi.

34. Seminar on Problems and Prospects of Rural Malaysia, 'Determinants of Rural Poverty and Underdevelopment: The Case of Malaysia' (Penang: Consumers' Association of Penang, 1985), p. 2. See also in this connection, 'The Nature of Poverty in Peninsular Malaysia: A Study of Baling District in the State of Kedah' (Birmingham: University of Birmingham, unpublished Ph.D thesis, 1983).

35. A. B. Shamsul, *From British to Bumiputera Rule: Local Politics and Rural Development in Peninsular Malaysia* (Singapore: Institute of Southeast Asian Studies, 1990), p. 242.
36. Ibid., p. 8.
37. K. S. Jomo, *Growth and Structural Change in the Malay Economy* (London: Macmillan, 1990), p. 9.
38. Ibid., p. 203.
39. Ibid., p. 240.
40. James V. Jesudason, *Ethnicity and the Economy: The State, Chinese Business, and Multinationals in Malaysia* (Oxford: Oxford University Press, 1989), p. vii.
41. Ibid., p. vii.
42. Ibid., p. 200.
43. Passim. pp. 161–3.
44. Alasdair Bowie, *Crossing the Industrial Divide: State, Society, and the Politics of Economic Transformation in Malaysia* (New York: Columbia University Press, 1991), p. 154.
45. R. S. Milne and Diane K. Mauzy, *Politics and Government in Malaysia* (Vancouver: University of British Columbia Press, 1978), p. 4. See also Harold Crouch, Lee Kam Hing and Michael Long (eds), *Malaysian Politics and 1978 Election* (Kuala Lumput: Oxford University Press, 1980); R. K. Vasil, *Ethnic Politics in Malaysia* (New Delhi: Radiant Publishers, 1980).
46. K. J. Ratnam, *Communalism and the Political Process in Malaya* (Kuala Lumpur: University of Malaya Press, 1965), p. 2.
47. Passim, pp. 111–12.
48. Dr Shaharuddin Maaruf, *Malay Ideas on Development: From Feudal Lord to Capitalist* (Singapore: Times Book International, 1988), p. 62.
49. Ibid., p. 121.
50. Ibid., p. 124.
51. Ibid., p. 143.
52. Mahathir Bin Mohamad, *The Malay Dilemma* (Kuala Lumpur: Times Book International, 1989 edn), p. 21.
53. Ibid., p. 3.

3 Indonesia

1. The first edition of this book was published in 1817. Subsequently Oxford University Press brought out its own edition in 1978. For our purpose we shall use the latter edition.
2. Ibid., p. vii.
3. Clive Day, *The Policy and Administration of the Dutch in Java* (Kuala Lumpur: Oxford University Press, 1966), p. 5.
4. See in this connection, Susan Abeyasekere, *Jakarta: A History* (Singapore: Oxford University Press, 1987).
5. Soetan Sjahriar, *Out of Exile* (New York: John Day, 1949), p. 67.

6. Ibid., p. 145.
7. Ibid., p. 135.
8. M. C. Ricklefs, *Modern Javanese Historical Tradition: A Study of Original Karta sura Chronicles and Related Material* (London: London School of Oriental and African Studies, 1978), p. 1.
9. M. B. Hooker, *Islam in South-East Asia* (Leiden: E. J. Brill, 1983), p. vii.
10. A. H. Johns, 'From Coastal Settlement to Islamic School and City: Islamization in Sumatra, the Malay Peninsula and Java', in J. J. Fox *et al., Indonesia: Australian Perspectives*, Mimeo (Canberra: Research School of Pacific Studies, Australian National University, 1980), p. 163.
11. Virginia Matheson, 'Sovereigns and Scribes: Life as Reflected in Some of the Literature of the Malays', in J. J. Fox *et al., Indonesia: Australian Perspectives*, p. 191.
12. M. L. Lyon, 'The Hindu Revival in Java: Politics and Religious Identity', in J. J. Fox *et al., Indonesia: Australian Perspectives*, p. 211.
13. Clifford Geertz, *The Religion of Java* (London: Collier-Macmillan, 1960), p. 5.
14. Ibid., p. 6.
15. Ibid., p. 309.
16. Allan A. Samson, *Concepts of Politics, Power, and Ideology in Contemporary Islam* (Cambridge, Mass.: Center for International Studies, 1974), pp. 5–6.
17. Clifford Geertz, *The Social History of an Indonesian Town* (Cambridge, Mass.: Massachusetts Institute of Technology Press, 1965), p. 113.
18. Ibid., pp. 125–49.

The anthropological writings of Clifford Geertz have become a subject of controversy throughout Indonesia. Indonesian scholars view his classification of society into *prijajis, santris* and *abangans* as an oversimplification of a complex social reality. Moreover, by his own admission, these three categories are different in their nature: the *prijajis* are considered to be largely a bureaucratic and elitist group; the *santris* are designated as a religious group; and the *abangans* as a residual category. While these three terms are widely used in Indonesia, there are many more which have escaped his examination and analysis. His critics also contend that Indonesia has nearly 13 600 islands. How can we therefore take his anthropological works in Java island, in a small radius, as representing the rest of the country?

As is always the case, Western scholars are reluctant to face the criticism of indigenous scholars when the latter acquire education and research training in Western universities, go back to where they came from, do reseach in areas where the former have established a scholarly reputation, and critically review those works with analytical depth and sophistication.

So far Indonesian scholars have published their scholarly material in *Bahasa* which might not be widely read. There are now some efforts to bring out such material in the English language.

Then there are unpublished Ph.D theses in the English language done by various scholars. One of them is Persudi Suparalan on Sumatra. In that he has argued that instead of the religious and semi-religious categories used by Geertz in order to classify the people of Indonesia, the term 'ethnicity' would have been far more useful because outside Java the Geertzian classification has much less validity. See in this connection: Parsudi Suparalan, 'The Javanese in Surinam: Ethnicity in an Ethnically Plural Society' (Urbana-Champaign: University of Illinois, unpublished Ph.D thesis, 1976).

19. Hildred Geertz and Clifford Geertz, *Kinship in Bali* (Chicago: University of Chicago Press, 1975), p. 10.
20. Zamakhsyari Dhofier, 'Islamic Education and Traditional Ideology of Java', in J. J. Fox *et al.*, *Indonesia: Australian Perspectives*, p. 263.
21. Mitsuo Nakamura, 'The Reformist Ideology of Muhammadiya', in J. J. Fox *et al.*, *Indonesia: Australian Perspectives*, pp. 273–5.
22. Ibid., p. 281. See also in this connection Alfian, *Muhammadiyah: The Political Behaviour of a Muslim Modernist Organization under Dutch Colonialism* (Yogyakarta: Gadjah Mada University Press, 1989).
23. Kuntowijyo, 'Religion, State, and Social Formation in Indonesia', reprinted from *MIZAN: Indonesian Forum and Social Studies*, vol. I, no. 3, 1984.
24. J. S. Furnivall, *Netherland's India: A Study of Plural Economy* (Cambridge: Cambridge University Press, 1967), p. xv, my emphasis.
25. B. Schrieke, *Selected Writings of B. Schrieke, Indonesian Sociological Studies, Part one*, 2nd edn (Bandung: N.V. Mij Vorkink-Van Hoeve, 1960), p. 225.
26. W. F. Wertheim, *Indonesian Society in Transition: A Study of Social Change*, 2nd rev. edn (The Hague: W. van Hoeve, 1964), pp. vii–viii.
27. Brian May, *The Indonesian Tragedy* (London: Routledge & Kegan Paul, 1978), p. 23.
28. Ibid., p. 47.
29. Ibid., p. 78.
30. Ibid., p. 159.
31. Ibid. Quoted by Brian May, *The Indonesian Tragedy*, p. 333
32. *Far Eastern Economic Review*, 1 April 1993.
33. The five principles embodied in the *pancshilla* were as follows: 'Belief in one Supreme Being, symbolised by the star in the center of the coat of arms; nationalism, symbolised by the revered banyan tree; internationalism or humanitarianism, emphasizing the broad common basis of human values of all men and women, symbolized by a golden chain with alternate square and round links; social justice, symbolised by a spray of cotton and stalk of rice, representing the basic necessities of life; and popular sovereignty or democracy, symbolised by the head of the *banteng* or wild buffalo, an animal patient and hard to rouse, yet when roused, prepared to fight to the death to protect his heard.' Christine Drake, *National Integration in Indonesia: Patterns and Politics* (Honolulu: University of Hawaii Press, 1989), p. 77.
34. Ibid., pp. 241–55.

35. Hal Hill and Terry Hull (eds), *Indonesia Assessment 1990* (Canberra: Australian National University, (1990), p. 7.
36. J. A. C. Mackie, 'Indonesian Conglomerates in Regional Perspective', in Hill and Hull, *Indonesia Assessment 1990*, p. 110.
37. *A World of Difference: A New Framework for Development Cooperation in 1990s* (The Hague: 1990), p. 237. See also Michael Vitikiotis, *Indonesian Politics under Suharto* (London: Routledge, 1993) for a balanced evaluation; and Michael Leifer, *Dilemmas of Statehood in Southeast Asia* (Vancouver: University of British Columbia Press, 1972) for an earlier perception of leadership in the region.
38. Yahya Muhaimin, 'Muslim Traders: The Stillborn Bourgeoisie', *PRISMA*, 1990, p. 84.
39. Yahya Muhaimin, 'Politics, National Business and the Indonesian Middle Class', *PRISMA*, 1986, p. 25.
40. See in this connection Leo Suryadinata, *The Chinese Minority in Indonesia: Seven Papers* (Singapore: Chapman Enterprises, 1978), pp. 63–80. Over the years the relationship between the Indonesians and the Chinese has significantly changed. See for the details of this Charles A. Coppel, *Indonesian Chinese Crisis* (Kuala Lumpur: Oxford University Press, 1983). See also J. A. C. Mackie (ed.), *The Chinese in Indonesia* (London: Nelson in association with the Australian Institute of International Affairs, 1976).
41. Bruce Glassburner, *Indonesia's New Economic Policy and Its Sociopolitical Implication* (Cambridge, Mass.: Center For International Studies, Massachusetts Institute of Technology, 1974), pp. 1–9.
42. Quoted by Brian May, *Indonesian Tragedy* (London: Routledge & Kegan Paul, 1978), p. 315.
43. Ibid., p. 322.

4 Thailand

1. John L. S. Girling, *Thailand: Society and Politics* (Ithaca: Cornell University Press, 1981), p. 19.
2. Ibid., p. 18.
3. Fred Riggs, *Thailand: The Modernization of Bureaucratic Polity* (Honolulu: East-West Centre Press, 1966).
4. See in this connection, Kavi Chongkittavorn, 'A New Japanese Image in Thailand', in *The Nation*, 9 December 1991.
5. See in this connection, Rawi Bhavilai, 'Buddhism in Thailand: Description and Analysis', *Proceedings of the International Conference on Thai Studies*, compiled by Ann Buller (Canberra: Australian National University, 1987), p. 615.
6. S. J. Tambiah, *Buddhism and the Spirit Cults in North-east Thailand* (Cambridge: Cambridge University Press, 1970), p. 62.
7. Ibid., p. 68. Edmund Leach also argued: 'Theological philosophy is often greatly preoccupied with the life hereafter; practical religion is connected

with the life here and now.' From Introduction by E. R. Leach to *Dialectic in Practical Religion*, edited by E. R. Leach. (Cambridge: Cambridge University Press for the Department of Archaeology and Anthropology, 1968), p. 1.

8.   Yoneo Ishi, *Sangha, State and Society: Thai Buddhism in History* (translated by Peter Hawks), Monographs of the Center for Southeast Asian Studies, Kyoto University (Honolulu: University of Hawaii Press, 1986), p. 10.
9.   Jane Bunnag, *Buddhist monk, Buddhist layman: A Study of Urban Monastic Organization in Central Thailand* (Cambridge: Cambridge University Press, 1973), pp. 1–2.
10. Hanten Brummelhuis and Jeremy H. Kemp (eds), *Strategies and Structure in Thai Society* (Amsterdam: University of Amsterdam, Publikatieserie Vakgroup Zud-en Zuidoost-Azie, Anthropologisch-Sociologisch Centrum, 1984), p. 13.
11. Ibid., pp. 13–14.
12. See John F. Embree, 'Thailand: A Loosely Structured Social System', *American Anthropologist*, vol. 52, 1950. Also reproduced in Hans-Dieter Evers (ed.), *Loosely Structured Social Systems: Thailand in Comparative Perspective*, Southeast Asian Studies; Cultural Report Series No. 17 (New Haven: Yale University Press, 1969), p. 4.
13. Hans-Dieter Evers (ed.), *Loosely Structured Social Systems: Thailand in Comparative Perspective*, Southeast Asian Studies; Cultural Report Series No. 17 (New Haven: Yale University Press, 1969), p. 1.
14. See in this connection Jack M. Potter, *Thai Peasant Social Culture* (Chicago: University of Chicago Press, 1976), p. 1.
15. See in this connection, Amara Pongsapich et al., *Traditional and Changing Thai World View* (Bangkok: Issued under the Joint Auspices of the Southeast Asian Studies Program and the Chulalongkorn University Social Research Institute, 1985), p. 5.
16. See in this connection, J. A. Niels Mulder, 'Origin, Development, and Use of the Concept of "Loose-structure" in Literature about Thailand', in Hans-Dieter Evers (ed.), *Loosely Structured Social Systems: Thailand in Comparative Perspective*, p. 17.
17. Boonsanong Punyodyan, 'Social Structure, Social System, and Two Levels of Analysis: A Thai View', in Hans-Dieter Evers (ed.), *Loosely Structured Social Systems: Thailand in Comparative Perspective*, p. 77.
18. Ibid., p. v.
19. Chai Podhisita, 'Buddhism And Thai World View', in Amara Pongsapich et al. (ed.), *Changing Thai World View*, p. 25.
20. Ibid., p. 182.
21. G. William Skinner, *Chinese Society in Thailand: An Analytical History* (Ithaca: Cornell University Press, 1957), p. iv.
22. Ibid., pp. 91–2.
23. Ibid., p. 299.
24. See in this connection Boonsanong Punyodhyana, *Chinese–Thai Differential Assimilation in Bangkok: An Exploratory Study*, Cornell Thailand

Project Interim Reports, No. 13 (Ithaca: Cornell University Press, 1971),
p. ix.

25. See in this connection, *Far Eastern Economic Review*, 18 February 1993,
p. 66.

26. Ibid., 4 February 1993, p. 25.

27. I am grateful to Professor Prudhisan Jumbala for allowing me to look
at his manuscript entitled *Political System and Nation-building in Thailand* (unpublished manuscript, 1992).

28. See in this connection A. H. Somjee, *Political Society in Developing
Countries* (London: Macmillan, 1984).

29. Clark D. Neher and Bidya Boworwathana, 'Thai and Western Studies of
Politics in Thailand', in *Thai Politics and Government Minority Groups*
(Bangkok: International Conference on Thai Studies, 1984), p. 1.

30. Ibid., p. 2.

31. Prudhisan Jumbala, *Political System and Nation-building in Thailand*,
p. 3.

32. Ibid., pp. 3–5.

33. Zakaria Haji Ahmad and Harold Crouch (eds), *Military–Civilian Relations in Southeast Asia* (Singapore: Oxford University Press, 1985).

34. Suchit Bunbongkarn, 'Political Institutions and Process', in Somsakdi
Xuto (ed.), *Government and Politics of Thailand* (Singapore: Oxford
University Press, 1987), p. 41.

35. Ibid., p. 42.

36. Suchit Bunbongkarn, 'Thai Military and Its Role in Society', in Viberto
Selochan (ed.), *The Military, the State and Development in Asia and the
Pacific* (Boulder, Col.: Westview Press, 1991), pp. 67–9.

37. Kanok Wontrangan, 'A Theory of Thai Politics: Situation and Power
Struggle', in John Girling (ed.), *What is Culture? Politics, Thought and
Action in Thailand* (International Conference on Thai Studies, 1984),
p. 3.

38. Likhit Dhiravegin, 'Thai Politics from June 1932 to the Coup of 1957:
The Struggle Between Bureaucracy and Democracy', ibid., p. 17.

39. See in this connection, Kanok Wontrangan, 'A Theory of Thai Politics:
Situation and Power Struggle', in ibid., pp. 5–13.

40. For the concept of political capacity see A. H. Somjee, *Political Capacity in Developing Societies* (London: Macmillan, 1982).

41. For a detailed discussion of civil society and political society see A. H.
Somjee, *Political Society in Developing Countries* (London: Macmillan,
1984).

42. See in this connection, Noriko Sakamoto, 'Grass-roots Movements Towards Social Development in Thailand Through Strengthening the Roles
and Activities of Non-Government Organizations', *Proceedings of International Conference on Thai Studies* (Canberra: Australian National University, July 1987).

43. Likhit Dhiravegin, *Demi Democracy: The Evolution of the Thai Political
System* (Singapore: Times Academic Press, 1992). See also David Morell

and Chai-anan Samudavanija, *Political Conflict in Thailand: Reform, Reaction and Revolution* (Cambridge, Mass.: Oelgeschager, Gunn & Hain, 1981).

5 The Philippines

1. Ledivina V. Carino, 'The Land and the People', in Raul P. De Guzman and Mila A. Reforma (eds), *Government and Politics of the Philippines* (Singapore: Oxford University Press, 1988), p. 6.
2. See in this connection one of the most moving accounts by O. D. Corpus, *The Roots of the Philippino Nation*, vol. I (Quezon City, Philippines: Akhlahi Foundation, 1989), p. xi.
3. Ibid., p. xiii.
4. Ledivina V. Carino, 'The Land and the People', in Raul P. De Guzman and Mila A. Reforma (eds), *Government and Politics of the Philippines*, p. 9.
5. Dennis Morrow Roth, *The Friar Estates of the Philippines* (Albuquerque: University of New Mexico Press, 1977).
6. Jose V. Abueva, 'Philippine Ideologies and National Development', in Raul P. De Guzman and Mila A. Reforma (eds), *Government and Politics of the Philippines*, p. 39. See also David Wurfel, *Filipino Politics: Development and Decay* (Ithaca: Cornell University Press, 1988).
7. Yasushi Kikuchi, *Uncrystallized Philippine Society* (Quezon City: New Day Publishers, 1991), p. iii.
8. See in this connection, Fred Eggan, 'Philippine Social Structure', George M. Gutherie (ed.), *Six Perspectives on the Philippines* (Manila: Bookmark, 1968), p. 44. See also, Virgilio G. Enriquez, *From Colonial to Liberation Psychology* (Diliman, Quezon City: University of Philippines Press, 1992), p. 4.
9. Ibid., p. 46. See also for an intensive case-study of interaction of religion and social structure in the Philippines, Raul Pertierra, *Religion, Politics and Rationality in a Philippine Community* (Honolulu, Hawaii: University of Hawaii Press, 1988).
10. Ibid., p. 14.
11. George M. Gutherie, 'Philippine Temperament', in George M. Gutherie (ed.), *Six Perspectives on the Philippines*, pp. 55–67.
12. Also see in this connection, *The Filipino Family, Community, and Nation: The Same Yesterday, Today and Tomorrow?* Final Report by Emma Porio, Frank Lynch, and Mary Hollsteiner (Quezon City: Institute of Philippine Culture, Ateneo de Manila University, 1975), p. 1.
13. George M. Gutherie, 'Philippine Temperament', in George M. Gutherie (ed.), *Six Perspectives on the Philippines*, p. 77.
14. Mark Turner and Lulu Respall Turner, 'Introduction', in Mark Turner, R. J. May, Lulu Respall Turner (eds), *Mindanao: Land of Unequal Promise* (Quezon City: New Day Publishers, 1992), p. 1.

15.	Ibid., p. 160. See also W. K. Che Man, *Muslim Separatism* (Singapore: Oxford University Press, 1990); Cesar Adib Mujul, *Muslims in the Philippines* (Quezon City: University of the Philippines Press, 1973); and Samuel K. Tan, *The Filipino Muslim Armed Struggle: 1900–1972* (Quezon City: Filipinas Foundation, 1977).
16.	Esther C. Viloria, 'Agrarian Reforms in the Philippines', in Sandra Sewell and Anthony Kelly (eds), *Social Problems in Asia Pacific Region* (Brisbane: Qld. Boolarong Publications, 1992), p. 305.
19.	Ibid., p. 307.
18.	See for a critique of economic policies of various colonial regimes and the Japanese occupation, Ranalto Constantino and Letizia R. Constantino, *The Philippines: The Continuing Past* (Quezon City: Foundation for Nationlist Studies, 1982).
19.	Benedict J. Tria Kerkvliet, *Every Day Politics in the Philippines: Class and Status in a Central Luzon village* (Quezon City: New Day Publishes, 1991), p. 6. Also published by California University Press, 1989).
20.	Richard J. Kessler, *Rebellion and Repression in the Philippines* (New York: Yale University Press, 1989), p. 7.
21.	Corinne Canlas, Edsell Sajor and Catherine Venzuela, 'Dynamics of the Philippine Rural Economy' (Quezon City: Philippine Peasant Institute for Philippine Working Group, unpublished paper), p. 2.
22.	See in this connection Jacques Amyot, Monograph Series No. 2 (Bangkok: Chulalongkorn University, Institute of Asian Studies, 1972), p. 25.
23.	Ibid., p. 43.
24.	*Far Eastern Economic Review*, 6 May 1993, p. 45.
25.	Ruby R. Parades, 'The Paradox of Philippine Colonial Democracy', in Ruby R. Parades (ed.), *Philippine Colonial Democracy* (Metro Manila: Ateneo de Manila University Press, 1989), p. 1.
26.	Ibid., p. 9.
27.	Charles C. McDougald, *The Marcos File: Was He Philippine Hero or Corrupt Tyrant?* (San Francisco, San Francisco Publishers, 1987), p. 89.
28.	Ibid., p. 240.
29.	William H. Oversholt, 'The Rise and Fall of Ferdinand Marcos', in *Asian Survey*, vol. XXVI, November 1986, p. 1138.
30.	Ibid., p. 1143.
31.	Ibid., p. 1153.
32.	See in this connection, Robert L. Youngblood, 'The Corazon Aquino "Miracle" and the Philippine Churches', in *Asian Survey*, vol. XXVII, no. 12, December 1987.
33.	Sandra Burton, 'Aquino's Philippines: The Center Holds', in *Foreign Affairs*, vol. 65, no. 3, 1987, p. 524.
34.	Robert L. Youngblood, 'The Corazon Aquino "Miracle" and the Philippine Churches', in *Asian Survey*, vol. XXVII, no. 12, December 1987, p. 1243.
35.	See in this connection, Carolina G. Hernandez, 'The Philippines in 1987: Challenges of Redemocratization', in *Asian Survey*, vol. XXVIII, no. 2, February 1988.

36. See in this connection, Carolina G. Hernandez, 'Philippines in 1988: Reaching Out to Peace and Economic Recovery', in *Asian Survey*, vol. XXIX, no. 2, February 1989.
37. Alex B. Brilliantes, 'Philippines in 1991: Disasters and Decisions', in *Asian Survey*, vol. XXXII, no. 2, February 1992, p. 142.
38. Ibid., p. 142.
39. *Far Eastern Economic Review*, 16 April 1992, p. 28.
40. *Far Eastern Economic Review*, 2 July 1992, p. 11.
41. Virgilio G. Enriquez, *From Colonial to Liberation Psychology* (Diliman, Quezon City: University of Philippine Press, 1992).
42. Patricia Licuana, 'Social Psychological Factors in Philippine National Development', in *Social Science Information*, vol. 12, no. 5, April–June, 1985.
43. A. Timothy Church, *Filipino Personality: A Review of Reseach and Writing* (Manila: De La Salle University Press, Monorgarph Series No. 6, 1988).
44. Manuel F. Bonifacio, *Images of Agriculture: Issues, Problems and Trends in Technology Transfer* (Manila: Philippine Council for Agriculture, Forestry and Natural Resources Research and Development, 1992).
45. Michael R. Walrod, *Normative Discourse and Persuasion: An Analysis of Ga'dang Informal Litigation* (Manila: Linguistic Society of the Philippines, 1988).

6 Brunei

1. Quoted by David Leake Jr, *Brunei: The Modern Southeast-Asian Sultanate* (Kuala Lumpur: Forum, 1990), p. 113.
2. D. S. Ranjit Singh, *Brunei 1839–1983: The Problems of Political Survival* (Singapore: Oxford University Press, 1984), p. 13.
3. For a historical account of the gradual grabbing of territory in this region see Nicholas Tarling, *The Burden, the Risk, and the Glory: A Biography of Sir James Brooke* (Kuala Lumpur: Oxford University Press, 1982).
4. Ibid., p. 106.
5. The discovery of oil was quite unexpected. One of the accounts of it describes it as follows:

> Two employees of Shell, a Mr. F. F. Marriott and the Hon. T. G. Cochrane, were in a remote part of Brunei called Kuala Belait, which at that time consisted of a few fishermen's huts. They had borrowed a couple of bicycles and used them to pedal along the coastline . . . They came to a stream called Sungei Seria and, exhausted, they lay down on the beach for rest.
> Suddenly Cochrane sat up and said 'I smell oil!'
> He subsequently persuaded Shell to search the area which is how the first major oil field, the 'Seria' oilfield, came to be discovered in 1929, James Bartholomew, *The Richest Man in the World: The Sultan of Brunei* (London: Viking, 1989), p. 13.

6. Ibid., p. 117.
7. David Leake Jr, *Brunei: The Modern Southeast-Asian Sultanate*, p. 87.
8. D. E. Brown, *Principles of Social Structure: Southeast Asia* (London: Duckworth, 1976), p. 185.
9. Ibid., p. 186.
10. David Leake Jr, *Brunei: The Modern Southeast-Asian Sultanate*, p. 87.
11. Lord Chalfont, *By God's Will: A Portrait of the Sultan of Brunei* (London: Weidenfeld & Nicolson, 1989), p. 13.
12. David Leake Jr, *Brunei: The Modern Southeast-Asian Sultanate*, p. 110.
13. Ibid., p. 113.
14. Ibid., p. 151.
15. Quoted by Lord Chalfont, *By God's Will: A Portrait of the Sultan of Brunei*, p. 188.

Index